Breadth and Balance in the Primary Curriculum

Breadth and Balance in the Primary Curriculum

Edited by

R. J. Campbell

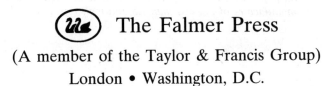

The Falmer Press

(A member of the Taylor & Francis Group)
London • Washington, D.C.

USA   The Falmer Press, Taylor & Francis Inc., 1900 Frost Road, Suite 101,
       Bristol, PA 19007
UK   The Falmer Press, 4 John St, London WC1N 2ET

First published 1993

**A catalogue record of this publication is available from the British
Library**

ISBN 0 75070 179 X Cased
ISBN 0 75070 180 3 Paperback

**Library of Congress Cataloging-in-Publication Data are available on
request**

Jacket design by Caroline Archer

Typeset in 10/12pt Times by
Graphicraft Typesetters Ltd., Hong Kong

*Printed in Great Britain by Burgess Science Press, Basingstoke
on paper which has a specified pH value on final paper
manufacture of not less than 7.5 and is therefore 'acid free'.*

Contents

Contents

A Note of Thanks

Alan Blyth

It was a great surprise to me when Dr. Ved Varma, who has been associated with *Festschriften* for several distinguished people in the educational world, invited me to suggest a theme for a similar volume for me, and a list of potential contributors. I responded to his invitation by proposing the title that the present volume bears, one that figures in current parlance but also has, I believe, a more timeless significance. The list of contributors was more difficult to propose, because I wanted to include people who had worked with me in different capacities and realized at once that the list could be a very long one, even if limited to the better-known among them. All the authors represented here fulfil that criterion, but so do others whose necessary omission I regret.

I am grateful for this opportunity to thank all who have written in this book and especially Jim Campbell for his persuasive editorship; Ved Varma for his enthusiastic support; and also Malcolm Clarkson of Falmer Press for making the venture possible. The others have been included for these special reasons:

MIKE ASHTON	as Head of the primary school at which I carried out my final research on assessment, and as a higher-degree student at the University of Liverpool.
JIM CAMPBELL	(again) for his long-standing interest in the political and administrative aspects of primary education and in humanities in the primary curriculum, matters in which he has generously involved me.
RAY DERRICOTT	as my fellow-worker in the Schools Council Project which he analyzes, and subsequently in many other situations in the University of Liverpool and beyond.
MAURICE GALTON	for his general contribution to primary teaching and particularly because we have collaborated in

	several enterprises including editing the Council of Europe data on primary education.
VIC KELLY AND GEVA BLENKIN	for their distinctive and widely-recognized contribution to thinking about the primary curriculum, and for my contact with them at Goldsmiths' College when I examined there.
BILL MARSDEN	for his insight into the history of the curriculum and primary geography, and also as a thoroughly dependable colleague at the University of Liverpool.
JENNIFER NIAS	because she was the first full-time tutor to the primary PGCE course at the University of Liverpool, and because of her subsequent studies of primary teachers' careers.
ANDREW POLLARD	as one of the most perceptive analysts of social relations in primary schools, a field in which I am still interested and have discussed with him.
COLIN RICHARDS	for his work as lecturer, writer, editor and organizer, and for his long collaboration with me in primary and middle-years education.
ALISTAIR ROSS	for his interest in primary humanities and especially in primary industry education, to which he and his research team have made major contributions.
NORMAN THOMAS	for his level-headed and admirable contribution as HM Chief Inspector for primary education and subsequently. I have had the privilege of working with him in a number of contexts.

ALAN BLYTH
Chester

Editor's Preface

Jim Campbell

This book had its origins in a proposal from Dr. Ved Varma, an educational psychologist, that there should be a *Festschrift* in honour of Professor Alan Blyth, until recently Professor of Education at the University of Liverpool and, since 1965, a major influence on the study of primary education in England and Wales. The theme and working title were suggested by Professor Blyth, as were the contributors, all of whom had collaborated, or enjoyed some other professional relationship, with him.

The concept of 'breadth and balance' was deliberately not defined in the same way for each contributor. Instead, contributors were asked to write using the phrase and the idea of 'breadth and balance' applied to an aspect of the primary curriculum related to their work. It is not surprising that several contributors wished to develop critiques of the National Curriculum in England and Wales, either concerned with its fundamental assumptions (Pollard, Kelly and Blenkin) or with manageability (Thomas and Campbell). But it is equally predictable that other contributors, reflecting the range of Professor Blyth's scholarship, should look beyond the National Curriculum to concerns with curriculum practice and thinking (Ashton and Nias), the social subjects (Derricott, Marsden and Ross), and to comparative dimensions of primary education (Galton). Even so, we have not been able to incorporate all Professor Blyth's interests; in particular we have certainly not done justice to his influence on thinking about initial teacher education or assessment.

Dr. Varma had to withdraw from involvement at a late stage in the book's development, but I should like to record my gratitude for his initiation of, and enthusiasm for, the project.

Colin Richards, HMI, in the Foreword that follows, articulates something of the debt that all engaged in studying primary education owe to Professor Blyth, and it is not my task to do that. However, I could not refrain from going back to my battered paperback version of Vol. 2 of *English Primary Education* (a Routledge paperback, 1965, 10s. 6d). In the final chapter, Blyth surveys the various aspects of research needing to be undertaken into the relationship between primary education and society. His sub-headings

Jim Campbell

were: The Social Class Aspect, The Religious Aspect, The Political Aspect, The Economic Aspect, The Cultural Aspect and The Comparative Aspect. It is a measure of his vision then, and the poverty of educational research and theory since, that, with the possible exception of the first, most aspects he identified remain only inadequately researched.

Foreword: An Enabling Man

Colin Richards

Even as skilled a craftsman as Alan Blyth would have difficulty writing this foreword. His teaching and writing have *en*abled many of us in primary education to see further, to see more widely and to see more clearly, yet the very scale and subtlety of his influence daunt, almost *dis*able, me as I try to characterize it, put it into elusive words and pin it down (an impossibility anyway as his thinking and influence continue to evolve). In attempting to assess his impact on the study of primary education, I am in danger of writing more about myself than about him — thus producing a very immodest introduction to a very modest man. That quality of his presents a very real difficulty. Since he began teaching in 1945, his work has been conducted with great modesty — appropriate to the significance and complexity of the enterprise in which he was engaged, but inappropriate in its commendable inability to recognize the value of his own contribution to the academic study of primary education. A foreword such as this cannot, should not, be modest in its appreciation, yet in *not* doing so, it runs the risk of doing injustice to a key and endearing quality of the man whom it seeks to characterize.

As a Cambridge graduate entering primary teaching in the mid-sixties, I was acutely aware of the unbelieving stance of college and friends to my taking such a 'low status job' and of the suspicion of some LEA officials that I could not seriously be contemplating staying on in that sector of the education service. But published in the same year that I began teaching was Alan's first book, *English Primary Education: A Sociological Description*. I read it. To my amazement, I found the Sydney Jones Professor of Education at the University of Liverpool taking primary education seriously, taking young children seriously, taking *my* self-chosen profession seriously. Two quotations from that book stand out: 'To regard the serious study of young children's society as trivial or puerile is a dangerous fallacy — the Lilliputian fallacy it might be called', and, 'If we do not concern ourselves with what takes place in these years, then we neglect the seed-bed of English society itself'. That seriousness is a pervading theme in all his writing, thrown into relief, paradoxically, by the lightness and playfulness of his touch (there are a multitude of examples similar in impact and insightfulness to the 'Lilliputian fallacy').

Respect for children also pervades his writing — a respect born not of sentimentality, still less with his eye to currying favour with the ultimate consumers of education, but rather rooted in his fascination with the complexities of human development, experience and their interaction and in his own values, particularly his espousal of personal autonomy. He views children neither as imperfect adults nor as soon-to-be-corrupted cherubim; he accords them respect as *developing persons* whose education should enable them to 'choose and to accept and to cope'. That enabling education has to take account of social contexts, processes and influences on children, so ably analyzed by Alan himself in his published work since the late 1950s, but also has to acknowledge that very importantly 'each individual child makes his or her own personal way, never quite smoothly, never on quite the same path as anyone else, sometimes protesting, sometimes dreaming, sometimes preoccupied with anything rather than the curriculum'. He accepts, almost celebrates, the inevitable (and even desirable?) limitations, both of primary education and its study; 'there is always more to be found out about children, however well one knows them'. Books such as *Development, Experience and Curriculum in Primary Education* illustrate the great range and depth of that 'limited' knowledge!

His work accords primary school teachers respect — by illuminating the subtle moral and social dimensions of their chosen profession, by contributing to the extension of their technical culture (through his work on curriculum planning and assessment) and by taking their development as thinking, feeling professionals seriously. It does so too, by *not* offering recipes, nostrums or ready-made prescriptions: 'schools are not places in which there are any ready answers'. It acknowledges the uniqueness of individual classrooms and schools but identifies sets of overlapping characteristics which enable practitioners to learn both from one another and from those involved in the study of primary education. He believes (both passionately and rationally) that individually and collectively teachers need to 'think deeply, systematically and reflectively' about their intentions and their practice. It was teachers' professional development that his Schools Council project (History, Geography and Social Science 8–13) sought to promote and to assist 'for their growth carries with it the promise of purposive growth for the children, development for the schools, and a social process leading to the improvement of their physical and social environments'. At times perhaps (as illustrated by his suggestions for assessment in primary humanities) he expects rather too much of hard-pressed ordinary teachers but he does so with a ready and sympathetic appreciation of each individual's imperfections and fragility (including his own).

As a young teacher, I tried to improve my classroom skills but at the same time I was curious to know more about the enterprise of primary education itself. I determined to read anything and everything that had been written about English primary education since the 1944 Education Act; I determined to become, if not the most skilled primary teacher, then the most widely read student of primary education. I soon realized the impossibility of both ambitions — a number of 'difficult' classes and Alan himself were to blame. I found, I still find, his knowledge of primary education to be encyclopaedic; he has read, reflected on and made his own virtually everything that has been written about primary education in English. Yet to characterize his knowledge as 'encyclopaedic' is in danger of belittling it.

He not only knows more about the study of primary education than the rest of us; he works on that knowledge, relating and cross-referencing its various strands and multiplicity of elements to arrive at two kinds of synoptic perspective — as befits his two-subject (history and geography) background. One perspective involves focussing on a topic — often of contemporary relevance (for example curriculum planning, assessment, or the National Curriculum), identifying and locating its various features and facets, mapping out hitherto undetected interconnections among different studies, adding personal insights and synthesizing such material into an overall, almost 'geographical' view as a basis for reflection and possible future action. In so doing he sometimes detects strengths and relevances in published work of which its authors were unaware.

Of particular, almost unique, importance is his ability to provide a historical perspective not just of primary education but of the study of education itself, drawing, in his own words, 'on prolonged, if limited, participant observation as consumer, purveyor and occasionally contributor' (for 'if limited' read 'substantial' and for 'occasionally' read 'frequently'). His own career as trainee teacher, secondary school teacher, college and university lecturer, university professor and, latterly, honorary senior fellow span the period since the 1944 Education Act formally established primary education as the first of three progressive stages in the statutory system of public education. He brings to the study of post-War educational issues, whether these be, for example, the significance of middle schools, developments in informal education, or approaches to curriculum planning and assessment, a deep, informed historical perspective, arrived at in part from his personal involvement in many of the topics he so insightfully and memorably analyzes. His synoptic views illuminate the past and give pointers to the future.

Alan, more than any other individual in England, has established and sustained the study of primary education as a legitimate area of scholarship; he has also become its first historian through his analysis of 'English primary education as a field of study: achievements and prospects'. It is clear from his own writing that he sees his work as part of a developing, increasingly autonomous, tradition of educational enquiry. Through his teaching, writing and personal contacts he has encouraged and helped many of us to contribute to that scholarly tradition. He continues to generate a wealth of ideas and tasks which practitioners in that tradition might pursue; he gives us the necessary self-confidence and optimism to believe that we 'will be able to carry those tasks forward with conspicuous success in the years that lie ahead'.

Despite my personal difficulties in writing this foreword, Alan is, and will remain, a very enabling man.

Part 1

Breadth and Balance in the National Curriculum

Chapter 1

Breadth, Balance and the National Curriculum

Norman Thomas

The title of this chapter touches on interventions by two Secretaries of State for Education and Science. Sir Keith (now Lord) Joseph spoke at the 1984 North of England Conference of the need for breadth and balance in the curriculum. Kenneth Baker steered the 1988 Education Act through the House of Commons and, with it, the establishment of a National Curriculum in England and Wales. There have been modified initiatives in Scotland and Northern Ireland. For the sake of simplicity, the rest of this chapter refers to English primary schools unless specific reference is made otherwise.

The Foundation Subjects

Breadth and balance require definition. The National Curriculum provides its own in the form of Statutory Orders. So far as primary schools are concerned, the first definition of breadth is that the curricula of all pupils (unless specially excluded) must include all of the Foundation Subjects other than a foreign language. They are English, mathematics, science, technology, history, geography, music, art, physical education, plus Welsh in some Welsh schools. Each of the subjects is, or will be, defined in terms of Attainment Targets, Statements of Attainment and Programmes of Study. The National Curriculum Council also provides 'official' but non-Statutory advice. The Council is concerned both with the legally required National Curriculum, and with the total, national curriculum, of which the National Curriculum is part.

A number of commentators have expressed dissent from the definition of the curriculum in terms of subjects. Some would prefer a description under headings such as knowledge, skills, concepts and attitudes — about the last of which the National Curriculum has little to say. Others are more attracted by a list of areas of experience such as those described by Hirst (1974) and echoed by HMI (DES, 1985) in *Curriculum Matters 2, The Curriculum from*

5–16. While the law does not direct the form of a school's timetables or the methodologies that teachers use — as is the case at the time this is being written — the choice of analytical form is probably not critical. Indeed, it is advantageous in schools to use at least two different forms of curricular analysis as a way of avoiding gaps and overlaps that occur all too easily if a single form is used. The subject tally has the advantage that many of today's teachers are familiar with it through their own school days, but the disadvantage that learning subject skills and concepts is still too often closely *and exclusively* associated with the divisions of the school day, for example, there is a presumption that children's mathematical development is something for the mathematics lesson even while accepting that mathematics should be applied during a scientific investigation. Further, a visit to a primary school at any time between 1900 and 1988 would almost certainly have revealed that much that was being done could have been parcelled out among the Foundation Subjects, leaving none empty. In addition attention would be being paid to religious education and, in a relatively small number of schools for some of the period, work in a foreign language. For the first fifty years or more of that period it would have been probable that each of the Foundation Subjects (not always under their present names or with precisely the same content) would have been represented specifically on the class timetable. I have compared elsewhere (Thomas, 1990) the changes in the curricular headings used by the Hadow Report (Board of Education, 1931), the 1967 Plowden Report (CACE 1967) and the 1988 Foundation Subjects. What is most striking is their similarity. The greatest change has been in the area of what is now called technology. In 1931 it was referred to as handicraft. In 1967 it (and more) was dealt with under the heading art and craft. Between 1931 and 1967, arithmetic and simple geometry became mathematics; and nature study became science. With a good deal of sense, Hadow singled out handwriting, which the 1967 and 1988 analyses lumped with English.

At this level of consideration, it would fly in the face of experience to suggest that the National Curriculum is so broad that primary schools, their teachers or their pupils cannot manage it. The question is: can that sanguine opinion be sustained when the National Curriculum is looked at in more detail?

Criteria for Choosing

Before going into more detail some general points need to be made, some of them by way of expanding what has already been inferred.

The advocacy of breadth and balance can be looked at from two points of view. In one way it is a call to think about what should be included in the curriculum and what place and priority various parts should have. Obversely, it is a plea to consider what should be left out. What are the criteria for choosing? Here, in a random order, is a possible list:

(i) Taken together, the things children are taught in school should broadly represent the range of experiences they have and are likely to have outside school — as far as one can foretell.

(ii) What is selected should be appropriate to the children's present levels of maturity.

(iii) Each aspect of experience should be represented sufficiently powerfully to enable a child to develop a proper confidence in participating in it at the level, at least, of an apprentice citizen. Most children will not become professional writers, mathematicians, physicists, anthropologists, musicians or sculptors, though we had better remember that some will.

(iv) It follows that what is chosen must be within the capabilities of a child who is to follow the chosen curriculum. There are two aspects to this:

   (a) each 'requirement' should, when met, be within the child's reach;

   (b) the child should be able to grasp the sum of the parts.

(v) The schools and their teachers must be able to teach what is chosen. As with the children, the requirement applies both to the separate 'items' of the curriculum and to their sum. (There is no presumption here that the whole is simply a sum of the parts). This partly questions what teachers can reasonably be expected to know (which is not the same as saying, 'what any one teacher may know'). It also questions what facilities and time the teachers and children have available for their work.

(vi) What is chosen must be regarded by society at large as commendable, or at the very least as tolerable — some desirable newcomers find entry at the 'tolerable' gate.

Readers will have noticed that I referred to the list as 'criteria for choosing'. It hardly begins the debate about what should be chosen. It does suggest some considerations to be kept in mind while debating choices and against which other people's choices, in the National Curriculum for example, can be set.

The Criteria and the National Curriculum

If we look at the way in which the detail of the National Curriculum is being formed in the light of the above criteria then some risks immediately become apparent. They are risks. They do not immediately and inevitably lead to injury.

The first in time was contained in the instructions to the Subject Working Groups. In the case of the core subjects, each Working Group was urged, in one connection or another, to take the 'good' or 'best' practice (actual or projected) as the basis for its recommendations. The Mathematics Working Group (DES, 1988b) was told to use the '1982 report (the Cockcroft Report) of the Committee of Inquiry into the teaching of mathematics in primary and secondary schools' as a starting point, and reminded that it also had HMI's discussion paper '*Mathematics from 5 to 16*'. The English Working Group (DES 1988e) was expected to 'build on' recommendations of the Kingman Committee; and the Science Working Group (DES 1988c) on the Department of Education and Science's publication, '*Science 5–16: A Statement of Policy*'. Both were recent publications. Additionally, the Science and the Mathematics Working Groups were expected to 'take account of good practice in those LEAs that have developed effective and well-founded policies for science' and the views of the main associations of teachers of the subjects. Additionally, to use the terms of reference of the English Working Group, 'it should take account of . . . best practice and the results of relevant research and curriculum developments'.

The point about all this is that the opinions and advice that the Working Groups were asked to use *as a basis for their recommendations* was itself opinion about improvements that people at the leading edge hoped that schools might achieve over some unspecified time, given support and in-service training. What was proposed for the future was not compulsory at the time it was proposed, and remained to be put to the test of practicality, both as a whole (within the subject) and in detail. Furthermore, in the National Curriculum the best, or at least the good, was to be achieved not just in English, or in mathematics, or in science, or in one or another of the Foundation Subjects as they came along, but in all of them; and the law says it *should* be done when the Statutory Instruments are established. To be best or even good at everything is not common in individual human beings or their institutions. If the Working Groups succeeded in meeting the terms of reference set by the politicians — as by and large they probably have — there was and is a certainty that virtually all schools would, to some degree, fail to meet the statutory requirements put upon them at the time of placement, and would be very unlikely to meet them ever. Schools in other countries commonly fail to meet the requirements of their national curricula, but it would be folly if the gap between aspiration and practice were wide.

A politician struggling to capture the imagination of the voters, in Parliament and outside it, might ask what else he/she could do. It is not easy to engender enthusiasm for a massive change of arrangements if what you have to offer is a slight improvement on the average. Someone running a business might have started from a different point: what is it that we do now; what is it that we wish to do; how do we move from here to there? S/he might have concluded that any changes would have to be based on an account of present practice and its variety and also have asked about any of the proposed changes (the local management of schools or the National Curriculum): what are the principal and subsidiary gains that I can expect from that initiative and what are the steps (rather than step) necessary to achieve them?

It is a tenable proposition, at the least and perhaps at the most, that the introduction of the National Curriculum would bring up towards the average those schools that had been offering an inadequate curriculum while encouraging those already adequate or better to go further. There is a hint of this in the Working Groups' terms of reference, already referred to, when it is said that what was recommended should 'leave scope for teachers to use their professional talents and skills to develop their own schemes of work, within a set framework that is known to all'. The starting points, however, are well beyond the present states of schools in the modal group — in that sense, average schools. As the studies by Bennett, Wragg and Carré (1991) have shown, primary school teachers felt and continue to feel most vulnerable with regard to technology, though interestingly their most recent survey indicates some loss of confidence in dealing with the English and mathematics orders and some gain in science.

While being urged to start from an elevated point when enunciating their requirements of schools, the Working Groups' terms of reference make it plain that the schools will have no more resources than already promised to them in their pre-National Curriculum state.

Revisions to the Statutory Orders

Given their starting points and the fact that the Working Groups were composed largely of enthusiasts for their subjects, what are the results?

In two important senses it is still too early to say, even though results of assessment have now appeared for the trial run of Key Stage 1 reporting. First, the National Curriculum is still being, and should continue to be, reviewed and adjusted. Second, whatever else they had at their disposal in the form of personal experience (not much of primary education) or research evidence, none of the Working Groups had national evidence as to what '7-year-old' children could do, especially not in the terms in which the Statements of Attainment are couched. The Working Groups, the present Secretary of State and the present Parliament cannot be blamed for the inadequate mathematical and English comprehension skills of those education correspondents who reacted to the first published results by saying that 28 per cent of 7-year-olds had failed to reach the standard expected of them. The Working Groups and the Task Group on Assessment and Testing had supposed that different 7-year-olds would reach different levels of achievement. Neither the correspondents nor Working Group members could do more than guess, beforehand, in what proportions and at what levels children would achieve in the terms prescribed in the Statutory Orders. In the light of the results and of wider experience in schools, it is as arguable that the Statements of Attainment should be changed as that work should immediately be put in hand to improve the children's performances. Both sides of that coin require examination and action.

7

The revision of Attainment Targets and Statements of Attainment that has taken place so far as mathematics and science are concerned is leading to their reduction. The history of modification up until 1991 is shown in the following table:

Table 1.1: Changes in the numbers of Attainment Targets (ATs) and Statements of Attainment (SoAs) in science and mathematics

Subject		ATs	SoAs
Science	1988	22	
	1989	17*	409
	1991	5	178
	1991	4	176
Mathematics	1988	12	
	1989	14	296
	1991	5	147
	1991	5	145

* 14 for Key Stage 1

Plainly, the argument is accepted by the National Curriculum Council, DES and Welsh Office, and the Secretaries of State, that there was too much itemized and compulsory detail in the 1989 Statutory Orders. I am in no doubt they are right: the main weakness of the National Curriculum is that it is over-itemized, even though much remains to be defined. Two techniques used to achieve reduction — identification of essential Statements of Attainment and combinations of the others — have been employed *within* science and *within* mathematics to reduce the detail. One technique identifies some items that are regarded as vital. The other combines items, an arrangement that allows teachers (and their pupils) more freedom of choice; they could, after all, satisfy the new more general item by selecting one of the parts out of which it was composed.

Taking the Revisions Further: More of the Same

Do the new proposals for the National Curriculum (as defined so far and as apparently intended) make it manageable by teachers, by children, by the schools as resourced? If not, must these techniques be taken further? Are there more techniques that could be used?

The following table shows the numbers of Attainment Targets and Statements of Attainment for six Foundation Subjects using the 1991 draft Standing Orders for Science and Mathematics and existing Statutory Orders for the others:

Table 1.2: *Statements of Attainment within each Attainment Target for six of the subjects of the National Curriculum, Levels 1 to 6 only*

AT:	1	2	3	4	5	Total
English	25	30	25	12	12	104
Mathematics	19	24	13	20	19	95
Science	17	22	23	33	*	95
Technology	18	20	23	18	24	103
History	17	6	6	*	*	29
Geography	28	28	23	26	15	*120*
Grand total to Level 6						*546*

* no AT in this subject

It is likely that a teacher wholly and singly responsible for a class containing year 5 children will have to be conscious of all of these Statements of Attainment (and those related to the other three/four subjects) in the course of his/her daily work. Even supposing that, as may well be the case, no children in Key Stage 2 in a school go beyond Level 5, the teacher should be aware of what the next step is. A teacher taking the older age groups in a two- or three-teacher school will certainly have to carry them in mind — or, at least, is being expected to do so by the law of the land; is expected to arrange work that will encompass them all for, probably, between 20 and 30+ disparate children; and to assess how well children have responded.

A cursory glance at table 1.2 suggests where first it might be worth looking for further reductions: English, geography and technology each make more than 100 demands. It would be rash to suppose immediately that their demands should be reduced, or that they are more easily trimmed than other subjects with fewer Statements of Attainment. Nevertheless, their apparent gluttony invites investigation.

It is not within the scope either of the present writer or this chapter to propose what a detailed redefinition of the National Curriculum should be. The examples that follow are included merely to illustrate a methodology for reducing the itemization. Individually the examples may well be contentious and require further debate.

Could the two techniques for reduction already identified — identification of the essential and conflation within a subject — be usefully applied to other subjects? The first, the identification of what is essential as it now stands, needs closer examination. What is meant by 'essential'? The obvious response is that the item is vital to children's further learning: it is one of a complex of items that together form a vital aspect of knowledge (including 'knowing how to') if a child is to operate reasonably effectively in his/her present circumstances and eventually as an adult citizen.

There is something else that should be borne in mind: no matter how useful, is the item something that need not be dealt with at school because there can be every expectation that it will be learnt outside? For example, many would regard it as essential to know how to turn on a television set or, if they live in Tottenham, that the local professional football team is Tottenham Hotspur and when its first team is playing at home. Whether they wish to go to the match on Saturday or avoid the High Street at about 5 pm, having the information may often affect their behaviour. Yet I doubt whether many advocates could be found for including the name of the local football team and its fixture list in the National Curriculum. Nor would parents expect to find a Statement of Attainment about turning on television sets. School is not a necessary, let alone an essential, medium for that learning.

How does being able to 'recognize rocks, soil and water and understand that they are part of the environment' (Geography AT3, Level 1) measure up to being essential in that sense.? Does anyone really suppose that the vast mass of children of 5, 6 or 7 will not be able to distinguish, by observation and in words, water from rock and soil? If the point is that they should be able to distinguish rock from soil, what is the nature of the distinction that is necessary at this stage and could not be picked up in passing at some later time? One has the impression that a conscientious Working Party felt that it ought to be filling an otherwise empty space in its tables of Attainment Targets. If that is all there is to say about physical geography at Level 1, why say anything? The other 'odd one out' in the same Attainment Target in Levels 1 to 3 is that children should describe a *familiar* landscape feature. The rest are concerned with the weather and, particularly, rain. There is hardly more to say for the whole of Key Stage 1 in this Attainment Target than:

Level 2 — Children's awareness of static and changing features in their local environment should be heightened, especially of the weather.
Level 3 — Children should know that these features differ from place to place.

There is, of course, a fundamental geographical notion on which Key Stage 1 teachers spend much effort but which is not sufficiently recognized in the National Curriculum at that Stage. It is the notion that place affects activity, and vice versa. The layout of the nursery or KS. 1 teaching area is, in a real sense, a simulation of a varied geographical region. It is one of the signs of a university-down approach to the National Curriculum that is not recognized and that the associated teaching time is not recognized, sometimes being referred to as part of the non-professional chores.

Taking the Revisions Further: Additional Techniques

But hold. The need to group materials according to observable features is already referred to in the new Science Attainment Target 3, Level 2. Furthermore, Level 3 calls for knowing that some materials occur naturally. The associated Programme of Study refers to rocks, soil and water. In Science Attainment Target 4, the Programme of Study requires the observation of the 'local natural environment' to detect seasonal and weather changes and for children to 'relate these to the passage of time'. And what about the new Mathematics Attainment Target 5? Level 1 includes: 'selecting criteria for sorting a set of objects and applying them consistently', and level 2 requires children 'to interpret data which has been collected' by the children; and an illustration in Level 3 suggests handling weather statistics. The fundamental ideas are that

- children should be able to differentiate between materials using two or more criteria such as colour, shape, texture, size, weight — in other words directly observable and directly measurable characteristics;
- they should recognize that some aspects of our circumstances are more changeable and/or more local than others.

There is clearly a need to add to the list of techniques for the reduction of the Statutory Orders by eliminating repetition across subjects. There should be some rationale for choosing where to place items, and perhaps it is here that the notion of the core subjects could be useful: wherever there is uncertainty about placement as between the core and the other Foundation Subjects, the former should be used, though reference across subjects might appear.

In the new, draft Orders, the Programmes of Study have been printed beside the Statements of Attainment. That has straightforward advantages for teachers using the materials, but it also raises more sharply the place and function of the non-Statutory advice. So as to avoid confusion about the requirements upon schools and to allow the easy development of new and more apposite examples, there are good grounds for publishing non-Statutory guidance separately from the Statutory orders. Now that the first rush is over and some illustrative material has been given to make meaning clearer, it might be sensible to let the educational publishers recover their traditional role and take the responsibility for producing illustrative material from which teachers can choose.

To sum up so far. There is room, maybe plenty of room still, for the items within the National Curriculum to be reduced still further and made to look more manageable to teachers. Six ways are:

(i)   identify and keep Statements of Attainment that are regarded as essential in their present form;

(ii)   either (a) omit Statements of Attainment that are not essential;[1]

(iii)   or, (b) combine them with others to cover a more general field that is essential;

(iv)   allow none to appear twice, but provide references across subjects where necessary;

     (v)   whenever in doubt, place the main reference in a core-subject Order;

    (vi)   publish the non-statutory illustrations under separate cover, but clearly referenced.

So far as the last is concerned, it is important to be sure that teachers are given great encouragement to use local examples as illustrations of more general ideas or historical movements. The issue of relevance continues to be important.

Could Teachers Manage a Streamlined National Curriculum?

If the reduction in Attainment Targets and Statements of Attainment in Science and Mathematics are any guide — and they may not be good bases for forecasting — then it might be possible to reduce the Statements of Attainment to between 40 and 50 per cent overall in other subjects; still a large number and, in sum, demanding considerable knowledge across a wide field from teachers. However many there are, they will continue to be the basis for assessment and, for the foreseeable future, the coinage for recording and reporting. The great volume of uneconomic effort required for such *universal* detail in recording and reporting will continue to be a drag on teaching time.

It is difficult to resist the conclusion that the fifth criterion above for choosing curricular items is not being and will not be met if we assume, for the time being at least, that a teacher is expected, alone, to manage not only each item, but also their sum: the National Curriculum, even allowing for intended amendments, contains more than an individual teacher should be expected to manage, certainly at the end of Key Stage 2. It must be remembered that a typical teacher in a secondary school will usually have to be concerned with the Statements of Attainment in only one, rarely more than two, subjects.

It would make no difference to the total load if each subject were taught separately rather than through topics. Each form of organizing the work has its advantages and disadvantages — like most forms of organization, neither should be treated as though it were a matter of principle. In both, the disadvantages increase as the form is taken towards the extreme. If too much is attempted via general topics either important elements get neglected, or tenuous and even absurd links are made to secure their presence. If a rigid subject division is manufactured, especially if each is taught by a different teacher, then overlap can be wastefully included or, once again, items can be missed because they are assumed to be covered elsewhere — faults that are easier to put right in a national analysis, as with the Foundation Subjects' Orders, than they are in daily practice in a school; perhaps even worse, the advantages can be lost of using examples from one field to illuminate and extend concepts in another.

If there is a solution for the teachers, then it must be that there are more to share the load and that arrangements can be made for sharing. That implies some degree of specialism with teachers in a school working together, supporting each other, and sometimes teaching children in other classes than their own. No form of organization is faultless. If the worst dangers are to be avoided, a teacher should be responsible for coordinating the work of the class as a whole and for teaching as much of it as he/she can. The case has been discussed many times. The extremes of splitting the curriculum into separate subjects, even the Foundation Subjects, and making a different teacher responsible for each is not advantageous for primary school children, especially the younger children. Nor is that a practice available to primary schools as they are presently staffed. Either they are too small, as the majority are, to employ 9 or 10 teachers; or the the number of teachers is too close to the number of classes to make the shifts between teachers and classes possible; or both. Something between the simple class-teacher system and the subject-teacher system is required. The issue has been written about many times before (for example, Campbell, 1985, House of Commons, 1986) and there is neither the need nor the room to go into it again here. Suffice to say that even this requires a class: teacher ratio closer to the 1:1.4 of secondary schools than the 1:1.17 of primary schools.

The three elements to be considered in (teacher) staffing standards are the number of teachers, the number of children and the number of classes. The common ratios used have been the numbers of children in a class (class size) and the number of teachers in relation to the number of children (teacher: pupil ratio). The third relationship, class:teacher ratio, was discussed by Edward Simpson in an address reported in *Assessing the National Curriculum: From Practice to Policy, Report of 1989*, (Campbell, 1989), and by me in *Primary Education from Plowden to the 1990s*, (Thomas, 1990). The ratio is a valuable operating ratio. It presumes a view about the likely size of a class but it is not intended to preempt decision at school level about how best to arrange either classes or staffing. Edward Simpson was previously the Deputy Secretary with responsibility for teacher training, inter alia, at the DES. The alternative is to reduce the requirements of the curriculum to the point where a single teacher is able to teach it all. I have deliberately not said a typical or normal teacher. The question that has to be faced is: is it so important that a child in Key Stage 1 or Key Stage 2 has only one teacher that that should be the limiting factor for the curriculum? The answer to that question must satisfy numbers 1, 2, 3 and 4 of the criteria for choosing, as well as criterion 6.

A Reduced Curriculum and the Children

If no child in a class is permitted to do more than the teacher can support through teaching, the dilemma disappears. I said, earlier, that no one had or yet has secure knowledge as to what children generally can do in terms of the

National Curriculum. We do not know what proportions of children of 11 at
the end of Key Stage 2 might reach level 3 or 4 or 5 or more in any of the
Attainment Targets in any of the subjects. What I, and I dare say many
others, can say is that we have met children of that age who can 'use estima-
tion to check calculations' (Maths AT2, Level 6), or 'understand the relationship between speed, distance and time' (Science AT4, Level 6), or 'describe
the different ideas and attitudes of people in an historical situation' (History,
AT2, Level 6), or 'explain the effect of recent changes on the home region'
(Geography, AT2, Level 6), or 'use knowledge of technical and symbolic
representations of materials, components and processes to assist making'
(Technology, AT3, Level 6). Add to these:

> the range and perception of art on which the National Curriculum
>   Working Party based its recommendations;
> the extensive view of physical education proposed;
> the variety of requirements in music;
> and the demands of the cross-curricular themes,

and the gap between the possibilities for the children and what might reasonably be expected of any one teacher increases well beyond the tolerable.

Changing from a consideration of what a teacher can be expected to
teach to what some children might be expected to learn brings to the fore
another argument for reducing the number of items in the National Curriculum. As was indicated earlier, one of the consequences of combining two or
more Statements of Attainment allows the possibility that one of the previous elements can be taken up and the other passed over. The scope for
option may allow a child to go further than he/she would if every stone must
be turned. The simplest parallel from within primary schools concerns the
teaching of reading. Some schools have amassed collections of graded readers
and insisted that every child reads through every one of the books at each
grade before going on to any in the later grades. For some children for some
of the time that might just be a sensible practice. It is undoubtedly not sensible for all of the children for all of the time.

Breadth, Depth and Precision

The critical questions are: how far can the first series of Statements of Attainment be conflated before:

(i)   the curriculum definition becomes too vague to be useful;
(ii) the curriculum as presented fails to represent the range of know-
      ledge and experiences that children need and will need to conduct
      their lives within the wider community?

There is no simple rule of thumb, but one safeguard is provided by the structure that combines Statements of Attainment vertically into Attainment Targets and Attainment Targets horizontally into Foundation Subjects. The necessary coverage of examples, which has implications for breadth and balance, might more easily be secured if the core subjects were the English language, mathematics, science, society[2], the arts, and personal health — with history, geography, literature, technology, art, music, dance and physical education being illustrative subjects. We are a long way, politically, from such a pattern, and it is hardly worth developing an argument for it.

In the meantime, we should recognize the value of retaining broad categories such as the Foundation Subjects. Be conscious that they are man-made and imperfect and that some important and cohesive aspects of learning such as economic and industrial awareness or health education cross the boundaries — they are cross-subject rather than cross-curricular. We should be parsimonious in legislating what, specifically, the children should be taught, but continue to require that no significant aspect of human experience is omitted simply because of poor resourcing, the inaccessibility of a teacher with the competence, or the temporary disinclination of the child. We should allow space for using a child's interests, a teacher's expertise and knowledge, and local opportunities especially so that children can learn more than the law requires.

Conclusion

The question is: is the National Curriculum broad and balanced? Perhaps the question ought to be: is its range and scale suited to its purpose? The analogy is with mapping. To produce a sheet that can be handled, the larger the area covered the smaller the scale of the map and the less detail it is possible to include if it is to be comprehensible. If I want to learn where Leeds is in the United Kingdom I do not begin my search by leafing through the Ordnance large-scale Seventh Series Maps, with a scale of about 1:63,000. Nor would a world map be any good at about 1:78,000,000. I need something between-a scale of about 1:30,000,000. On the other hand, when I get to Leeds I shall want a map closer to 1:18,000 if I am to find the address I want. The National Curriculum map covers, reasonably well, the territory it needs to cover. The detail currently included is too great for comprehensibility and intelligent use. Even when it is reduced as far as it should be, the demand on a teacher of year 4, 5 or 6 children to interpret it will be too great. On the other hand, there will be a significant number of children ready and able to go further than expected. The solution of simple subject specialist teaching in the secondary school sense is unnecessarily crude and reduces the possibility of adapting teaching to children's actual learning requirements. The decision when to introduce a teacher additional to the class teacher is a pragmatic matter: it should be taken when the class teacher is unable to meet a curricular demand,

and for that purpose. If the achievements of the children are to be increased significantly, the class: teacher ratio in primary schools must be increased to much the same level as in the first five years of secondary schools.

Notes

1 I have travelled about England more than most by car, train and aeroplane. In seventy years I can only twice remember finding it helpful to use a six-figure map reference (Geography AT. 1/L4, four-figure coordinates; L5, six figure coordinates), and those were when directions were given by a geography specialist. The use of map referencing would be more useful as a non-statutory illustration of the use of coordinates than as a Statement of Attainment. If a child understands the principles of coordinates well enough, the application to map reading is not likely to cause difficulty.
2 'Society' would include history and what is sometimes called human geography and also the teaching that Key Stage 1 teachers spend much time and effort on, namely, teaching children to live and work in a larger community than the family.

References

BENNETT, N., WRAGG, E. and CARRÉ, C. (1991) 'Primary teachers and the National Curriculum', *Junior Education*, 15, 11, November.

BOARD OF EDUCATION (1931) *Report of the Consultative Committee on The Primary School* (The Hadow Report) London, HMSO.

CAMPBELL, R.J. (1985) *Developing the Primary School Curriculum*, London, Holt Rinehart & Winston.

CAMPBELL, R.J. (1989) *Assessing the National Curriculum: From Practice to Policy*, Leamington Spa, Scholastic Publications.

CENTRAL ADVISORY COUNCIL FOR EDUCATION (1967) *Children and their Primary Schools* (The Plowden Report) London, HMSO (2 volumes).

DES (1985) *Curriculum Matters 2, The Curriculum from 5–16*, London, HMSO.

DES (1988a) *English for Ages 5–11*, London, HMSO.

DES (1988b) *Mathematics for Ages 5–16*, London, HMSO.

DES (1988c) *Science for Ages 5–16*, London, HMSO.

HIRST, P.H. (1974) *Knowledge and the Curriculum*, London, Routledge & Kegan Paul.

HOUSE OF COMMONS EDUCATION, SCIENCE AND ARTS COMMITTEE (1986) *Achievement in Primary Schools*, Third Report, Session 1985–86, HC. 40-1, Volume 1, London, HMSO.

THOMAS, N. (1990) *Primary Education from Plowden to the 1990s*, Lewes, Falmer Press.

Chapter 2

A Dream at Conception:
A Nightmare at Delivery

Jim Campbell

Introduction

For anyone attempting to understand the curriculum of the primary school in the period from 1944 up to the early 1990s, the *locus classicus* is Alan Blyth's *English Primary Education*, Vol. 2, pages 20–43 (Blyth, 1965). In a few lucid pages, and without any of the jargon that has marred much sociological writing about education since, he analysed the ideologies ('traditions' as he called them, with proper respect for the history of education) competing to dominate curriculum thinking and practice.

Blyth identified three traditions: the elementary, the preparatory and the developmental. The elementary had its roots in the latter decades of the last century, concentrating narrowly upon the basic skills of number, reading and writing, topped up with some religious instruction. The social function of the primary curriculum in this tradition was, or is, to ensure functional literacy, minimum arithmetical competence and moral docility. Gradgrind was its icon, and histories of education portray its popularity. The elementary tradition, however, is not a thing of the past; its ghost rattles still in think-tanks of the New Right. Letwin (1988), for example, argued that the state should be entitled to impose only a basic 'grounding' of literacy and numeracy upon pupils, but that the grounding itself, being the key that unlocks the rest of the curriculum, was so important that even the neo-liberal mind had to accept that it could not be left to the market. More generally, the tradition survives in the high priority given in primary schools to literacy and numeracy at the expense of other areas (Alexander, 1984). It found expression in a DES discussion paper (Alexander *et al*, 1992): 'Whatever else they do, primary schools must get their policies and practices right for teaching the basic skills of literacy and numeracy' (para. 50).

The second tradition is one in which the primary curriculum is mainly an anticipatory socialization device for the secondary school. Through it the pupils are prepared to meet the requirements of the secondary school curriculum, irrespective of its appropriateness to their needs and developmental stages. Its historical model is the English preparatory school 'serving' a public school, but a contemporary critique by one of the contributors to this book (see Kelly, 1990), suggests that it is the dominant model underlying the National Curriculum. The National Curriculum in this interpretation imposes an alien requirement on the primary school curriculum to adapt to the subject frame of the secondary school and beyond that to the requirements of the economy. Penetrating right down the age range it has led to contemporary infant children being taught history, geography and science and technology in preparation for the secondary curriculum, even though some teachers and heads think it might be adversely affecting standards in literacy at Key Stage 1, (DES, 1991a; Campbell *et al*, 1991; Alexander *et al*, 1992).

The third tradition concentrates upon the alleged developmental needs of children, rather than those alleged to be the needs of society or the next school stage. Although epitomized by the Plowden Report (CACE, 1967) it has a long tradition generated in the practice of private or independent schools, according to the analysis by Skidelsky (1967). Often characterized by a romantic interpretation of childhood combined with a simplistic reading of Piaget, the developmental tradition in the 1970s and 1980s was designated 'child-centred' or 'progressive'. In this tradition, curriculum practice draws on children's interests as a starting point for learning, encourages 'discovery' learning, celebrates the significance of first-hand experience, and gives high priority to the expressive arts. The developmental tradition has provided the foundation for contemporary definitions of 'good practice', especially in the early years of primary education, (see Pascall *et al*, 1989; Campbell and David, 1989; Alexander, 1992; David *et al*, 1992). It appears to have influenced the thinking of the working groups set up to formulate the subjects in the National Curriculum in which pupils' investigations, choices and definitions have considerable significance. Examples are in the programmes of study, and the ATs numbered 1, in mathematics, science and technology.

The basic ideological analysis of Blyth has been developed in alternative and more sophisticated versions. Richards (1986) usefully added 'liberal pragmatism' in order to recognize an approach, often associated with HMI (for example, DES, 1985a), in which the ideals of classical humanism were tempered by the realities of school context and provision. Blyth himself (1984) sought to unite elements of the differing traditions into an ambitious analysis combining, or matching, the needs of the curriculum with the development of children and their social experience. These advances have helped draw attention to the ways the three traditions mingle in classroom practice and curriculum policy alike. Their values and purposes conflict, but the primary curriculum, whether framed in policy or realized in schools, embodies elements of them all. It is the ***emphasis*** upon one or other tradition where the distinction lies, and political contention has developed.

The Promotion of the Broad and Balanced Curriculum

I have argued elsewhere (Campbell, 1989) that, compared to the curriculum for secondary schools, the primary curriculum in the period from 1944 until the mid-1980s suffered from a policy vacuum. This vacuum was filled by the sub-texts of a series of surveys, discussion papers and other documents written by Her Majesty's Inspectorate. I accept that, technically, HMI do not *make* policy, (Raynor Report, 1982). An important and consistent part of the argument and evidence presented in this series was that the primary curriculum needed to be broadened. *Primary Education in England* (DES, 1978) had claimed that practice was dominated by a narrow emphasis on basic skills, and that standards were higher in classes where skills were applied to practical tasks across a broader curriculum.

A cause and effect relationship was implied, though not demonstrated; the broad curriculum was the cause and higher standards were the effect. The possibility that the association was the reverse — that teachers with high achieving pupils would feel free to broaden the curriculum, whereas those with low achievers would concentrate narrowly on the basic skills — was not raised. A similar position was taken in later surveys of first and middle schools (DES, 1982 and 1985b). The picture from HMI surveys was consistent with findings from researchers (Bennett, 1976; Bealing, 1972; Galton and Simon, 1980; Barker-Lunn, 1982 and 1984) that teaching concentrating narrowly on the basics was the typical approach. Next, in a series of influential discussion papers known as the Curriculum Matters series, and especially in *Curriculum Matters 2: The Curriculum from 5–16* (DES, 1985a), the argument for the broad and balanced curriculum was most forcefully raised. Although presented as discussion papers, their explicit aim was the creation of 'broad agreement about the objectives of the curriculum'.

The Inspectorate's attempts to quantify the curriculum in primary schools have been bedevilled by definitional problems, but the quantitative picture provided by the 8–12 survey (DES, 1985b) and the Primary Staffing Survey (DES, 1987) was consistent with other studies. They showed some 40–45 per cent of time given over to language and mathematics, about 10 per cent each for history/geography or topic, PE and art/craft, leaving about 25 per cent of the week for science, technology, music, RE and anything else. The broad brush picture confirmed the findings of the 1978 survey, that the heavy emphasis on basic skills meant too little time being available for the rest of the curriculum. The underlying assumption that the curriculum should be broadened was thus explicitly linked to the notion of balance. If the curriculum was to comprise the 'nine areas of learning and experience' promoted in the Curriculum Matters series (DES, 1985a), it could not continue to provide only token amounts of time for the scientific, technological, social and aesthetic areas. To do so would be to leave the curriculum unbalanced, i.e., weighted too heavily towards literacy and numeracy.

It is difficult to read these documents from the Inspectorate as anything else than a deliberate attempt to redefine the basics of primary education (see Richards, 1986), to provide the grounds for arguing that a curriculum that did not make adequate provision in all nine areas was deficient.

After 1985 the political pressure for a broad and balanced curriculum intensified. The House of Commons Select Committee 3rd Report (House of Commons, 1986) made the case for an entitlement to a common curriculum with formal responsibility for it being placed unambiguously in the hands of the Secretary of State. The 1988 Education Act required a 'balanced and broadly based curriculum' and Circular 5/89 (DES, 1989c) emphasized breadth and balance (p. 17), requiring from August 1989 that each core and foundation subject should be allocated 'reasonable' time for worthwhile study. Over the next four years, the various working groups proposed the details of syllabus (programmes of study) and the graded criteria (Attainment Targets and Statements of Attainment) for assessment. As they became serially statutory, the broad and balanced curriculum began to be established in practice.

The Failure of Resistance

Resistance to the National Curriculum at Key Stages 1 and 2 was multidirectional, short-lived and in the main politically motivated. Those hoping for a narrow specification in the elementary tradition (for example, Lawlor 1988; Letwin, 1988; IEA quoted in Haviland 1988, pp. 28–9) were disappointed, but the distinction between the core subjects and the other foundation subjects, with the former only being statutorily assessed, may have gone some way towards defusing any serious conflict.

Initial opposition within the teacher associations was quickly overturned into motions of approval or acceptance of the National Curriculum at annual conferences in 1990 and 1991. Egalitarian analysts (for example, Lawton, 1988; White, 1988) critical both of the accretion of central control and the dangers of an assessment-led curriculum, found themselves hoist with their own curricular petard. For it was egalitarians who, in effect, had been pushing for a common curriculum and now had to seek refuge in the distinction between 'a' and 'the' National Curriculum. Much egalitarian analysis shifted towards the impact of market forces and grant-maintained status, with the possibility of their leading to a three-or two-tier system, (for example, Tomlinson, 1986).

There were, of course, substantive analytical critiques of the appropriateness and worthwhileness of the nine subject frame as a model (for example, Kelly, 1990), and the validity of the cognitive hierarchy built into the levels of attainment (for example, Schwarzenberger, 1989), and the nature of the content balance, especially in history, music and art. Moreover, the consideration about how the nine subjects might cohere in relation to each other was sketchy (see Thomas in this volume). There were also concerns about serious apparent omissions, and the relegation of some important objectives to the status of cross-curricular themes (see Ross in this volume). There were widespread doubts about the seriousness with which the interests of children with special needs had been catered for (see Lewis, 1991). Many of these issues are raised in other contributions to this book. Nonetheless, in comparison to the typical curriculum practice in primary schools before 1988, the new conception of the primary curriculum as needing to be broad and balanced, with common objectives for all children, was a dream.

The Character of the Dream

There were five features of the proposed broad and balanced curriculum that proved seductive to most of those working in primary education.

First, there was the concept of entitlement. Articulated most clearly in the House of Commons 3rd Report (House of Commons, 1986), a broad and balanced curriculum would provide a legal framework of common entitlement for children that would remove the inconsistencies of curriculum provision (see Richards, 1982), which had arisen arbitrarily from class teacher autonomy. For the first time since 1944 pupils and parents would be able to know what the school should provide in curriculum terms. It was, of course, coupled with the establishment of a complaints procedure, to be used if the curricular provision was considered inadequate and so helped introduce consumer interests into primary education. But it, nonetheless, promised greater equality of curricular experience for children.

Second, and linked to the concept of entitlement, was the promise of real breadth. A statutory curriculum in which all foundation subjects, not just the core, would be allocated reasonable amounts of time and emphasis seemed to offer a once-and-for-all opportunity to destroy the elementary curriculum whose persistence, noted by Alexander (1984), had remarkably survived the previous non-statutory discouragement of HMI and others.

Third, included in the legal definition of the curriculum, was a set of assessment arrangements which would require a radical rethinking not merely of assessment but also of teaching itself. The TGAT report (DES, 1988) was sold to the profession by its emphasis on the formative purposes of assessment, most clearly articulated by Shipman (1983). Before 1988, most assessment in primary schools had employed narrowly focussed tests of reading comprehension and number, predominantly at the end of the infant and junior stages, (see Gipps, 1988 and 1990). The TGAT report went as far as to separate out conceptually assessment from testing and proposed that the former should replace the latter.

On this model, continuous assessment would involve diagnosing individual pupils' needs through observing them learning, talking with them about their learning and using the observations for planning the next steps in learning.

Its appeal to the value-system of the developmentalists was obvious and immediate (for example, Smith, 1991).

Fourth, it was a modernizing curriculum. It was not merely that science was included in the core but that the kind of science involved acknowledged advances in biology, physics and chemistry; technology, including information technology, was in the foundation; mathematics included the handling of data, and most other subjects called for applications using computers. English called for literature that was global. The broad and balanced criterion had been used not simply to attack the narrow focus on the basics but also to haul the primary curriculum into a state of relevance to knowledge and information processing in the latter decade of the twentieth century.

Finally, there was the relationship of the curriculum to standards. Primary education in England and Wales had been characterized by relatively low standards, especially in relation to children judged to be able (DES, 1978 and 1990; Alexander *et al*, 1992). The common and facile explanation for this state of affairs was that teacher expectations were too low, especially in inner cities and other areas of poverty. Following a series of important observational studies at the University of Exeter (Bennett *et al*, 1984; Bennett and Dunne 1992; Bennett, 1991 and 1992), the demonstration of poor match between tasks set by teachers and pupil capacities (or, to be precise, sometimes poor pupil understanding of the task) lent force to the argument that the broad and balanced curriculum would lead to raised standards in two ways. First, expectations of able children would be raised through the explicitly differentiated levels in which the attainment targets would be specified. Able children at the end of Key Stage 1 would be operating at Levels 3 or 4, and at the end of Key Stage 2 at Levels 5 or 6. Secondly, standards would be raised simply by virtue of teaching being planned, delivered and assessed, often for the first time, according to systematic programmes of study and set targets right across the nine subject areas. Standards would no longer be defined mainly by reference to English and mathematics.

Thus the promotion of the broad and balanced criterion held out the promise of a radical transformation of the primary curriculum. Its promise crossed ideological boundaries. To the preparatory tradition it offered a common entitlement, consistent from 5 through to 16, to a broad and aggressively modern curriculum. The curriculum was to be integrated with a developmentally focussed assessment system, and key demands in the core subjects, (ATs 1 in science, mathematics and English), were concerned with processes. Previously neglected subjects such as history and geography had to be given a suitable place, and new subjects and material such as technology and information technology were also incorporated. Even those in the dismissed elementary tradition could cast fond eyes on the end-of-Key Stage statutory assessment tasks focussed on the basics (though these now included science) which thereby gave them highest priority. As a conception of the curriculum for contemporary primary schools at the end of the twentieth century it was a dream package.

Delivering the Broad and Balanced Curriculum:
The Emerging Nightmare

The evidence about what it was like to be delivering the National Curriculun was, in 1992, patchy and suggestive rather than comprehensive and certain, not least because the published evidence related to the introduction of the statutory orders for the core subjects only. There were surveys by HMI (DES, 1989a, 1989b, 1990a and 1991a) and research reports on the early implementation stages (Campbell and Neill, 1990; Silcock, 1990; Campbell *et al*, 1991; Coopers and Lybrand Deloitte, 1991; Core Subject Association, 1991; NUT, 1991; Osborn and Pollard, 1991; Osborn and Broadfoot, 1991; Taylor and Stanley, 1991; Acker 1992; Muschamp *et al*, 1992; NCC, 1992). But what evidence there was suggested that, for classteachers, delivering the broad and balanced curriculum had become, or would become, not a dream but a nightmare. It was simply not manageable even for experienced and able teachers. The reasons for believing this are different at Key Stage 1 and Key Stage 2, mainly because the empirical evidence refers to the former only. The problems, and possible solutions, need to be considered separately for each Key Stage.

Key Stage 1

At Key Stage 1 there appear to be four clusters of problem.

First, evidence from the Teaching as Work project at the University of Warwick, (Campbell and Neill, 1990; Campbell *et al*, 1991) showed conscientious teachers committed to implementing the curriculum but having to work unreasonably long hours combined, in their view, with intense pressure during the school day. One teacher caught the perceptions of most others by her use of the metaphor of a 'Running Commentary':

> Well, what is frightening now is that we are being blinkered now into the National Curriculum ... I am noticing it far more now that I never complete what I hope to achieve. There is always, like, a carry-forward so that you never get the feeling at the end of a session or day, 'Great, I've done this that I hoped we would do' ... there is this Running Commentary, really, in the background saying that, 'You haven't done this' or 'You haven't done that', which I find very annoying considering that you work so hard. (Campbell *et al*, 1991, para. 2.14)

Delivering the curriculum was seen as an enervating treadmill in which the teachers worked very hard but obtained little sense of achievement. The overload had carried over into their personal and domestic lives and most of the teachers were experiencing stress. Evidence from the PACE project at Bristol (Osborn and Pollard, 1991; Osborn and Broadfoot, 1991) and from the Core Subject Association (CSA, 1991) supported this view.

Second, and despite all this, the broad and balanced curriculum was not being delivered. Our evidence (Campbell *et al*, 1991) showed that the three core subjects were taking, on average, at least half the timetabled time and, at the very most, about fifteen minutes a day was left for each of the other foundation subjects and RE. Most of these subjects at Key Stage 1 are practical, time-consuming activities, for example, art, PE, music and technology fifteen minutes per day (seventy-five minutes a week) seems inadequate for full treatment. The core was squeezing out the other parts of the basic curriculum. This view was supported by Muschamp *et al* (1992). At the same time and, paradoxically, teachers claimed to be spending less time hearing children read so as to cover the new subjects such as technology, and manage assessment. This was also reported in Alexander *et al* (1992).

Third, the formative purposes of assessment had been subverted by the pressure to provide accurate and fair end-of-Key Stage results for summative purposes, though part of the problem was the inability of teachers to internalize the integration of teaching and assessment (Harlen and Qualter, 1991). Confusion over the expectations for assessment and record-keeping, allied to a fear of inspection and accountability, had led to the teachers abandoning formative perspectives in fearful and frantic attempts to get summative results 'right', whatever that meant. The publication of LEA 'league tables' towards the end of 1991 did little to allay the pressure on teachers to concentrate on the summative.

The picture emerging from our research was supported, or not contradicted, by other early studies (for example, DES, 1991b; Taylor and Stanley, 1991; Smithers and Zientek, 1991; Coopers and Lybrand Deloitte, 1991). It shows, despite the commitment of hard-pressed teachers, that the curriculum at Key Stage 1 in 1990/91 had few of the features of the dream package: it was not providing the entitlement to breadth and balance, assessment was not integrated diagnostically into teaching, and if it was being modernized it might be at the expense of the rate of progress in pupils' achievement in reading.

It has been argued (Alexander *et al*, 1992) that this analysis is both misdirected and premature. It is misdirected because counting the time available is less important than how available time is used. High quality learning experience in small amounts of time is better than low quality in adequate time. Moreover, this early research picture might be a 'blip' created by novelty and uncertainty. Although there is some truth in both points, neither would lead automatically to the view that the whole curriculum will at some time in the medium-term future become more manageable. The high quality time argument only makes sense within an overall framework of adequate time and it is this that is in question. The blip argument would be more convincing if:

(i)   the arrangements for curriculum and assessment were not being subject to continual change;

(ii)   the whole broad and balanced curriculum was already in place in 1990/91, the period to which the evidence refers. It was not, and since the following two years would see further subjects in statutory form brought on stream, problems of manageability had yet to reach their peak.

Key Stage 2

The argument about unmanageability at Key Stage 2 is based on task analysis rather than empirical evidence since little of the latter is yet available. There are three elements here: the nature of the task facing the teacher, the expertise in the system, and the support available. Thomas (in this volume) provides one analysis of the task facing the teacher, even in a slimmed down version of the National Curriculum. With over 500 statements of attainment to manipulate, detailed and confusingly presented programmes of study, poorly defined cross-curricular themes and religious education, the tasks demanded of classteachers are realizable only by Renaissance men and women. In this perspective, the assertion (Alexander *et al*, 1992) that, 'Teachers must possess the subject knowledge which the statutory orders require' (para. 120), begins to sound like a plea of desperation.

Secondly, there are few Renaissance men and women in the primary teaching force. The Primary Staffing Survey (DES, 1987) found fewer teachers qualified as main subject Mathematics teachers than there were schools and, even using the most generous definition of qualification, only 400 teachers in the system qualified in technology. The study by Bennett (1992) showed serious problems of perceived competence and confidence to teach and assess many foundation subjects, especially technology. Evidence about standards in a number of the subjects such as history and geography, (for example, DES, 1978 and 1989), and in activities set in art lessons (for example, Alexander, 1992) should not lead us to be sanguine about confidence and competence in other subjects.

Thirdly, the infrastructure of support for in-service training that might have helped bridge some of the gap between the task demands and the competencies of the teachers has been eroded (see Keep, 1992, for a fuller analysis). Thus, classteachers at Key Stage 2, and especially in the latter two years of it, are facing statutory obligations that they cannot, even with high levels of commitment and effort, meet, because hardly any individual teacher has the range and depth of knowledge required. In years 5 and 6, where the range of performance within a class in each of the nine subjects is expected to be at least from Level 2 to Level 5 or 6 in each of the nine subjects of the National Curriculum, the classteacher's task of delivering the broad and balanced curriculum looks dramatically impossible.

Discussion

This nightmare at Key Stage 2 has been recognized obliquely (Alexander *et al*, 1992) and four solutions have been proposed. The first, in Alexander *et al* (1992), is that there should be greater flexibility in staff roles, with greater use of specialist, semi-specialist and coordinator roles, especially at the top end of Key Stage 2. This would make more use of existing specialized curricular expertise within a staff group. The problem with this idea is that coordinator roles were developed (Campbell, 1985 and 1988) in some schools with great difficulty but limited success, given the lack of non-contact time. The use of specialist or semi-specialist teaching, even if in a limited form, cannot be adopted except where schools have more non-contact time. In any case, for the one in five small schools (with ninety or fewer pupils) in the system the options for exchanging specialisms are extremely circumscribed.

A second solution is to use activity-led staffing models (Simpson, 1988 and 1989) so as to fit staffing in primary schools to the tasks now required of them. Where this was modelled (Kelly, 1991) it tended to equalize staffing across the 5–16 age range. The problem here is that decisions about staffing have been devolved to schools, and the only way forward would be to develop a central policy to improve primary staffing through the funding formulae in the LMS schemes. These require approval from the Secretary of State so, in theory, it would deliver what is needed, but its implementation would run directly counter to the principle of devolved management and is unlikely to be attractive to DES policy-makers. In any case, it is unclear whether improved staffing levels in themselves can help with the problems of expertise in the primary teaching force as a whole, or with the task demands facing most classteachers, even after some specialist support has been provided.

The third solution is to modify the demands of the National Curriculum so as to make them realizable for the majority of classteachers. There are two approaches here; the radical and the ameliorative. The former position (for example, Oliver, 1984; Wicksteed, 1987) is that the broad and balanced curriculum is undeliverable and that a less broadly-conceived approach would be more realistic. Whatever its attractions to those in the elementary tradition, this radical option seems politically impossible. The Conservative government has committed itself to nine subjects and asserted that standards will rise across all of them. The ameliorative position is represented in this book by Thomas's chapter. The position here is that the teachers' task will become more reasonable if some major tidying-up of the existing curriculum were to be undertaken. Overlapping and inessential material could be excised, a standard format for all subjects be introduced, and a less-detailed specification of curriculum items put in place. The revision of the mathematics and science orders for 1993 have led the way; other subjects could follow. This approach would help teachers, particularly with their use of documents for planning, but would still leave substantial problems of curricular expertise for most teachers.

A fourth solution would be for schools to introduce standard texts in all, or most, subjects, in which the intellectual content would be provided for teachers, together with examples of learning and assessment tasks in differentiated levels. The advantage here is that the teachers could have a reasonable degree of confidence that the intellectual demands were appropriate in those areas where their own intellectual background was shaky. There will be understandable opposition to such a move from two quarters. First, there are those who believe that 'good practice' cannot be based on class texts in which learning tasks are fairly standard and progressively sequenced. Yet mathematics schemes of work, and reading schemes, are very close to such a format and are widely adopted.

The second source of opposition would be from those who fear state-approved texts. Although these are common in other systems I would argue that there is no reason for state approval in our system. Market forces are already operating and the emergence of new schemes and texts tailored to the current National Curriculum requirements are emerging. Schools would have choice, assuming they have access to the kind of information needed to make it.

The major problem here is in the culture of primary schools, where teachers have been made to feel guilty about widespread use of class texts because they do not appear to meet the developmentalists' conceptions of 'good practice' where first-hand experience is at a premium.

The four solutions are not mutually exclusive. In some combination they could go a long way toward protecting the dream of the common broad and balanced curriculum, and simultaneously making it realizable, without subjecting teachers to unmanageable workloads and a profound sense of failure.

References

ACKER, S. (1992) 'Teacher relationships and educational reform in England and Wales', *The Curriculum Journal*, 2, 3.

ALEXANDER, R. (1984) *Primary Teaching*, London, Holt Rinehart & Winston.

ALEXANDER, R. (1992) *Policy and Practice in Primary Education*, London, Routledge.

ALEXANDER, R., ROSE, J. and WOODHEAD, C. (1992) *Curriculum, Organization and Classroom Practice in Primary Schools: A Discussion Paper*, London, HMSO.

BARKER-LUNN, J. (1982) 'Junior schools and their organizational policies', *Educational Research*, 24, 4.

BARKER-LUNN, J. (1984) 'Junior schoolteachers and their methods and practices', *Educational Research*, 26, 3.

BEALING, D. (1972) 'The organization of junior school classrooms', *Educational Research*, 14, 3.

BENNETT, S.N. (1976) *Teaching Styles and Pupil Progress*, London, Open Books.

BENNETT, S.N. (1991) *Group Work*, London, Routledge.

BENNETT, S.N. (1992) *Managing Learning in the Primary Classrooms*, ASPE Paper No. 1, Stoke, Trentham Books.

BENNETT, S.N., DESFORGES, C., COCKBURN, A. and WILKINSON, B. (1984) *The Quality of Pupil Learning Experiences*, New York, Lawrence Erlbaum.

BENNETT, S.N. and DUNNE, E. (1992) *Managing Classroom Groups*, New York, Simon and Shuster.

BENNETT, S.N., WRAGG, E.C., CARRÉ, C.G. and CARTER, D.S.G. (1992) 'A longitudinal study of primary teachers' perceived competence in, and concerns about, National Curriculum implementation', *Research Papers in Education*, 7, 1, pp. 53–78.

BLYTH, W.A.L. (1965) *English Primary Education*, Vol. 2., London, Routledge & Kegan Paul.

BLYTH, W.A.L. (1984) *Development, Experience and Curriculum in Primary Education*, London, Croom Helm.

CAMPBELL, R.J. (1985) *Developing the Primary School Curriculum*, London, Holt, Rinehart & Winston.

CAMPBELL, R.J. (1988) *Cashmore School*, Block ED. 352, Milton Keynes, Open University Press.

CAMPBELL, R.J. (1989) 'HMI and aspects of public policy for the primary curriculum' in HARGREAVES, A. and REYNOLDS, D. (1989) *Education Policies: Critiques and Controversies*, Lewes, Falmer Press.

CAMPBELL, R.J. and DAVID, T. (1989) *In Search of Depth and Quality*, Coventry, Warwick University Education Department.

CAMPBELL, R.J., EVANS, L., NEILL, S.R.StJ. and PACKWOOD, S. (1991) *Workloads, Achievement and Stress*, London, Assistant Masters and Mistresses Association.

CAMPBELL, R.J. and NEILL, S.R.StJ. (1990) *1330 Days*, London, Assistant Masters and Mistresses Association.

CENTRAL ADVISORY COUNCIL FOR EDUCATION (1967) *Children and their Primary Schools*, Vol. 1., London, HMSO.

COOPERS AND LYBRAND DELOITTE (1991) *Costs of the National Curriculum in Primary Schools*, London, National Union of Teachers.

CORE SUBJECT ASSOCIATION (1991) *Monitoring the Implementation of the National Curriculum*, Sheffield, NATE.

DAVID, T., CURTIS, A. and SIRAJ-BLATCHFORD, I. (1992) *Effective Teaching in the Early Years: Fostering Children's Learning in Nurseries and Infant Classes*, an OMEP (UK) Report, Coventry, Warwick University Education Department.

DES (1978) *Primary Education in England: A Survey by HMI*, London, HMSO.

DES (1982) *Education 5–9: An Illustrative Survey*, London, HMSO.

DES (1985a) *The Curriculum from 5–16: Curriculum Matters 2*, London, HMSO.

DES (1985b) *Education 8–12 in Middle and Combined Schools*, London, HMSO.

DES (1987) *Primary Staffing Survey*, London, HMSO.

DES (1988) *Task Group on Assessment and Testing: A Report*, London, HMSO.

DES (1989a, 1989b and 1990a) Series of reports called: *The Implementation of the National Curriculum in Primary Schools*, summer 1989, autumn 1989, summer 1990.

DES (1989c) *Circular 5/89*, London, HMSO.

DES (1990b) *Standards in Education 1988–90: Annual Report of HM Senior Chief Inspector of Schools*, London, HMSO.

DES (1991a) *The Implementation of the Curricular Requirements of ERA: An Overview by HM Inspectorate of the First Year*, London, HMSO.

DES (1991b) *Assessment, Recording and Reporting: A Report by HMI on the First Year*, 1989–90, London, HMSO.

GALTON, M. and SIMON, B. (1980) *Inside the Primary Classroom*, London, Routledge & Kegan Paul.

GIPPS, C. (1988) 'The debate over standards and the uses of testing', *British Journal of Educational Studies*, XXXVI, 1, pp. 21–37.

GIPPS, C. (1990) *Assessment: A Teacher's Guide*, London, Hodder and Stoughton.

HARLEN, W. and QUALTER, A. (1991) 'Issues in SAT development and the practice of teacher assessment', *Cambridge Journal of Education*, 21, 2, pp. 141–53.

HAVILAND, J. (Ed.) (1988) *Take Care, Mr. Baker!*, London, Fourth Estate.

HOUSE OF COMMONS (1986) *ESAC 3rd Report: Achievement in Primary Schools*, Vol. 1., London, HMSO.

KEEP, E. (1992) 'The need for a revised management system for the teaching profession', *National Commission on Education* — Briefing No. 2.

KELLY, A. (1991) 'Toward objective funding: An activity-led model of teacher staffing in primary and secondary schools', paper presented at the annual meeting of the *British Educational Research Association*, Nottingham.

KELLY, V. (1990) *The National Curriculum: A Critical Review*, London, Paul Chapman.

LAWLOR, S. (1988) *Correct Core: Simple Curricula for English, Mathematics and Science*, London, Centre for Policy Studies.

LAWTON, D. (1988) 'Ideologies of education' in LAWTON, D. and CHITTY, C. (Eds) *The National Curriculum*, London University, Bedford Way, Papers No. 33.

LETWIN, O. (1988) *Aims of Schooling: The Importance of Grounding*, London, Centre for Policy Studies.

LEWIS, A. (1991) *Primary Special Needs and the National Curriculum*, London, Routledge.

MUSCHAMP, Y., POLLARD, A. and SHARPE, R. (1992) 'Curriculum management in primary schools', *Bristol Polytechnic*.

NATIONAL CURRICULUM COUNCIL (1992) *Regional Primary Seminars: Report to Delegates*, York, NCC.

NATIONAL UNION OF TEACHERS (1991) *'Miss, the Rabbit Ate the Floating Apple': The Case Against SATs*, London, NUT.

OLIVER, D. (1984) 'Is primary education possible?', *Education 3–13*, 12, 2.

OSBORN, M. and POLLARD, A. (1991) 'Anxiety and paradox: Teachers' initial responses to change under the National Curriculum', *Working Paper 4, PACE Project*, Bristol Polytechnic.

OSBORN, M. and BROADFOOT, P. (1991) 'The impact of current changes in English primary schools on teacher professionalism', paper presented at the annual meeting of the American Educational Research Association, Chicago.

PASCALL, C. (1989) (for the Early Years Lobby) *National Curriculum and Early Years*, Stoke, Trentham Books.

RAYNOR REPORT (1982) *A Study of HMI in England and Wales*, London, HMSO.

RICHARDS, C. (1982) 'Curriculum consistency' in RICHARDS, C. (Ed) *New Directions in Primary Education*, Lewes, Falmer Press.

RICHARDS, C. (1986) 'The curriculum from 5 to 16: Background content and some implications for primary education', *Education 3–13*, 13, 1, pp. 3–8.

SCHWARZENBERGER, R. (1989) *Attainment Targets in Mathematics*, Stoke, Trentham Books.

SHIPMAN, M. (1983) *Assessment in Primary and Middle Schools*, London, Croom Helm.

SILCOCK, P. (1990) 'Implementing the National Curriculum: Some teachers' dilemmas', *Education 3–13*, 18, 3, pp. 4–11.

Jim Campbell

SIMPSON, E. (1988) *Review of Curriculum-led Staffing*, Windsor, NFER.

SIMPSON, E. (1990) 'The stubborn statistic', *Education*, 21, April.

SKIDELSKY, R. (1967) *English Progressive Schools*, Harmondsworth, Penguin.

SMITH, R. (1990) 'What doesn't Anita know?', *Education 3–13*, 18, 3, pp. 11–13.

SMITHERS, A. and ZIENTEK, P. (1991) *Gender, Primary Schools and the National Curriculum*, Birmingham, NAS/UWT.

TAYLOR, P. and STANLEY, J. (1991) *Early Days: Primary School Teachers and the National Curriculum*, Birmingham, Primary Schools Research and Development Group.

TOMLINSON, J.R.G. (1986) 'Public education, public good' *Oxford Review of Education*, XII, 3.

WHITE, J. (1988) 'An unconstitutional National Curriculum' in LAWTON, D. and CHITTY, C. (Eds) *The National Curriculum*, London, London University, Bedford Way, Papers No. 33.

WICKSTEED, D. (1987) 'Curriculum matters, enough to reduce it', *Education 3–13*, 15, 2.

Chapter 3

Balancing Priorities: Children and the Curriculum in the Nineties[1]

Andrew Pollard with
Marilyn Osborn, Dorothy Abbott,
Patricia Broadfoot and Paul Croll

Introduction

In this chapter, I aim to consider the interaction of children, teachers and curriculum, with particular reference to patterns of practice and perspective at an early point in the introduction of the National Curriculum as it progressively impacts on Key Stage 1. In so doing I shall reflect many of the issues which Alan Blyth has himself considered during his long and distinguished career. For instance, his classic two-volume study, *English Primary Education* (1965), was distinctive for its careful treatment of children, their cultures and interests, as well as for being the first comprehensive sociological account of the field of primary education. This chapter will also draw heavily on accounts of children as we consider the influence which the National Curriculum is having on their classroom experiences. In addition, I shall draw specifically on Alan Blyth's work to conceptualize 'curriculum' and its place in the process of education.

In *Development, Experience and Curriculum in Primary Education* (1984), Alan Blyth argued that curriculum should be seen as 'planned intervention in the interaction between development and experience' (p. 43). Curriculum, in this view, contributes to both development and experience. However, whilst development and experience are both continuous and will occur naturally in one form or another through each person's life, curriculum is the outcome of deliberate decisions by others about appropriate provision for a learner. As Blyth put it regarding primary schools, 'Curriculum ... is designed to make a positive impact on children' (p. 44). This, of course, is exactly what the National Curriculum is intended to do — to provide the broad and balanced education which, for the first time, is described as system-wide aims in the 1988 Education Reform Act.

However, whilst most teachers and educationalists have endorsed the principle of the National Curriculum and the entitlements which it offers for children, many, particularly in primary education, also have some reservations over the particular form of its introduction. I will dwell on just two of these concerns here.

First, there is an issue of balance. Is primary education only to concern itself with academic achievement? What place is there for the development of the person, for the social development of children? This issue has certainly received very little public attention in recent years.

Second, there is the question of how young children learn and its associated issues of classroom pedagogy and pupil experience. Some teachers have been concerned that the curriculum could become overcrowded and that the equality of pupil learning experiences will suffer. It is certainly the case, in my view, that policy-makers have generated the National Curriculum on the basis of 'what knowledge it is thought that "society" requires young children to acquire' rather than on any serious consideration to learning processes or to social and personal development.

Alan Blyth's view of curriculum (1984) was rather different. He tied it to a firm set of values stemming from his Christian faith and his beliefs in democracy and the dignity of individuals. He was thus led to advocate a curriculum which would, above all else, be *enabling*. It would thus support learning, 'a systematic process of construction of reality'; it would 'enable each individual to become a person with an emerging set of values and ideals'; and it would enable people to exercise choices themselves, to appreciate the conditions in which choices have to be made and to accept the choices of others.

The enabling curriculum which Alan Blyth described so lucidly in 1984 was no pipe-dream, and I would argue that there were many developments through the 1980s which could be used to illustrate its attainment. In my judgment these occurred where teachers reflected carefully on their practice and really got to close grips with the issues involved in learning, irrespective of the particular curriculum areas in which they may have been working. However, for the moment the question has been superseded by the daily demand simply to cope with the new curriculum.

We cannot tell at present what the outcome of the introduction of the National Curriculum will be for our children in the 1990s. What will be the balance of advantage between competing priorities for intellectual and for social growth and development? What will turn out to be the most appropriate balance in competing priorities to teach existing knowledge and to support children in constructing their own? It is much too early to make any serious, empirically-based statements about the overall balance of advantage on such issues. However, research activity provides some early indicative data of an essentially descriptive sort on the *initial* effects of the introduction of the National Curriculum, and it is on this which I have drawn, tentatively, in this chapter.

In the first part of the chapter I will attempt to identify some features of what I take to have been an emergent professional model of teaching and learning over the last decade. This seems to me to have a great deal of affinity with Alan Blyth's conception of an enabling curriculum which I reviewed briefly above. I will analyze some sociological aspects of this approach to teaching and learning by drawing on some ethnographic work in which I am engaged.[2]

In the second part of the chapter I will draw on empirical evidence from the PACE Project (Primary Assessment, Curriculum and Experience)[3] to review some of the apparent effects of the introduction of the National Curriculum on classroom practice. In particular, I will consider some early evidence of how young children themselves perceive the forms of pedagogy and curriculum which they experience.

I will conclude by revisiting both Blyth's 'enabling curriculum' and the emergent professional model of teaching and learning which I will have introduced. I will relate both the classroom and pupil data to them and will speculate about some of the possible longer-term consequences of the apparent trends.

A Model of Teaching and Learning

Over the past decade or so there have been considerable professional developments in teaching methods regarding the curriculum subjects which make up the primary school curriculum. In almost every case the innovations embraced a move away from individualized work towards group work, a concern to make the active and skilled role of the teacher more explicit and a growing recognition of the capacity of children to construct their understanding together. The idea of problem-solving in small groups was widely adopted in subjects such as mathematics, design technology and science. Thus 'starting points' for investigation were offered, with the teacher being on hand to monitor, support and extend the thinking, experimentation and exploration which followed. Model processes for teaching/learning episodes also came to be outlined. For instance, the National Writing Project endorsed 'process writing' in which young children were encouraged to draft, share and discuss, redraft and eventually 'publish' their stories. In design technology a process for producing hand-made objects evolved. This incorporated conceptualizing, planning, testing, discussing, revising and eventually 'realizing'. Such trends in pedagogy and curriculum provision have been powerfully sponsored by subject associations such as the Association for Science Education, the National Association for the Teaching of English and the Maths Association. A new, idealized form of 'effective professional practice' thus emerged through the 1980s, and it did so with powerful new legitimation from child psychology available in the wings.

Whilst theoretical influences and innovations in psychology have not always been explicit in these curricular and pedagogic developments, the work of people such as Bruner, Wood, Edwards and Mercer, Gallimore and Tharp, with the strong influence of Vygotsky, have an underpinning significance. Indeed, such ideas, which I have termed 'social constructivist', (Pollard, 1987), can be seen as gradually replacing the legitimation for 'good primary practice' which was previously provided by Piaget.

We thus seem to have experienced almost two parallel but complementary streams of development in the generation of new forms of teaching and learning. Professional teachers have developed through curricular and pedagogic refinement — work which has shown the enormous commitment of the profession in the face of almost continuous public critique. Meanwhile, academic psychologists have worked away too, whilst the understanding of the ramifications of their basis analysis has gradually grown amongst professional educators.

Of course, I must clarify that I am focussing here on what might be termed 'exceptional practice' — that is, practice which is identified and respected for its quality and effectiveness in facilitating children's learning and may be offered as a 'model' which other teachers might emulate. To some extent, too, we may have to recognize this model as being ideological — a representation of a form of practice to which many teachers can aspire but relatively few may achieve, at least across the curriculum. We certainly know that much practice would not conform to the model. Indeed, among the findings which have emerged regularly in recent research and in HMI surveys has been that of the routine and weakly-matched nature of many of the activity structures and classroom tasks in which children engage. Nevertheless, innovations and new ways of conceptualizing practices are of vital importance in exploring future directions and influencing opinion. Whilst realism is important there is a very important role for ideals.

For my own part, I have spent several years trying to think through the sociological contribution to this emergent theory of learning. The empirical focus of this effort has been through a longitudinal ethnography of a small cohort of children as they pass through a primary school. My main concern has been to identify the ways in which the social context, and relationships within it, influence the opportunities which children have to construct their meanings and understanding. As Galton (1987) has suggested, we need to concentrate:

> . . . on the social factors affecting pupil learning and (on) the ways in
> which teachers can create classroom climates which allow situations of
> 'high risk' and 'high ambiguity' to be coped with successfully. (p. 44)

This statement underlines what is, for me, a key point in social constructivist models of learning about *control* of the learning process. Since understanding can only be constructed in the mind of the learner, it is essential that learners exercise a significant degree of control over the process. In particular, they must feel both motivated by the subject matter and able to try things out and to make mistakes in an atmosphere of security and support.

In my ethnographic work I have attempted to draw on symbolic inter-actionist sociology to elaborate the 'social' dimension of social constructivism. One result was the simple formula below, which I have found very useful in analyzing data from different settings:

Figure 3.1:   Individual, Context and Learning — An Analytical Formula

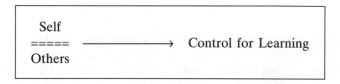

The relationship between 'self' and 'others' expresses the key symbolic interactionist focus, with its recognition of the importance of social context in the formation of meaning and self. A sense of control in social situations is seen as a product of this. It is an indication of the success, or otherwise, of a child's coping strategies in the politico-cultural context of any particular social setting — home, classroom, playground — and thus reflects the inter-play of interests, power, strategies and negotiation. However, it is also a necessary element of the learning process as conceived by social constructivist psychologists. Only children themselves can 'make sense', understand and learn. They may be supported and instructed by others, but once their under-standing has been scaffolded in such ways, it must stand on its own foundations — foundations which can only be secure when the child has been able to control the construction itself.

Teaching and other forms of support by adults are necessary for effective learning, but they are not sufficient. Learning also requires conditions which enable each child to control and manage the assembly and construction of *their* understanding.

I have elaborated a model by Rowland (1987) in order to express this process visually (see figure 3.2).

The suggestion here that objectives be negotiated should be noted, for this model should not be confused with an entirely open child-centredness. Negotiation may well encompass making the children aware of constraints such as the National Curriculum requirements and discussing how these may best be satisfied. Indeed, such a state is important to establish clarity in goals and, implicitly at least, criteria for success.

It is also worth dwelling a little on the importance of the role of an adult as a 'reflective agent' in this model, providing meaningful and appropriate

Andrew Pollard

Figure 3.2: A social-constructivist model of the teaching/learning process

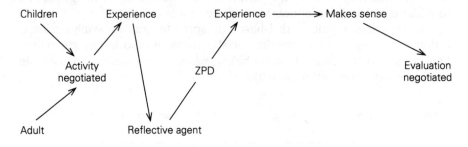

guidance and extension to the cognitive structuring and skill development arising from the child's initial experiences. This, it is suggested, supports the child's attempts to 'make sense' and enables them to cross the zone of proximal development (ZDP). Their thinking is thus *restructured* in the course of further experiences.

The model above describes a pedagogic process, a process which is dependent on a number of important factors. For instance, carrying out the role of a reflective agent effectively is dependent on accurate knowledge of each child's needs and on being able to respond to them appropriately. In addition to creating the social conditions in which fruitful dialogue can take place, it thus places a premium on formative teacher assessment and on having appropriate subject knowledge at one's disposal.

There are thus three important conditions for this model of teaching to be put into effective practice:

— provision of a classroom context in which children are enabled to control and manage the construction of meaning and understanding;
— effective assessment and communication with the children so that relevant adult support and instruction is identified;
— provision of appropriate adult support and instruction for the subjects which form the curriculum.

We thus see the need for assessment, teaching and subject knowledge and their relationship to children's control over their learning. The elements are not contradictory — though they are sometimes in tension when any one is seen to be dominant over another. I would argue that each is necessary but that neither is sufficient for high quality learning. Of course, such an argument is very close to Alan Blyth's view of the role of curriculum in relation to development and experience. The whole-person will learn and develop most effectively when the conditions are right, when the balance of structure, opportunity and support are appropriate.

Once again, I want to emphasize that, whilst such a model of teaching/

learning processes represents a basic idea which I think has widespread support within the teaching profession, most people recognize the difficulties in actually realizing it. Of course, too, it is located among a repertoire of teaching strategies. In the development and realization of this approach, teachers face formidable constraints in the form of class size, lack of non-contact time, the extent of assessment skill and subject knowledge required, and the range of the demands on classroom organization. These difficulties are so great that there is real argument about the degree of realism in maintaining such idealistic ambitions on a system-wide basis. Should we settle for something less? I do not know but, to anticipate the thrust of my report of findings from the PACE study, it does seem that the introduction of the National Curriculum and assessment procedures could be driving teachers' practice in directions which could make the realization of this model — or of Alan Blyth's 'enabling curriculum' — even more difficult.

Indeed, I would suggest that we are in danger of producing an imbalance in the factors which I identified above because of a misplaced confidence in the primacy of subject 'teaching' and of summative assessment for external audiences. Furthermore, I would suggest that changes in classroom practice being introduced as a consequence of the National Curriculum appear to be likely to reduce the provision of opportunities for children to control and manage their own learning. Such matters are the subject of the second part of this chapter.

Changes in Classroom Practice — The Views of Children

The PACE Study, on which this part of the chapter is based, aims to monitor the impact of the National Curriculum and assessment on schools, teachers and children in Key Stage 1. It is very wide-ranging and embraces issues such as teacher professionalism, school change, assessment, classroom pedagogy and pupil experience. The research design provides for two basic cycles of data gathering, each cycle to consist of interviews with a national sample of teachers from forty-eight schools, classroom studies of pedagogy in nine classrooms and assessment studies in nine classrooms. There is a considerable emphasis on pupil behaviour and perspectives in both the classroom and assessment studies.

The data used here are based, first, on the analysis of the first round of interviews with eighty-eight classroom teachers in infant schools, conducted in May 1990, and, second, on the analysis of interviews with fifty-four 6-year-old children conducted in the autumn of 1990. In each case the data are based on answers to specific questions and these preliminary findings will, in due course, be triangulated with observational and documentary evidence. Findings reported here should be regarded as being preliminary.

Teaching Organization

As part of our initial round of interviews, the PACE team asked teachers about their classroom practice and how this was being affected by the National Curriculum and assessment, as well as how they thought it might be further affected in future.

It was striking that, when asked about their approach to teaching, only 23 per cent described their approach as 'child-centred', while 71 per cent saw their teaching style as a mixture of child-centredness and more traditional, formal approaches, described in such ways as 'firm but fair' or 'structured but flexible'. The picture presented was of a mixture of philosophies with professional judgment being applied to draw on different approaches as appropriate. Almost half (48 per cent) of the teachers said that they worked with a variety of different sorts of activities taking place at the same time, and half also said that they emphasized 'group-based' work compared with only 34 per cent who emphasized whole-class work.

Of course, the teachers were very aware of changes following the implementation of the National Curriculum; 77 per cent mentioned that there had been some degree of change and 23 per cent saw their approach as *very much* changed. This was felt to be having a direct effect on their work with the children.

For instance, many teachers expressed frustration and even anger over the amount of time now apparently demanded for record-keeping and assessment. There were fears that this was beginning to 'take over from teaching!', that the heavy burden demanded in time and effort left too little time for planning, for responding to children, for display work, for all the things which were seen by many as 'real teaching'. As one teacher put it:

> If we collect all the National Curriculum documents and we are supposedly implementing them as it's stated, I feel that you might as well stop breathing, because are we going to be able to cope? And, if we do cope, in what way will we be coping? ... I'd hate to get to the point where I think, 'I must do that do-day' and 'I'm sorry if Emma comes in crying but she's just got to sit and do it because the law says I must be doing it'.

This strong feeling that, in spite of the reforms, the greatest sense of satisfaction and achievement in teaching came from children's response was emphasized by the 85 per cent of teachers who said that a 'really good day' for them would be one when the children had responded 'with interest and enthusiasm', or 'with a desire to learn'. One teacher said:

> A good day is when the children are relaxed, happy and have achieved something they have found difficult for a long time. That's something that is really satisfying. It's a circular thing. Children pick up your

relaxation and things go well. If you are not relaxed, everything goes badly.

The teachers thus retained a very strong commitment to the children. They were sensitive to their feelings and aware of what they saw as the dangers of new requirements.

We also asked teachers how they handled classroom organization methods. Mostly teachers used a combination of whole-class teaching, group work and individual work, but group work was clearly reported as the main approach:

	Whole Class	Individual	Groups
Predominantly used	13%	21%	52%
Used some of the time	74%	62%	47%

We also asked how far such organizational practices had changed as a response to the Education Reform Act. As the table below indicates, more group and whole-class teaching were reported with less individual study:

Percentage of teachers indicating changes in methods of grouping children for teaching purpose

	Whole Class	Individual	Groups
More	21.6	9.1	28.4
Same	64.8	65.9	65.9
Less	12.5	23.9	3.4

Interestingly, many teachers felt that they should be doing more individual work as a result of the reforms but that, paradoxically, the time pressure generated by the demands of the National Curriculum and assessment did not allow this.

The teachers then, in response to the pressures of the National Curriculum and assessment, seem to be adapting by tightening their classroom control and by providing more direction to the children's activities through group or whole-class activities.

How then are such developments likely to be appreciated by the children? We interviewed fifty-four year 1 children, drawn from each of the nine schools in the 'classroom studies' sample. In answer to the question, 'Do you like it best when you choose what to do or when your teacher does?', over 80 per cent of the children recorded that they preferred to control their own activities. Their answers were direct, simple and unified on this point.

Those children who said they preferred to choose themselves were then asked to explain their reasons. They gave the following types of account:

Reasons given by children for wishing to choose activities themselves

	Number of responses	%
Because it's easier to do	2	5
Because it's more interesting	14	32
Because it's *my* choice	16	36
Because it's good for me	1	2
Don't know	3	7
No answer	8	18

Though the numbers are small, the patterns are clear. The children preferred to engage, autonomously, in activities which *they* regarded as interesting.

Those who emphasized *autonomy* said things like:

I like to choose my very best things I like doing.

Because you can do what you want.

Because you don't have to wait.

'Cos you can choose to play.

Those who appreciated *scope to choose 'interesting' things to do* said:

Because Miss gives us boring things ...

'Cos you can make things.

'Cos I can choose nicer things.

'Cos I like it. More fun. I play with dough.

I think it might be because I like playing.

'Cos you can get at the polydroms and you can stick 'em together.

The children appear to appreciate opportunities to take decisions, to follow and develop their own ideas, to be creative, have fun and to 'do things'. Their concern for the intrinsic value of activity was contrasted with their view of many teacher-directed activities as being 'boring' and as 'things which we have to do first'.

However, when asked, 'Do you choose what you do at school or does your teacher choose for you most of the time?', the children confirmed the teachers' views presented earlier by indicating a high degree of teacher control.

Children's views of who chooses what to do in school

	Number of responses	%
Teacher chooses most of the time	29	54
Teacher or children choose	17	31
Children choose most of the time	5	9
No answer	3	6

The few children who felt that they chose themselves most of the time all came from the same class and, as with the children who reported shared choice of activities, their views reflected the nature of the organizational system in the classrooms. In many cases a degree of child choice was overtly provided for in these classroom systems as an attempt to be appreciative of children's needs and to encourage 'independent learning'. The majority of children, however, recognized their experience of classroom life as being framed by tighter teacher control. As we have seen, they were not universally appreciative of this.

The 30 per cent of children who said that they preferred their teacher to choose their activities gave two types of reason. Two-thirds simply explained that they liked the activities which the teacher chose. For example:

I like it when the teacher chooses 'cos she's nice and chooses good things. She lets us do good work — colouring, playing on the computer, playing in the Wendy house, construction, Lego.

The other main reason concerned acceptance of teacher authority and gratitude for the clarity of goals which might be provided:

Well, she's the teacher, so if she chooses we know what to do.

Curriculum Balance

We had anticipated that as a result of the requirements of the National Curriculum the balance of the infant school curriculum was likely to shift towards the 'core' subjects laid down by the Act — mathematics, English and science — and possibly away from some of the 'creative' areas — art and music — which traditionally were seen as an important part of infant children's daily activities. This expectation was largely borne out by teachers' responses. Although the majority (80 per cent) said that they had always done a lot of maths and English, most teachers (84 per cent) said that they were now doing more science, while 60 per cent were doing more technology. There was also a less pronounced move to a more specific emphasis on the humanities, with 34 per cent saying they now did more history and 36 per cent saying this about geography, although many teachers argued that these areas had always been covered in topic work without being *called* history and geography. It was suggested that what was happening now was a more conscious labelling of the history and geography areas of topic work rather than an increase in 'real' terms.

As we had suspected, it was music and art which appeared to be suffering in the move to embrace science. Thirty per cent of teachers said they were now doing less art and 30 per cent said the same of music. However, there were other, more subtle ways in which the 'creative' side of the curriculum appeared to be affected. Although the time spent on English had not changed for most teachers, the type of activity upon which children were engaged as part of English work *had* altered. Many teachers said that they were doing less creative writing with their children. Similarly, art may well have been eroded more than is apparent from the (30 per cent) response cited above. A large number of teachers said that they were doing less 'Art for art's sake' with their children. Most said that writing, painting and drawing were now related to topic areas which formed part of their National Curriculum work rather than being open to children's free choice.

As one teacher put it:

It's less fun now. Everything has to be specifically related to the topic.

Apart from the change in curriculum balance there was a real issue of curriculum overload for many teachers. With the pressure to do more in the core subjects and the humanities, cutting down the time allocated to music and art did not, in itself, create enough extra time since these subjects had never occupied a large proportion of the time available. There was an overwhelming feeling amongst teachers of being constantly pushed for time, of never quite enough time to get in all that was required.

The issues of breadth and overload have also evidently been concerning HMI, who draw attention to the 'continuing need to offer children an appropriate range of experience in the arts and physical education' (HMI, 1990, p. 13), and, from the interview data which we gathered with the 6-year-old children, it seems that many of them will be grateful to HMI for expressing such concerns. The children were shown a collage of various common infant school activities and were asked to say which activities they liked doing best and which they did not like. Choice was unrestricted and yielded the table which follows:

Children's preference for common infant school activities

	Number of responses	
	'Like'	'Don't like'
Physical education	22	2
Painting	20	2
'Home corner' play	19	6
Sand	12	1
Stories	9	4
Construction	7	7
Reading alone	6	2
Singing	4	4
Science	2	7
Reading with teacher	0	8
Maths	2	9
Writing	5	12

The pattern of the children's feelings is clear and it is also rather unfortunate, in view of the pressures which teachers are evidently feeling to emphasize aspects of the curriculum which children seem to 'like' least. Interestingly, each of the core subjects of the National Curriculum is represented at the least liked end of the children's choices.

Further analysis of the data which will identify the reasoning behind these choices has not yet been completed. However, it is already clear that children value activity, autonomy, stimulation, engaging with other children, things they can succeed at and opportunities to be creative. For instance:

I like painting — it's not really work, I hate work, I like talking to people.

You can play in the sand but you can't in science and writing.

I like PE 'cos you can climb things, and do all sorts of things.

I like dressing up ... 'cos you can play schools and stuff in here.

One might draw particular attention to the release of the imagination and the connection with previous experience which is implicit in many of the priorities given by the children. For instance, one child said that playing in the sand was her best activity. She went on:

Because I like making sandcastles when it's wet ... 'cos I've been down to the seaside before and last year I done a big sandcastle ... and me Mum did a big flag so I could do a big flag sandcastle, and some people played with me, and I had a 'Turtle' spade and bucket and we dig right to the bottom and we found treasure and silver.

Egan's (1988) argument that the understanding of young children should be linked through curriculum to their interest and facility in fantasy and imagination takes on a direct significance here. The children whom we interviewed confirm his priority. However, the teachers whom we interviewed felt increasingly unable to respond to such concerns and were, in fact, beginning to move in the opposite direction.

Teacher-Pupil Relationships

An area central to the PACE research was the question of whether the imposition of external requirements on teachers, as embodied in the National Curriculum and assessment procedures, would affect the relationships between teachers and children.

Would the 'loss of fun' referred to by one teacher above, and the pressure to relate everything to planned National Curriculum topics, affect the warm, informal relations which many teachers had previously seen as lying at the heart of good English primary practice?

When asked if they felt that the quality of teacher-pupil relations had been affected, 45 per cent of teachers said that there had been no change and 21 per cent argued that they would hotly defend their existing relationship with the children against any outside influences, since it was of such central importance to the teaching/learning process. One teacher insisted:

> I haven't let it change me. I still try to be a person for the children, someone they understand and who tries to understand them.

Another teacher in an inner city school saw it as a collective response:

> We've tried very hard not to change and I think that's where we've been torn apart, to be frank. I feel very strongly that it should not change, but it's getting harder ... With our children, if they don't get a close relationship with their teacher they won't have a relationship with anybody. And if they haven't got somebody to give them some attention at school then they're not going to get any from anywhere else and they won't learn.

In contrast, 9 per cent of teachers felt that there had been an improvement in the teacher-pupil relationship and suggested that the National Curriculum required them to have more contact with individual pupils. However, a far greater number (31 per cent) felt that there had definitely been a change for the worse and that their relationship with children was affected adversely by pressures on teacher time or by feelings of stress on the part of the teachers. Fourteen per cent felt that contact with children had become more formal as a result.

A number of teachers (one-fifth) expressed a feeling of sadness that things which had been seen as central to good primary practice — spontaneity, flexibility, the ability to respond to topics introduced by children, and to create teaching activities around them — were being eroded because of pressure to cover everything laid down in the programmes of study.

In one local education authority this was widely referred to as the 'dead pigeon' syndrome, and there was a general feeling that the learning experiences provided by unpredictable, but immediate, child experiences — such as finding a 'dead pigeon' — were now having to be ignored rather than utilized in teaching. A teacher responded:

> I just feel less relaxed now. The other day one child brought in some bird's eggs, but there was so much to get through that I couldn't make time to show them to the class or talk about them. At the end of the day I still hadn't managed to show them and he burst into tears. I felt so bad ... really bad. It's terrible if we don't have time to respond to children any more.

The children's responses when we interviewed them in the autumn of 1990 did not convey the teachers' sense of foreboding, but they did map almost exactly onto their concerns.

In the first place, the quality of existing classroom relationships was attested by the children, with fifty-one out of fifty-four interviewed giving positive responses to the question, 'How do you get on with your teacher?'

To elicit their perspectives a little more, the children were then asked, 'What do you like best about your teacher?' The breakdown of responses was as follows:

Children's views of what they like best about their teachers

	Number of Responses	%
Personal characteristics	3	6
Provision of interesting activities	18	33
Provision of 'easy work'	2	4
Opportunity to choose activities	11	20
Quality of interaction	13	24
Don't know	5	9
No answer	2	4

Of the three main areas of child concern — interest, choice and interaction — children said such things as:

Provision of interesting activities:

'I like my teacher best when she ...

'does good work with us'

'the way she reads'

'I like her stories'

'gives you work you like'

'When she comes and she's doing things with us, like when she had a big table and we have all things to taste and we dip papers in and it goes different colours'.

Opportunity to choose activities:

'I like my teacher best when she ...

'lets us play games and read books and go out to play'

'lets us go over to dinners and we can sit by somebody'

'says we can choose'

''cos she lets us do painting'

''cos she lets me play'.

Quality of interaction:

'I like my teacher best when she ...

'says something nice, like "Well done, Sarah" '

'bestest is that she like doing things with us. When I can't do it she writes it for me — helps me'

'doesn't shout, that's when I like her'

'when she's not mad'

'when she gives me a smiley face on my hand'

'if you cry or fall over she tells someone to take you in, and if you feel sad she cuddles you'.

Of course, such patterns in children's concerns are not unexpected for they are very similar to findings reported by studies such as Davies (1982) and

Pollard (1985). However, in the context of teachers' concerns regarding the impact of the National Curriculum and assessment procedures, the children's views have particular force. In the future the quality of children's experiences — measured in their own terms — will be adversely affected on grounds of *interest*, if teachers are less able to respond spontaneously to children's immediate concerns, on grounds of *choice*, if teachers feel that they must tighten their classroom control in order to 'cover' more curriculum, and on grounds of the *quality of interaction*, if teachers become stressed, preoccupied with record keeping and assessment and unable to sustain the good relationships with children which they currently achieve.

Conclusion

In this chapter I began by reviewing Alan Blyth's concept of the 'enabling curriculum' and I associated it with innovative forms of teaching and learning, underpinned by social constructivist psychology which have developed during the 1980s. Such approaches appeared to offer a great deal for the 1990s.

However, the introduction of the National Curriculum and the many other educational innovations of recent years is, it appears, having effects on teacher practice which, whilst entirely understandable, seem unlikely to be welcomed by most children. Teachers' efforts to protect classroom relationships are a notable success but they remain under threat. Classroom organization and forms of pedagogy appear to be tightening whilst the curriculum, despite some counter-tendencies, may be narrowing overall. It is certainly becoming more specified and thus less responsive to children's ongoing interest.

Alan Blyth's work has always been characterized by its appreciativeness, humanity and integrity and his conception of an enabling curriculum offered a fine analytical framework for balancing the priorities of society and the learner in the 1990s. Consideration of development, experience and curriculum together is salutary and moderating in itself. It delimits thinking and ambition with regard to any one element and sets it in the context of the others. It is unfortunate that the National Curriculum which has been created for the 1990s does not reflect such a balanced understanding of children, their learning and development. Of course, there are many differences between plans and execution and there will be adaption of the National Curriculum at many levels and in diverse ways over the next few years. The professional judgment of teachers as they work with parents and governors will make a vital contribution to this, and the outcome, I predict, will eventually be an approach to the primary curriculum which is more appreciative of the whole-child, of personal and social development as well as intellectual growth and of the importance of the process of learning.

Notes

1   A version of this chapter was presented at the annual conference of the Association for the Study of Primary Education, Cambridge, September 1991.
2   For a fuller account of the argument in the first part of the chapter, see my article, 'Towards a sociology of learning in primary schools', *British Journal of Sociology of Education*, 11, 3, 1990. The ethnography from which this work has developed tracks a cohort of children throughout their primary school careers and began in 1987. The study is now funded by the Leverhulme Trust and has a team working on it of Ann Filer, Kath Henry and Andrew Pollard, all at the University of the West of England (formerly Bristol Polytechnic).
3   The material in the second part of this chapter has been developed from the PACE Project. In particular, it draws on a paper delivered at the annual meeting of the American Educational Research Association in April 1991, 'Classroom change and pupil experience' by Andrew Pollard and Marilyn Osborn, with Paul Croll, Dorothy Abbott and Patricia Broadfoot.

The PACE Project is the largest independent funded research project investigating the impact of the National Curriculum and assessment on Key Stage 1. It is funded by ESRC and is based at the Universities of Bristol and the University of the West of England. Members of the team are: Dorothy Abbott, Patricia Broadfoot, Paul Croll, Marilyn Osborn and Andrew Pollard.

References

BLYTH, W.A.L. (1965) *English Primary Education*, Volumes I and II, London, Routledge.

BLYTH, W.A.L. (1984) *Development, Experience and Curriculum in Primary Education*, London, Croom Helm.

BRUNER, J. (1986) *Actual Minds, Possible Worlds*, London, Harvard.

DAVIES, B. (1982) *Life in the Classroom and Playground*, London, Routledge.

EDWARDS, D. and MERCER, N. (1987) *Common Knowledge*, London, Methuen.

EGAN, K. (1988) *Primary Understanding*, London, Routledge.

GALTON, M. (1987) *Teaching and Learning in Primary Schools*, London, David Fulton.

HMI (1990) *The Implementation of the National Curriculum in Primary Schools*, London, DES.

OSBORN, M. and BROADFOOT, P. (1991) 'The impact of current changes in English primary schools on teacher professionalism' paper presented at the annual meeting of the American Educational Research Association, Chicago, April.

POLLARD, A. (1985) *The Social World of the Primary School*, London, Cassell.

POLLARD, A. (Ed) (1987) *Children and their Primary Schools*, Lewes, Falmer Press.

POLLARD, A. (1990) 'Towards a sociology of learning in primary schools'; *British Journal of Sociology of Education*, 11, 3.

ROWLAND, S. (1987) 'Child in control' in POLLARD, A. (Ed) *Children and their Primary Schools*, Lewes, Falmer Press.

WOOD, D. (1988) *How Children Think and Learn*, Oxford, Blackwell.

Chapter 4

Never Mind the Quality:
Feel the Breadth and Balance

Vic Kelly and Geva Blenkin

There are several reasons why the notions of 'breadth' and 'balance', or the apparently single notion of 'breadthandbalance', as used in current policies, although asserted as devices for securing both entitlement and a raising of standards, are likely, in the event, to lead to a diminution in both of these areas. This chapter seeks to explore some of these reasons.

In particular, it will address what seem to us to be the most important of these reasons. It will seek to show that the use of terms such as these as part of a political rhetoric renders them less useful than they might, and ought to, be as concepts to move forward educational debate and planning. For, first, the use of rhetoric itself must lead to reduction in the quality of educational provision, as that must be conceived in a democratic context. Second, the hijacking of such terms and their location within that rhetoric diminishes their value as planning tools, particularly because it is a process which seeks to conceal their problematic nature and thus to inhibit and discourage exploration of their many nuances, potential meanings and implications. And, third, the particular, non-problematic meaning which they seem to bear in current officially approved discourse and official pronouncements itself contributes further to this process of quality diminution.

These three issues, then, will constitute the main points which this chapter will seek to argue and explore.

The Use of Rhetoric in the Legitimation of Educational Discourse

Among the many disturbing features of the current educational scene in the United Kingdom, quite the most disturbing, at least from a long-term perspective, is the degree to which rhetoric has come to replace reasoned argument in pronouncements about education from all kinds of official sources, within the profession as well as outside it. For, as a consequence, what was once a continuous educational debate, designed to clarify and elucidate educational

practice with a view to improving it, has been replaced by the issuing of ideological assertions from these official sources in a manner and form calculated
to discourage challenge or questioning. And, as a further consequence of this
process, the quality of educational practice, which depends crucially on continuous and open evaluation and on the intellectual level of its theoretical
underpinning, has itself been put at risk.

One expects politicians to spout rhetoric. From the birth of democracy
in ancient Athens, is has been their stock-in-trade. For their purpose in life
is not to seek fearlessly after 'truth', but to further their own personal ends
and those of their party. Success at the next election is their main and only
goal. In the knowledge of this, one learns to cope with their rhetoric, to see
beyond the facade which it seeks to erect. The ability to penetrate it is a
crucial quality for anyone who wishes genuinely to function as a free person
in a free society — and, incidentally, it must be a central purpose of education
in a free society to develop this quality in everyone.

However, it is a prime function and responsibility of those who accept
professional duties in any sphere to recognize that those duties must embrace
and extend to the maintaining of a proper level of professional debate, as the
only sound basis for professional development — not only in the sense of
their collective development as a profession but also, and more importantly,
in the sense of the continuous improvement in the quality of their professional
contribution to the life and health of their society.

It is therefore especially disturbing that what characterizes present-day
policies in education (and elsewhere too) more than anything else is that such
professional debate has been, and continues to be, seriously inhibited, and, in
particular, that the rhetoric of the politicians has been permitted to infiltrate
all levels of policy and planning. This begins with the law itself. The 1988
Education Act is not merely an Education Act, it is the Education *Reform*
Act, so that its very title not only describes it, it also seeks to sell it to us. And
its wording is littered with similarly rhetorical terminology, of which of course
'breadth' and 'balance' are salient examples.

What characterizes such terminology is that, first, it is emotive (and thus
has no place in a legal document), it uses what have been called 'pro' words
(Nowell-Smith, 1954), 'hurrah' words, words that are designed to fill us with
positive, warm feelings of approval; and, second, it offers such terminology as
non-problematic — definitions are never given and analysis of underlying
meanings is discouraged. It is this that constitutes the essence of that process
of the legitimation of discourse which an increasing number of people has
identified as a worrying current feature of so-called 'free societies'. For the
concern of such rhetorical devices is to establish a new dominant form of
discourse which will 'determine what counts as true, important, relevant and
what gets spoken' (Cherryholmes, 1987, p. 301), and to oust all alternative
forms of discourse, especially those which explicitly encourage challenge and
continuing debate; in short, to determine not only 'what can be said' but also
'what must remain unsaid' (*ibid*).

The degree of success the politicians have enjoyed in this process is evidenced by the extent to which this rhetoric, this new dominant form of discourse, has permeated many levels of the education profession itself. For not only is it a feature of the 1988 Education Act, it is also a prominent characteristic of all the official publications which preceded and have followed that Act, not only from the 'educrats' of NCC and SEAC, who have after all a purely executive role and thus may be excused for adopting whatever devices, rhetorical or otherwise, seem likely to assist them in fulfilling that role, but also from HMI and from other members of the profession whose responsibility it is, or ought to be, to promote educational standards by maintaining that professional debate we referred to earlier as essential to the continued development of the quality of educational provision. The role of the professional is not to transmit but to challenge the rhetoric of the politician.

There are many dangers inherent in what is thus being permitted to happen. At the macro level, it threatens the very fabric of democracy, the moral essence of which is that it provides, or should provide, the context for self-determination in the fullest possible sense of maximum participation in the making of social policy. This was a major element in John Dewey's definition of a democratic society. 'A society which makes provision for participation in its good of all its members on equal terms and which secures flexible readjustment of its institutions through interaction of the different forms of associated life is in so far democratic' (1922, p. 115). And conversely, 'an undesirable society ... is one which internally and externally sets up barriers to free intercourse and communication of experience' (*ibid*). Yet, through the replacement of open debate by rhetoric, it is towards this second, 'undesirable' form of society we are moving, as policy-making becomes an act of social control rather than of social development or advancement.

Next we should note that this creates a particular difficulty for education in a democratic society. For it is a major function of education in a democratic society to prepare children and young people for this kind of active participation in policy-making, this kind of self-determination. Indeed, the political rhetoric itself enjoins this upon us. To meet the requirements of the 1988 Act, a school's curriculum must be 'a balanced and broadly based curriculum' of a kind which 'prepares ... pupils for the opportunities, responsibilities and experiences of adult life' (1988 Act, Section 1(2)). And the National Curriculum 'must also serve to develop the pupil as an individual, as a member of society and as a future adult member of the community with a range of personal and social opportunities and responsibilities' (DES, 1989, para. 2.2).

And so, we, as teachers, are required, or rather cajoled, by means which are themselves inimical to the development of democracy, to prepare our pupils for life in a democratic society — unless, of course, it is acknowledged that the society for which we are to prepare them is not democratic. It is perhaps not without significance that the term 'democracy' is seldom, if ever, seen in the documentation. However, there is much there to suggest the characteristics of democracy and thus to create similar problems for the teacher. We are told, for example, in the HMI 'Curriculum Matters' series, that one of the educational aims set out in earlier DES and HMI publications continues to be 'to help pupils to develop, lively, enquiring minds, the ability to question and argue rationally' (DES, 1985, p. 3). There is a serious and debilitating professional problem there for teachers, who are required to develop lively, enquiring minds in their pupils but not to display, and certainly not to employ, such minds in relation to their own professional concerns. And it is even more of a problem for those who, like HMI, offer these recommendations to teachers for the education of pupils, while accepting, and indeed in some cases promoting, the denial of such freedom of thought and speech to themselves. The legitimating process thus creates a reality which is at odds with its own rhetoric, a discourse which is, in a fundamental sense, self-contradictory.

In being self-contradictory, it must also of course be self-defeating. And this is where the rhetoric can be seen to have the effect on practice of diminishing rather than enhancing its quality, of reducing rather than raising standards. The very fact that these requirements are offered as injunctions rather than as arguments, and are enforced by the subtle control mechanisms of rhetoric rather than by the democratic methods of persuasion through rational debate, that they are imposed by power-coercive strategies, however sophisticated, rather than by empirical-rational or normative-re-educative means (Bennis *et al*, 1969), ensures that they cannot be effectively implemented since they display this inherent self-contradiction.

The very use of rhetoric itself, then, must lead to a reduction in the quality of education, at least while education is defined in the terms which a democratic context must dictate. It does so both by inhibiting free and open debate of educational issues and by creating an insuperable conflict and contradiction between what the rhetoric itself enjoins and the climate which its use as a device for implementation and control must create.

It is not only the nature of rhetoric as an irrational form of communication, however, which causes these difficulties. It is also what it actually does to the terms and concepts it hijacks. It is to a consideration of this that we next turn.

The Rhetoric of 'Breadth and Balance'

The second point of concern we identified at the beginning of this chapter is that what the rhetoric does to the terms it hijacks is to emasculate them, to render them of no further value to educational debate or planning and thus to deprive us of useful tools for raising the quality of both.

There are many examples of this to be found in the official literature with which we have been bombarded over the last decade or so. One of them is the way in which the whole debate over the use of aims and objectives in curriculum planning, a debate which led to a major break through in our understanding of the complexities of curriculum, has been lost, even stifled, by the superficial way in which these terms have been used in the rhetoric of officialdom. The two have been conflated into a single notion of 'aimsand-objectives', so that the most important issues that debate raised, namely the distinctions and the interrelationships between the two concepts and the implications of these for conceptions of the school curriculum, and of educa-tion, have disappeared. The clumsy attempts of publications such as the HMI 'Curriculum Matters' series to separate them out reveals, through its very incoherence and unintelligibility, what the loss of this important conceptual distinction has led to (Kelly, 1989). And, as a direct result, a major advance in our understanding of the complexities of curriculum planning has been lost, only to be replaced by the antiquated simplicities of the curriculum currently being imposed on schools (Kelly, 1990). The manner in which these terms and concepts have been hijacked has thus led to a serious set-back in our thinking about curriculum, a consequent loss of depth of analysis and perception in the educational debate and an inevitable loss of quality in curriculum planning and implementation.

The same de-activating process can be seen in relation to the concepts of 'breadth' and 'balance'; and that process warrants closer examination.

To begin with, as we suggested earlier, the two terms have been collapsed into one, 'breadthandbalance', even more comprehensively than has happened with 'aimsandobjectives', since in this case we cannot even identify attempts, however clumsy, by HMI or others to distinguish them. It seems to be being assumed that breadth entails balance and *vice versa*. Yet a moment's thought will tell anyone who cares to give the matter that amount of thought that this is not so — in any walk of life. Within education, the distinction has long been an important one. Awareness of it has led us to address questions such as 'What kind of breadth leads to a balanced education?', 'Does a 'broadly based' curriculum necessarily lead to balance?', 'What might be the advan-tages of a 'broadly based' (as opposed to 'balanced') curriculum?' and so on. All of these questions are of interest and importance not only intellectually to those who find satisfaction in theorizing about education, but also practically, since clarity of thinking about such issues is a *sine qua non* of effective practice. Yet all of them are questions which can no longer be asked within the prevalent discourse.

The same is true of the individual concepts themselves. The concept of 'balance' in particular has been a lively concern of educationists since the time of Plato. His notion of 'harmony' was central to his theory of education, a balance of 'music' and 'gymnastic', the arts and physical education, the mind and the body, designed to bring about a balance within the 'soul' of its three major elements, 'reason', 'the appetites' and 'spirit'. Thus, from the beginning, theorizing about education required that we address the related issues of what makes a balanced curriculum and what kind of curriculum is likely to produced the balanced person. The *trivium* and *quadrivium* of

Quintilian and, much later, the Humanists, such as Elyot and Erasmus, reflected a continuing interest in the notion of educational balance. And that interest and concern has persisted to the present day, as is evidenced by the debate over 'the two cultures' (Snow, 1959 and 1969), the notion of 'forms of knowledge or understanding' (Hirst, 1965), the parallel view of 'realms of meaning' (Phenix, 1964), the '6Cs' of the Royal Society of Arts' 'Education for Capability' project, and, at the practical level, the principle of the School Certificate's 'subject grouping' system, the matriculation requirements of universities and the concerns expressed by HMI over the 'unbalanced' curricular experiences of so many pupils at Secondary level as a result of their survey of *Aspects of Secondary Education in England* (DES, 1979). The debate was taken even further, in what may have been the last HMI publication to contribute significantly to an open debate about education and curriculum, by the notion of 'areas of experience', as described by the 'eight adjectives' of *Curriculum 11–16* (DES, 1977).

This has, therefore, been a lively debate, as well as a long-lived one. And it has thrown up along the way a number of interesting issues and questions for debate (Kelly, 1986). Is balance to be determined by reference to subjects or to processes, to areas of experience? Is balance to be sought in the 'planned', the 'official' curriculum or in the 'received', the 'actual' curriculum, i.e. is it what is on paper or its impact on the pupil which is crucial? Are we seeking to balance arts and sciences, or the cognitive and the affective, or the theoretical and the practical (White, 1973), or the intellectual and the physical, or subjects and interdisciplinary study (James, 1968)? Further, is there potential conflict between these different dimensions of balance? What are the relative claims of breadth of study and specialist study? How might we balance vocational and 'liberal' aspects of schooling? Should the concern be to balance methods and approaches rather than subjects, since too many teachers seem to adopt the same methods and approaches regardless of subjects or 'disciplines' (Schools Council, 1981), 'the true balancing agent lies not in the subject content but in the methods and approaches of the teacher and his (*sic*) interaction with the pupils' (Petter, 1970, p. 43) and 'the way in which something is taught affects profoundly the form that it assumes in the consciousness and behaviour of learners' (Schools Council, 1975, p. 16)? Should we be seeking for balance every day? every week? every month? every year? or over the whole period of compulsory schooling? How many different dimensions of balance are there anyway? And how are we to 'balance' their relative demands?

A lively debate indeed, and one that must lead us to the conclusion that 'the balance the educational planner needs is not that of the scientist or mathematician, nor even that of the judge. It is that of the juggler' (Kelly, 1986, p. 142).

All of this lively debate, however, is lost in the offering of the notion of 'breadthandbalance' in the form in which it is offered in the current rhetoric, and, in particular, the presentation of it as a non-problematic concept. For, not only are the many dimensions and the many uncertainties of this debate unrecognized and unacknowledged in that rhetoric; it has not even been felt necessary by those responsible for these official pronouncements to offer any kind of definition or indication of the meaning they attach to it. Further than this, some of the claims which are made, or, rather, the prescriptions which are offered, demonstrate a lack of coherence which is directly attributable to this lack of clarity of analysis. To assert, for example, as a 'principle' that each pupil should have a broad and balanced curriculum which is also relevant to his or her particular needs' (DES, 1989, para. 2.2), and, further, that this 'principle' 'is now established in law' (*ibid*) is not merely to raise but also to beg some of those very questions we have just listed. For, when we look at the law which establishes this, we find it does so by listing the subjects which are to constitute this 'broad and balanced curriculum' (not to mention sub-sequently the 'attainment targets', 'programmes of study' and 'assessment arrangements'), so that we can be in no doubt that we are faced with an unchallenged, unexplored and highly questionable assumption that such a common form of subject-based curriculum will be relevant to the *particular* needs' of every individual pupil. The incoherence and unintelligibility, not to mention the self-contradiction, of this 'principle' thus becomes manifest. That incoherence, that unintelligibility and that self-contradiction are the direct result of a lack of awareness, of clarity of definition, of depth of analysis of the complex concepts which are being used. And all of this arises from the rhetorical and non-problematic use of these terms.

Such intellectual incoherence must inevitably lead to comparable con-fusions in practice. For loss of quality at the level of theory must always lead to loss of quality at the level of practice, a principle illustrated perhaps most vividly by the practice of so-called 'progressive' education. When the under-pinning theory of our practice is little more than a string of rhetorical asser-tions, that practice cannot hope to achieve a satisfactory level of quality. The loss of that clarity (not of course certainty) which has been a feature of the debates over curriculum 'breadth' and 'balance' must lead, therefore, to a matching loss of quality in the practice of any form of education or curric-ulum which claims or sets out to achieve these. In practical terms, then, the rhetoric must again be ultimately self-defeating.

Thus the notions of 'breadth' and 'balance' are prime examples, perhaps in many ways the most important examples, of how the use of rhetoric, and especially its refusal to recognize the problematic nature both of its utterances and of the concepts used in those utterances, must lead to a loss of quality not only in our thinking about education but also, as a direct consequence, in our practice of it.

The fact that the rhetoric refuses to offer openly a definition of these terms does not of course mean that we cannot detect, discover or deduce the meanings that it gives to them. And this, as we indicated at the beginning of this chapter, is the third source of our concern and unease. It is to this that we now turn.

The National Curriculum in Primary Schools:
A Broadly Balanced Entitlement?

The task of educating young children is not merely a practical or a technical matter. There is a number of reasons why we should hold to this view. Firstly, it is difficult to deny that planning an educational curriculum, especially one that will best serve a democratic and pluralist society, requires that choices be made from a range of very different views or ideologies, all of which compete in their attempts to define what a curriculum actually is. Alexander (1988) describes seven such competing ideologies, all of which have some currency in British primary education, and, although there is not space here to elaborate on these different views, each offers a particular and distinctive perspective on notions such as 'breadth' and 'balance' in the curriculum. The questions which we posed earlier give some indication of these different perspectives.

Secondly, no-one can demonstrate with scientific accuracy which of these perspectives is the 'correct' one to adopt. Each must be judged on its merits, and choices must be made between the different ideas about, for example, the kinds of experiences that are educative, or between the different characterizations of the nature of human learning and human development that each espouses and promotes. And these judgements and choices are crucial, since they will lead to the advancement of one particular kind of schooling at the expense of others. And, in doing so, they will shape what children actually experience in their schools and classrooms. It is not unreasonable, therefore, to expect, and, indeed, require, that such important decisions should be based on well-informed judgments and should be defensible.

It must follow from this, thirdly, that professional teachers have a responsibility to help in the making of such judgments and decisions. Indeed, if teachers are to be accountable as educators, they must be given some power to exercise such choices, whether they desire this responsibility or not. In this sense, then, they can never be cast in the role of mere technicians. For, as Eisner (1982) has pointed out, although knowing how to do the job may be what the public employs educators for, 'not to know what jobs are worth doing or to know but not to speak is a serious form of professional dereliction' (p. 20). Further, while it may be compelling to argue that it is the community and not professional educators who have the right to determine the goals and norms of education through political debate, Eisner warns us that such an approach 'denies the public access to more studied views concerning educational ends' (*ibid*), and one responsibility of the professional teacher is to provide such a studied view and to draw attention to the disadvantages of other views which might be being promoted.

It is a fallacy, therefore, to assume that education will be best served by teachers who are highly skilled technicians but who are discouraged from reflecting on the value and worth of what they are using their skills to offer to children in schools. As professionals, their responsibility must be to act as advocates for an entitlement curriculum which will offer truly educational experiences to all children. They must be encouraged, therefore, to expose any view that is offered or imposed under the disguise of rhetoric by drawing attention to the implications of that view and by setting those implications alongside other interpretations which might be made, making public, in particular, the potential conflicts, and hence enabling the community to make informed policy decisions.

All of this may seem to be self-evident in a democratic society. And yet the National Curriculum is prefaced on the assumption that teachers are merely technicians. For it is structured around the premise that the framework of the school curriculum and the goals towards which all children must work should be determined only by the national community, with teachers regarded as part of that community but as having no special contribution to make beyond skilled 'delivery'. Indeed, any teacher who challenges the sense and the validity of this limited role is undermined by politicians and all such criticism is defused through the use of what has been called the 'discourse of derision' (Ball, 1990).

It might be conceded that the use of such rhetoric by politicians, and their refusal to acknowledge the problematic nature of the educational concepts they trade in, have enabled them to achieve general acceptance in society of the idea that it is every child's entitlement — at least, the entitlement of every child in maintained schools in England and Wales — to have a broad and balanced curriculum. Such an idea is, after all, unobjectionable in itself. That rhetoric and that stance, however, have led also to the acceptance of a particular notion and form of such a curriculum. And it is when the meanings which are attached to these terms in current legislation are made apparent that many Primary teachers, particularly those who work with the youngest children, begin to feel and to express disquiet. And they object to this form of curriculum not out of perversity but out of a conviction that it is the least appropriate form of a broad and balanced curriculum which is about to be introduced into the primary school. For the National Curriculum is subject-based, it equates entitlement with sameness, it is content-, rather than learner-centred, and it is content rather than educational experience or learning which it seeks to broaden and to balance.

It is to a closer consideration of these features of the National Curriculum for young children that we now turn.

Breadth and Balance Defined by Subject Study

Both the statutory and advisory documentation of the National Curriculum make it clear that subjects will dictate the broad and balanced experiences of children in school. Indeed, it is clearly stated that the 'basic curriculum' is the ten subjects of the National Curriculum together with religious education, augmented by 'cross-curricular elements' (dimensions, skills and themes) and by 'extra-curricular activities' (outdoor pursuits). Continuity of schooling between the ages of 5 and 16 will be achieved by requiring that the primary curriculum, like that of the secondary school, adopts a content model that is subject-led.

There is some evidence in the documentation that the policy-makers are aware that other approaches to an entitlement curriculum were open to them, and have indeed been developed in schools. We read, for example, in the guidance to the whole curriculum, that 'traditionally primary schools have adopted a curriculum framework which has supported integrated and cross-curricular approaches' (NCC, 1990, p. 15). Such a statement itself reveals a gross misunderstanding and misinterpretation of those other approaches, since it characterizes them merely as cross-curricular or as the integration of subjects, thus revealing that this awareness of other approaches is tempered, and even distorted, by an entrenched belief that a curriculum is fundamentally a collection of subjects.

Inevitably, therefore, teachers are warned that 'if such topic work is not well planned, or if too many elements of different subjects are attempted, the work often lacks coherence, (and) . . . pupils receive a superficial experience of the subjects involved' (*ibid*). Not only does this fail to do justice to other views, it actually does violence to them by assuming the sanctity of subject divisions and assuming that mastery of them is the point and purpose of every approach to curriculum. A belief in these divisions is further evinced and reinforced by the formal assessment of pupils' performance in the core subjects, English, mathematics and science, and by the appraisal of schools and teachers through 'content and skills' audits.

What, then, are the problems that emerge when a subject-led curriculum is adopted in the primary school? The first is implicit in the arguments of those teachers who object to making the primary curriculum more like that of the secondary school, who object, in short, to the top-down pressure on the primary curriculum or, to use the more graphic American terminology, 'the push-down phenomenon' (Katz and Chard, 1989, p. 41). For a curriculum divided into subjects is, potentially, the most alienating form of curriculum for young children because it formalizes experience too soon and, in doing so, makes it distant from the everyday, common-sense knowledge and learning that the young child is familiar with and responsive to.

In this context the term 'formal experience' is used in a conceptual, not a methodological sense. It has long been known that, in certain circumstances, formal teaching methods can be effective in promoting the development of even the youngest children in school. Nursery teachers, for example, will have a planned programme of literature (rhymes, stories and picture books) — admittedly not usually English literature — which will be presented to the whole class (at story time). The experiences of story and rhyme, however, are linked to narrative form and to the playful and pretend approaches to organizing human experience and language. Narrative and playfulness are both very powerful ways of organizing, controlling and reflecting on experience.

And both are apparent in the earliest stages of human development. It is for this reason that children of three and four years are able to respond to, and profit from, the class story lesson (Whitehead, 1990). More abstract ways of organizing experience, however, create more difficulties for the young learner. And not all subjects are as accessible as literature.

As a result, attempts have been made to teach subjects to young children using informal methods of teaching. It has usually been found, however, that, even when the methods of teaching are informal, the subject content remains inaccessible to young or inexperienced learners. The research into the teaching of number to young children in the United States (Gelman and Gallistel, 1978) and in Britain (Hughes, 1986), for example, has shown the difficulties that young children get into and the perplexity that ensues if mathematics is presented to them too formally and divorced from their everyday experiences and interests too soon.

The main problem is that experience defined as subjects is often too abstract for young children. Subjects are, after all, the products of the academic community and the members of this community have had time and experience to shape and refine human understanding within their own sphere of interest. This refined experience, however, is usually a long way from the personal, social and cultural experiences that the children bring to their classrooms.

It is for this reason that those who have attempted seriously and thoughtfully to apply the concepts of 'breadth' and 'balance' to the learning of young children have recognized the necessity of interpreting these concepts in terms of the development of the child's understanding rather than in terms of the content, and especially the subject-content, of what is offered to him/her. For to use the subject as the measure of breadth and balance leads to 'the tendency to overestimate children's academic ability and to underestimate their intellectual capacities' (Katz and Chard, 1989, p. 41).

There is a further aspect of this which it is important to note, not merely because it reinforces yet again what we have said earlier about the inherent self-contradiction within the rhetoric of current policies but also because it has crucial implications for Primary practice. To see 'breadth' and 'balance' in terms of subject-content is, as we suggested just now, to create a curriculum which is alienating to many children and thus, far from offering equality of entitlement, has quite the opposite effect (Kelly, 1990).

Breadth and Balance as Entitlement

It is probably not an exaggeration to say that current official policies for the curriculum are founded on the two notions of 'breadth and balance' and entitlement. And these two notions are clearly seen as inextricably interlinked, in that we are told that every child is entitled to a broad and balanced curriculum and also that the offering of such a broad and balanced curriculum will ensure equality of entitlement for all pupils.

At the level of generality, there is little here to which one might take exception. Again, however, it is the precise definition of 'breadth and balance' which we can see in the kind of curriculum which is subsequently laid down and set before us on the basis of these principles that leads us to a strong sense of dissatisfaction over the likely, indeed certain, practical effects that this will have on the quality of educational provision and experience for many pupils of primary age.

Alienation is a phenomenon in education with which we have long been familiar. Research over several decades has left no room for doubt that many pupils have, and do, become disaffected and have thus gained little value from their educational experiences because of the wide cultural gap which exists between the experiences they bring from their social and ethnic backgrounds — their homes, their cultures, their peers — and those they are expected to respond to in their schools. Such research has offered conclusive evidence that quality of achievement in education owes far less to intellectual ability than it does to social and ethnic background. Furthermore, it has been for a long time equally clear that this phenomenon is explicable in terms of the subject/content-based form of curriculum such pupils have been offered. This is one major reason why it has not been anything like as evident in the primary sector, where the subject/content-based approach to curriculum has been far less common. Put simply, a curriculum framed by reference to the content and subjects regarded as important in a Eurocentric, white, middle-class ideology must be alienating to the majority of pupils whose social and/or cultural background is founded on different systems of values; and the imposition of such an ideology on these pupils plainly leads to unjustifiable inequalities in educational provision rather than to the opposite. The phenomenon of alienation, then, has been a major feature of secondary education for many years; and it is on that sector of education that the research has focussed.

The first point to be made here, then, is that the 'top-down pressure', the 'push-down phenomenon' to which we referred earlier will bring into the primary curriculum not only the subject/content base of the secondary school but, along with it, the alienating features of that form of curriculum which we have just briefly noted.

However, the problem goes further than this. For at primary level it is not merely the *kind* of content that the curriculum seeks to 'deliver' that is likely to have this alienating effect. It is also the very *nature* of the subject/content-based curriculum. For the reasons we gave earlier, the very organization of learning experiences into subjects will have the same kind of alienating effect on pupils who are of an age when, for sound developmental reasons, they are not yet ready to handle or respond to learning in this way. Thus a broad and balanced curriculum defined in terms of subjects and the content of those subjects cannot bring with it entitlement in anything but the most trivial sense, or in the sinister sense of entitlement to fail. And, for children of primary age, the problem will be doubly compounded, since not only is the actual content of this broad and balanced curriculum likely to prove alienating to many pupils, but the manner in which the learning experiences are offered is inappropriate and must lead to comparable problems — perhaps for all pupils.

And so, we must conclude by noting that the definition given to the notion of a broad and balanced curriculum in current policies leads not only to that internal self-contradiction to which we have referred on several occasions, since it is incapable of adhering to both of its proclaimed principles. It also, and more seriously, must lead to a debilitating impact on the primary curriculum and a resultant lowering of the standards of children's learning by imposing on them a body of content which may be inappropriate, and indeed unacceptable, to many; moreover if does this in a manner which is not properly matched to the learning styles of most, and perhaps, all. In short, it ignores what we know about how human beings, and especially young human beings, develop and make sense of the world.

Summary and Conclusions

Several issues of crucial relevance to the quality of educational provision have emerged from this discussion. First, an attempt has been made to demonstrate why rhetoric should have no place in educational policy-making in a free and democratic society. Second, it has been shown that, when it does so, its effect is to diminish the quality of the thinking behind that policy-making and thus, by a natural extension, the quality of educational provision itself, not least as a result of its own inherent self-contradictions. Third, the chapter has illustrated this claim by reference to the use, within the rhetoric of current discussions, of the concepts of 'breadth' and 'balance', showing that the adoption within the rhetoric of these two important concepts, and especially their conflation into one, have led to a loss of their value and usefulness as tools of educational planning. Finally, it has been shown that the particular, supposedly non-problematic, meaning which has been given to them within current policies represents an ideology which is antithetical not only to what a great deal of research evidence suggests are the natural learning styles and modes of understanding of young children, but also to the rhetoric's own declared aims and intentions.

A further general point of extreme significance has been discernible behind and throughout the whole discussion. In a democratic society, it is not the role of the professional merely to carry out the instructions of society in his/her own field of professional expertise and responsibility — and especially not when those instructions are issued by politicians on the basis of an assumed consensus or, worse, a consensus generated by skilful manipulation and the use of rhetoric. The professional has the further responsibility to make her/his expertise available to society as a source of deepened understandings of the issues lying within his/her own field in order to support the process of making informed choices and well-substantiated decisions.

Vic Kelly and Geva Blenkin

At present, the education profession in the United Kingdom has lost, or, rather, been deprived of, this role. (And we should not lose sight of the fact that perhaps it has never hitherto fulfilled it with total conviction.) It is important, however, that it be recovered, if only to ensure that there is a proper breadth and balance not only in the curriculum nor even only in the education system, but also in society itself where it is equally important.

References

ALEXANDER, R.J. (1988) 'Garden or jungle? Teacher development and informal primary education' in BLYTH, A. (Ed) *Informal Primary Education Today*, Lewes, Falmer Press, pp. 148–88.

ARCHAMBAULT, R.D. (Ed) (1965) *Philosophical Analysis and Education*, London, Routledge.

BALL, S. (1990) *Politics and Policy Making in Education: Exploration in Policy Sociology*, London, Routledge.

BENNIS, W.G., BENNE, K.D. and CHIN, R. (1969) *The Planning of Change* (2nd edn), New York and London, Holt, Rinehart & Winston.

BLYTH, W.A.L. (Ed) (1988) *Informal Primary Education Today*, Lewes, Falmer Press.

CHERRYHOLMES, C.H. (1987) 'A social project for curriculum' *Journal of Curriculum Studies*, 19, 4.

DEPARTMENT OF EDUCATION AND SCIENCE (1977) *Curriculum 11–16*, London, HMSO.

DEPARTMENT OF EDUCATION AND SCIENCE (1979) *Aspects of Secondary Education in England: A Survey by HM Inspectors of Schools*, London, HMSO.

DEPARTMENT OF EDUCATION AND SCIENCE (1985) *The Curriculum from 5 to 16, Curriculum Matters 2*, London, HMSO.

DEPARTMENT OF EDUCATION AND SCIENCE (1989) *National Curriculum: From Policy to Practice*, London, HMSO.

DEWEY, J. (1922) *Democracy and Education*, New York, Macmillan.

EISNER, E.W. (1982) *Cognition and Curriculum: A Basis for Deciding What to Teach*, New York, Longman.

GELMAN, R. and GALLISTEL, C.R. (1978) *The Child's Understanding of Number*, Cambridge, MA, Harvard University Press.

HIRST, P.H. (1965) 'Liberal education and the nature of knowledge' in ARCHAMBAULT, R.D. (Ed) *Philosophical Analysis and Education*, London, Routledge, pp. 113–38, also in PETERS, R.S. (Ed) (1973) *The Philosophy of Education*, Oxford, Oxford University Press, pp. 87–111.

HUGHES, M. (1986) *Children and Number: Difficulties in Learning Mathematics*, Oxford, Blackwell.

JAMES, C.M. (1968) *Young Lives at Stake*, London, Collins.

KATZ, L.G. and CHARD, S.C. (1989) *Engaging Children's Minds: The Project Approach*, Norwood, NJ, Ablex Publishing corporation.

KELLY, A.V. (1986) *Knowledge and Curriculum Planning*, London, Harper & Row.

KELLY, A.V. (1989) *The Curriculum: Theory and Practice* (2nd edn), London, Chapman.

KELLY, A.V. (1990) *The National Curriculum: A Critical Review*, London, Chapman.

NATIONAL CURRICULUM COUNCIL (1990) *Curriculum Guidance 3: The Whole Curriculum*, York, National Curriculum Council.

NOWELL-SMITH, P.H. (1954) *Ethics*, Harmondsworth, Penguin.

PETERS, R.S. (Ed) (1973) *The Philosophy of Education*, Oxford, Oxford University Press.

PETTER, G.S.V. (1970) 'Coherent secondary education', *Trends in Education*, 19.

PHENIX, P.H. (1964) *Realms of Meaning*, New York, McGraw-Hill.

SCHOOLS COUNCIL (1975) *The Whole Curriculum 13–16*, Working Paper 53, London, Evans/Methuen.

SCHOOLS COUNCIL (1981) *The Practical Curriculum*, Working Paper 70, London, Methuen.

SNOW, C.P. (1959) *The Two Cultures*, London, Cambridge University Press.

SNOW, C.P. (1969) *The Two cultures* and *A Second Look*: an expanded version, *The Two Cultures and the Scientific Revolution*, London, Cambridge University Press.

WHITE, J.P. (1973) *Towards a Compulsory Curriculum*, London, Routledge.

WHITEHEAD, M.R. (1990) *Language and Literacy in the Early Years: An Approach for Education Students*, London, Chapman.

Part 2

Breadth and Balance in the School Context

Chapter 5

Influences on Curriculum Balance at School Level: A Case Study

Mike Ashton

Introduction: Factors in the School Setting

Although the establishment of a primary curriculum which is both broad and balanced in its composition is central to the educational debate, its successful translation from the design board to action programmes is determined to a large extent by other factors. Any base for planning, therefore, must consider the age, design and condition of school premises, the experience and potential of its teachers and the income generated by its pupils. Failure to do so will produce a school development plan that is idealistic and does not acknowledge the real school situation. What, therefore, are the issues that affect and determine a balanced approach to the management and delivery of the primary school curriculum?

It may seem logical to start the discussion with school premises. Undoubtedly, these will affect class size, pupil groupings, teaching approaches and curriculum provision such as physical education and music, but it is the school's budget that offers opportunities for change, including the internal design of the building. The major part of a school's income is pupil-related and will, to some extent, reflect its status in the neighbourhood. This popularity may be rooted in tradition or through the expectations and achievements expressed in a glossy school brochure. It may, on the other hand, represent the ebb and flow of population and the changing socio-economic climate of the community. Whatever the size of a school's budget and however it has been generated, conflicting demands will impose the need for a balanced approach to financial planning. Minor improvement projects cannot be seen in isolation from programmes of planned, preventative maintenance, and teaching materials must be balanced with the provision of other curriculum resources.

The teaching establishment to some extent is influenced by local and national agreements on pupil/teacher ratios. These may need to be considered alongside the expansion of non-teaching staff to meet the administrative demands of a delegated budget. What must not be compromised, however, is the belief that teachers are the most valuable resource, even if the most expensive.

Within a framework through which teachers carry out their professional and management responsibilities, a number of points of tension are likely to emerge which are worthy of further consideration. Promotion structures in the short-term must be designed around the current range of expertise and should represent the reality of the school environment. In contrast, long-term staffing plans identify a range of areas for development and specify a series of desirable management skills and experience which may or may not present promotion opportunities for teachers within the school. The rationale would seem to be a balance between availability and opportunity. Where teachers aspire to positions which carry curricular or departmental responsibilities, the requirement to carry out related management tasks may be in some conflict with their duties as classroom teachers. The provision of non-contact time is currently limited in primary schools and will need to be identified and resourced in the school's development plan. Within this allocation of time the balance between preparing curriculum plans and implementing them alongside colleagues in their classrooms may be difficult to achieve.

Further elements which profoundly affect the quality and delivery of the curriculum are the complexities of staff development. These are to do with meeting school needs and addressing personal preferences and career intentions. Whilst curriculum development is essentially about staff development, there are fundamental differences between the two activities. School needs can be met either through whole-staff programmes of learning, or by resourcing the curriculum through the development of an individual teacher. It is much more difficult to service the career paths of individual teachers. Solutions to these INSET dilemmas may be found in the area of curriculum identified for development in the plan and closely linked with the budget priorities and allocation.

However, such arrangements do not take account of the time that teachers give to participating in courses outside normal school hours and attending numerous curriculum and departmental meetings. Senior management must constantly monitor the frequency and purpose of meetings, otherwise there is likely to be an imbalance between the professional duties of teachers and their domestic responsibilities.

The final and most important notion of balance refers to the preparation, delivery and evaluation of the school's curriculum. By necessity it must be an integral component of the planning process, although intermediary audit at the forecasting, tracking or assessment stages will monitor whether balance is being maintained. It will determine time allocation for national curriculum, core and foundation subjects in the short-term, and focus on demand within individual subjects when weightings have been specified.

Where consideration is given to progression and continuity within the primary phase, planning for balance will need to examine the range of pupil groupings and teacher deployment throughout Key Stages 1 and 2. Whether these plans distinguish between generalist teaching and subject specialism will be for each school to decide. Attempts to blur the distinctions between schools either side of the traditional point of transfer will require teachers from all schools to initiate development plans to this end. The National Curriculum will provide the framework on which these plans and the vehicle for delivery can be built. A successful outcome will depend on a collective and positive attitude by all participants.

Accountability for curriculum plans and their delivery is now invested in the powers and responsibilities of school governors. They will need to balance the findings of institutional self-reviews with reports and surveys carried out by the local education authority. Quality assurance will be further validated through inspections by HMI, or the inspection teams franchised by them.

So far, discussion has focussed on issues that influence the planning and delivery of the curriculum, either to enhance its quality or inhibit the good intentions of those charged with its design. This is because it is essential to acknowledge the influence that human and physical resources bring to bear on the school balance sheet, otherwise the construction of a development plan that seeks to ensure breadth and balance in the curriculum may be no more than a theoretical exercise.

I must now turn to the heart of the matter and address some practical issues that relate directly to a balanced curriculum.

Balance: The Use of Time

A starting point for a definition of a balanced curriculum is outlined in *Curriculum Matters 2* (DES, 1985). The document expresses the need to ensure that each area of learning is given appropriate attention in relation to others and the curriculum as a whole. When designing a balance sheet, this requires the allocation of sufficient time and resources for each area and element to be fully developed.

In their survey (DES, 1989a), HMI reported that most schools spent a very large proportion of their time on core subject work and that many schools would meet difficulties in providing the full range of core and foundation subjects. If reasonable time is to be allocated to the other foundation subjects, schools will need to reappraise current forms of curriculum organization (NCC, 1989) and apply more rigorous methods of curriculum planning and evaluation. Implicit in this recommendation was the need for schools to examine their current practice and know how much time is allocated for the different curriculum areas and what it proposes to devote to each subject as a result of its audit.

The Annual Curriculum Return required by the Department of Education and Science (DES, 1989b) sought to provide information on total lesson time for each age group of children and the implementation of the National

Table 5.1: Curriculum balance

Mathematics	152 modules ave. 4 per week
English	152 modules ave. 4 per week
Science	114 modules ave. 3 per week
Technology	38 modules ave. 1 per week
Geography	47 modules ave. 1.24 per week
History	47 modules ave. 1.24 per week
Art	38 modules ave. 1 per week
Music	38 modules ave. 1 per week
Physical education	76 modules ave. 2 per week
Religious education	19 modules ave. 0.5 per week

Curriculum. Although clinical in its composition and presentation, it did as-sist schools in forward-planning of curriculum provision. Using a year as a uniform time frame, it claimed to enable schools to represent their curriculum with some degree of accuracy and, at the same time, retain flexibility to allow a variety of provision from one part of the year to another. One could not disagree with the theory that by translating priorities into real time schools could make a commitment to managing and teaching their curriculum. The above example, Table 5.1, illustrates how this might be done by expressing the annual curriculum potential in terms of multiples of one hour modules. If, however, time allocation produces an unnecessary, fragmented curriculum and commits pupils to detailed timetables, it is likely to be counter-productive and unhelpful to the child. To deliver all subjects in independent modules of time in a week may not lead to effective and efficient use of time.

This audit exercise has raised a number of interesting issues which are fundamental to the planning and delivery of the primary curriculum. Firstly, whilst lessons can be planned on a daily basis with appropriate time allocation, equally patterns of timing can be planned across longer periods. A particular strength of an analysis of time is recognizing the difference between those curriculum elements that require a regular input and others that might be delivered over a longer period of time. Planning for balance needs to take several forms and must stand examination across the primary phase. This does not, of course, assume that all work for a year or more should be planned in detail. To do so would produce a sterile syllabus and leave no room for the child to negotiate or be guided into areas of learning which arise spontaneously.

The second point refers to the framework provided by the National Curriculum. Although it is expressed in terms of subjects and it is necessary, therefore, to plan subject-specific work, it does not preclude flexibility of delivery across subject boundaries. What is important, according to NCC (1989), is to structure the curriculum, in a manageable and efficient way.

Some of the work that takes place in primary schools, particularly at Key Stage 1, is through a thematic, topic-based or cross-curricular approach. Indeed, Clemson and Clemson (1989) argue that it is likely to be difficult to meet all the requirements of the National Curriculum without using carefully planned topic work. They suggest the possibility of developing a framework based on the grouping of subjects under areas of knowledge and experience; children tackling aspects of several attainment targets at one time, a process that Harrison and Theaker (1989) refer to as 'multiple accounting'.

Before the National Curriculum was specified, many schools had devised and sequenced a skill-based curriculum which could be taught through a combination of topic and subject lessons. It required the separation of the process skills of a subject from its knowledge content. With the National Curriculum this is easier to do with subjects where these skills are contained in specific attainment targets, for example, Exploration of Science and Using and Applying Mathematics.

Teachers frequently use the opportunities presented by topic work to observe whether knowledge assimilated in one context can be applied to new situations in other areas of learning. They also acknowledge the role topic work has to play in the mastery of study skills. Whether it is possible to deliver two or more subjects at the same time will be a decision that schools will have to make as they become familiar with the National Curriculum. What is clear is that there are many links between the foundation subjects, so that work in one subject contributes to work in others. This does not argue for a wholly integrated curriculum nor the core subjects being taught entirely separately. It merely serves to highlight the difficulties when considering the time element in a school's documentation of curriculum planning. One such example might be the allocation of time in English where it is taught both separately and through other curricular areas. In a similar example, DES (1989a) reflected considerable variations in how schools described what they did in mathematics and the difficulties they experienced when estimating time allocation in integrated work.

The Annual Curriculum Return did offer some guidance here by stressing the need to avoid double-counting of lesson time, expressed as a percentage of the total lesson time for an average week. For example, if the planned purpose of science lessons was to meet the requirements of National Curriculum Science, the total time spent on science lessons should be allocated wholly to National Curriculum Science. On the other hand, if the planned purpose of science lessons was to teach National Curriculum science and also elements of National Curriculum English and mathematics, then the total time spent on science lessons should be divided approximately between these three subjects. It is important to remember here that any such plans are set out for each class as a whole and do not prescribe the curriculum time for individual children. They must be flexible enough to accommodate the range of pupil needs, differentiated by tasks, and by the varying amount of time individual children will need to spend to achieve the same objectives. In any event, the balance of time spent on individual subjects within a week or year can only be expressed in average terms. Anything else may require the curriculum to be delivered in unmanageable packages and impose major constraints.

The Curriculum Return was successful in that it required schools to undertake a curriculum time audit in some considerable detail so as to provide information on subject/time allocation that would be helpful with future planning. It was less successful when theory and reality became incompatible and the actual curriculum provided differed considerably from that planned. The announcement that time allocation for particular subjects would not be centrally prescribed came as no surprise and was greeted with considerable relief by teachers.

There is, of course, a further dimension to the question of balance in the curriculum, namely balance *within* each area and element of learning. Teachers have traditionally sought to include in their weekly timetables pupil activities for each element of a curriculum discipline. Reading, spelling, comprehension and creative writing, with perhaps some attention given to oral communication skills, have traditionally been the ingredients of a language curriculum. Whilst these elements have not diminished in their importance and are now expressed as attainment targets in the National Curriculum, there is a greater awareness of the contributions that they have to the curriculum as a whole. Clemson and Clemson (1989) argue that a broad and balanced language programme is the best way of ensuring awareness of the total curriculum. It is, they say, the mortar that binds the curriculum together.

Proposals (DES, 1991a) regarding weightings and profile components offer some guidance to schools when addressing the task of establishing balance within a curriculum area. Particularly significant are the variations and differences in weightings between profile components and from Key Stage 1 to Key Stage 2. When drawing up schemes of work according to the proposals, schools should be guided by the weightings recommended. However, maintaining a balance within each area and element of learning (DES, 1985) cannot be maintained if undue emphasis is placed on the mechanical aspects if language and mathematics.

A further example of establishing balance in the delivery of activities within a subject appears in the draft orders for physical education. Clearly, not all areas of activity require an equal share in each Key Stage. Children's physical development demands different emphases on different activities at different times. If children are to progress to recognized forms of games and athletics in later years they must have pursued in depth the foundation of basic movement and skills at Key Stages 1 and 2. The context in which these can be established is a balanced programme of gymnastics, dance and games. The key to their success, however, as has been argued earlier may depend on resources including buildings and the availability of staffing expertise rather than the amount of curriculum time that can be allocated to them.

How, then, are schools to address these issues? The following account is the case study of one school. Information gathered about the real school situation offers evidence in support of the belief that a broad school balance sheet is determined to a large extent by factors other than generalized plans for curriculum or time use.

The Case of One School

The Context

The case study school is a large primary school of over 750 pupils, situated in a densely-populated, urban area. Its pupils are crowded into an aging, two-storey building, used originally as a boys' grammar school. Very few of its classrooms are of a uniform size and the movement of pupils around the building is a major problem. There is, however, a very friendly and positive atmosphere within the school, based on good relationships and high expectations. Within a budget of almost £1m, I have, as Headteacher, been able to establish a framework for the delegation of responsibility based on a range of incentive allowances, with each post carrying management responsibilities commensurate with the position. Large primary schools are distinctly advantaged in terms of planning and in the variety of management strategies available to them (DES, 1989a). This is mainly as a result of formula funding and such establishments are more likely to benefit from opportunities presented by a delegated budget than suffer the constraints imposed by its cash limitations.

Curriculum Leadership

All curriculum areas are led by a Coordinator who is supported by a team of teachers representing every age group. These curriculum leaders operate within job specifications which reflect local and national demands and management tasks which are proportionate to the experience of the postholder. They are dynamic and form the basis of an annual review. Whilst they carry a degree of negotiation, each specification is closely linked to the agreed curriculum development plan and its associated activities. Each Coordinator is responsible for translating the programmes of study into schemes and guidelines, advising teachers on the teaching content, organizing resources and disseminating information about current legislation and local education authority policies. These key people perform a vital role in the presentation and delivery of the curriculum. Harrison and Theaker (1989) rightly argue that there is no way headteachers can hope to provide the detailed knowledge and understanding of each area of the curriculum. They must recruit and promote teachers to positions of curriculum leadership which will determine a structure through which curriculum needs and personal development can be met.

Structures are, therefore, an amalgam of curricular demands and teachers' capacities. They cannot be a fixed entity, independent of, and imposed on, the people in the school, but must respond to school needs and have identified teachers' individual skills and qualities.

The priorities identified through the curriculum development plan determine a programme of management support where curriculum co-ordinators are released from teaching duties, either to support colleagues in their classrooms or to carry out other management tasks. It was not assumed that teachers would willingly accept colleagues into their classrooms and function in a subordinate role when, in other circumstances, they held a senior position. Credibility had first to be established through coordinators making vital contributions to staff meetings and leading curriculum groups and discussions. The emphasis, therefore, was placed on partnership rather than an unnecessary and inappropriate hierarchy.

When such classroom support is requested or deemed necessary, consideration is given to whether this would be for a short term or extended over a longer period. Where long-term classroom support has proved necessary is with curriculum areas that require new skills or specialist knowledge. Support within the classroom for technology is now in its second year and its duration is likely to be challenged by demand for music and physical education. Programmes of support are tailored to meet the needs of pupils and teachers. They enable the strengths and expertise of curriculum coordinators to be accessible to a wider range of pupils; they provide, by example, the skills required to deliver the unit of work; and they establish a base on which the confidence of colleagues can be developed.

In addition to working alongside colleagues, curriculum co-ordinators are responsible for arranging school-based INSET and evaluating curriculum development. They arrange workshops for parents and present policy statements and curriculum documents to committees of the governors.

Two senior members of staff are responsible for monitoring the provision and continuity of curriculum within, and between, early years and the junior department. One of the two deputy heads coordinates teaching and learning activities across the whole school in order to monitor curriculum breadth and balance from within Key Stage 1 through Key Stage 2. The other deputy is responsible for the management of resources and financial planning.

All teachers meet weekly in their year groups to prepare detailed planning record information and consider assessment procedures. Policy options and recommendations are discussed at full staff meetings and decisions and action plans are made as a result of these consultations. A point worth making here is that, although the overriding theme of the school is one of involvement of staff in the decision-making process, in reality the staff meetings and sub-committees may be simply forums for the exchange of information. If this is so then Southworth (1989) is right and a partnership of equals may not necessarily be on offer. What is clear, however, is that a principal aim of involving staff in the management of the school through staff, curriculum and departmental teams, is to assist in the preparation of plans for the school.

Budget Setting

A small group of senior staff form a management team which meets to consider and formulate policy options for whole-staff discussion. Included in their brief is the determination of a 'Resource Budget Allocation Plan', although the overall budget setting is the responsibility of a governors' sub-committee. This allocation plan represents a cycle of curriculum submissions, a programme of consultation and the determination of a resource budget. It draws its funding from the capitation allocation of the overall school budget and additional sources of income, including sponsorship, parent/teacher association and local and national grants. The plan seeks to establish balance, in terms of finance, between the day-to-day requirements of the school and the specific curriculum areas for development which have been prioritized in response to school-focussed and external demands. It is my belief that when curriculum responsibility is delegated and endorsed with a specific budget allocation for which the coordinator is the budget holder responsible, it often results in a greater awareness, motivation and willingness to identify ways to improve the service and reduce wastage.

Staff Sub-committees

The management structure within the school is designed to encourage staff contributions to the decision-making process. Smaller groups work to specific briefs, either planning the teaching and learning activities within an age group or preparing policy options for whole-staff discussion. These groups of four or five teachers recognize the limits of people's participation and are intended to encourage more active staff involvement. All meetings work to an agreed agenda and minutes and action plans are distributed to appropriate groups and individuals. Table 5.2 illustrates the range of sub-committees, the compositions, brief, objectives and frequency of meetings:

Table 5.2: Management structure within school

	Number of participants	Brief	Cycle	Objectives
Whole staff	*36	Consider policy options Decision making	Four-weekly	
Curriculum Sub-committee	8	Consider and disseminate current legislation, prepare guidelines and policy documents	When necessary	Short, medium and long term. Specified in agendas. Development plan and responding to local and national demands.
Year group leaders	3	Whole-school planning, curriculum balance and continuity	Three-weekly	
Finance Sub-committee	3	Determine budget options for governors and staff	Weekly	
Senior staff	6	Prepare policy options for whole-staff discussion	Weekly	
Year group meetings	*4–7	Detailed planning and evaluation	Weekly	

* Includes Classroom Assistants

School Development Plan

The Audit Commission (1991) suggested that the approach to the school planning and decision-making process could be summarized in the following way:

   (i)   setting aims;
  (ii)   identifying possible actions to meet these aims;
 (iii)   identifying resources needs;
  (iv)   selecting actions which are achievable within the funding allocations;
   (v)   implementing;
  (vi)   evaluating.

Prior to this, of course, is the need for an outline audit of the areas selected for development and their relative priority. Woven into this framework will be the consultation process between teachers, governors and link inspectors, timescales, publications and internal and external reviews. It should also contain the success criteria which specifies outcome and the standard to be expected. One school management plan, (LMS, 1989), identified eight elements which determined the actual school programme:

> School objectives
> Staffing (including development)
> Physical resources
> Finance
> Teaching and learning strategies
> Curriculum needs
> Pupil numbers (class organization)
> Pastoral care and policies

It is unrealistic to assume that schools can undertake a full scale review of all areas each year. The plan should be neither too ambitious nor insufficiently demanding (DES, 1991b). It is likely that schools will prioritize a number of areas for development that are achievable within a year.

With these guidelines in mind we sought to identify a framework through which a plan of needs for development could be set in the context of the aims and values of the school. We recognized that developing a plan is a complex but challenging task and has two major advantages (DES, 1991b); those that improve the quality of education for pupils and those which are by-products of the planning process and are about the benefits derived form people planning together. The Deputy Head produced a model based on a system of hexagons, each of which tesselated with the child at the centre who represented the core of the plan.

Connected to each core hexagon are smaller satellite hexagons that contain objectives and strategies which need to be implemented in order to satisfy the aims of the school. Year group leaders were asked to identify resource needs and say whether their requests were short-medium-or long-term. Similarly, each curriculum coordinator was required to carry out a subject audit, prioritize requirements and targets together with their cost implications.

From these exercises, areas for development were classified under four major headings:

(i) home/school relationships
(ii) alterations and furnishings
(iii) curriculum planning
(iv) curriculum time allocation (with particular reference to science)

The first area had little or no cost implications and required the staff to consider a range of written reports, meetings and classroom visits.

The second arose out of an 'accommodation crisis', although it proved to be an imaginative use of space. It required the conversion of a small balcony and corridor into an open-plan teaching area. Here, the cost implications were considerable in that a dividing wall had to be removed and a whole new area carpeted. What became evident from staff discussion was the need to reconsider pupil groupings, classroom organization and methods of teaching within this proposed teaching area. Additional furniture, free-standing display boards and storage units had to be included in the costing. A further point was the consideration that would have to be given to the staffing of this unique area. It became necessary to examine the relevant experience of this team of teachers and balance this with their ability to adapt to new circumstances. It created a climate and philosophy of its own which required the approval of governors and the understanding of parents.

The local education authority had provided schools with a range of forecasting and tracking guidelines which would enhance curriculum design and aid implementation of the National Curriculum in the context of the whole-school curriculum. They sought to inject rigour into some activities and make others more meaningful in relation to all the subjects taught in primary classrooms. They predicted that the planning sheets would provide a map of the experiences children have had in other classes and other years. Schools across the authority naturally adopted a range of these suggestions through which the face of planning was to change for ever. Whilst there was uniformity within the case study school in terms of planning, there developed a growing unrest about the appropriateness of the forecasting sheets.

It became necessary to consider where there might be duplication, gaps or general weakness. To this end we embarked upon a programme which involved many meetings and a good deal of discussion but, through a careful selection of forecasting devices, could lead to a planning process for the whole school.

By this time it had been agreed that two-thirds of the planning for the school year should be completed by September to ensure balance of emphasis in lead subjects. To carry out this requirement it was necessary to:

(i) determine teaching teams for the coming year;
(ii) provide two days during the summer term for team planning;
(iii) make available reprographics and other resources to complete this task.

This activity was managed financially by using a proportion of our budget underspend to engage a team of supply teachers to provide the classroom cover. The deliberations produced nine planning sheets, although these were later reduced to five, which would be kept in a year group master file (see Table 5.3). Three stages of this process are worth elaborating on, in that they present a visual account of the extent to which curriculum balance has been considered in the planning:

(i) The Curriculum Balance Check Sheet, (Figure 5.1), plots the core and foundation subjects against a three-term year. Teachers are required to indicate lead and secondary subjects and update at subsequent planning meetings. This sheet was not popular as it duplicated information found elsewhere. For this reason it was discarded when the planning process was reviewed:

Figure 5.1: Curriculum balance check

	TERM 1		TERM 2		TERM 3
English	L.S.	Tasks	Tasks		
Maths	Scale & Plans Measurement Angles	Money Graphs Number-Division Multiplication	Time Area/Volume	Fractions Decimals	
Science	L.S.	Module	Module	L.S.	
DT	Task	L.S.	Task	Task	
History	Module	Module		Module	
Geography	Module	Module	Module	Task	
Art	Tasks	Tasks	Tasks	Tasks	
Music			L.S.		
PE	Drama Unit	Aerobics Gym	Drama Dance Unit	Skills PE	
RE	P.S.E. Module			Module	

1. Theme or topic (inc. Lead Subject)
2. Project
3. Task
4. Module
5. Unit
6. Free Standing Subject

Table 5.3: Planning process
Planning included in master file will be passed on at end of year. Photocopies of all sheets can be kept individually if required. Base files may be passed on if required.

	Cross Reference	Planning Level:	File
1 *Year Planner* (Two-thirds) Complete before September to ensure balance of subject lead emphasis.	2	As Year Group	Master File
2 *Topic Matrix* Complete before September.	1	As Year Group	Master File
3 *Curriculum Balance* Plot lead subjects, modules, tasks. Complete during planning for every new project/topic, etc.	1,2,4,6	As Year Group	Master File
4 *Key Stage Planners* Complete during planning for every new project, etc. Highlight ATs to be visited.	All	As Year Group	Master File
5 *Brainstorms* To contain *all* ideas for planning period. All thoughts & ideas which are generated on theme be put down. Highlight areas which are to be developed. *Not to put into subject areas. Use Curriculum Balance sheet and National Curriculum Key Stage Planners to guide highlighting.	3,4	As Year Group	Master File
6 *Curriculum Squares* Using Brainstorm, indicate which curriculum areas are led by theme and those which stand alone. Ring ATs to be considered. Some squares will be left blank.	5,4	As Year Group	Master File

7 *Pruner Planner*
Identify links with C/Areas. Look at specific content:
    Programmes of study/skills
    Resources needed
    Possible starting points
D.T. * Use special sheet.
	3,4,5,6	As Year Group	Master File

8 *Detailed Planning* Plan weekly/fortnightly specific content. Highlight ATs covered in forecasted work. * Use D.T. Sheet.	7,8	As Year Group	Base Individual Files
9 *Special Needs* Specific aims/objectives for special needs pupils to be identified at outset of project and up-dated, planned regularly on special sheets, and all to be done with liaison with S.N.C.	Use relevant/ appropriate sheets	Year Group Individual S.N.C.	M.F./ Individual Files

(ii) The year planner, similar in layout to the balance sheet, presents at a glance a clear picture of what work is to be covered across a Key Stage. Like all other elements of the planning process it provides additional information that will be useful when the children transfer from one age group to the next and from Key Stage 1 to Key Stage 2.

(iii) Information contained in the 'topic matrix', (figure 5.2), offers at a glance, horizontally, the range of topics covered in a school year. Topics covered and recorded in subsequent years provide, as an instrument of balance, the total experiences of a single age group throughout the primary phase:

Figure 5.2: Topic matrix

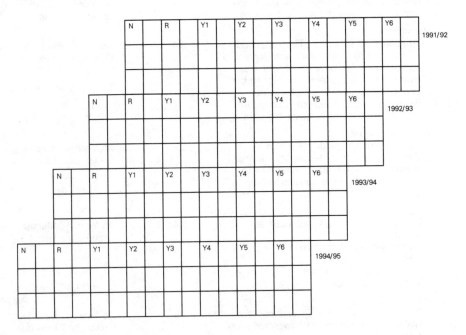

The fourth area which had been identified for development was specifically concentrated on curriculum provision. We had prepared a curriculum development plan in 1988/89. Having first identified the current position and specified the area for development, priority was assigned within the area and a timescale for implementation was agreed. Further to this, the planned expenditure and the financial year under which the budget heading was to be set were decided. A named member of staff was responsible for the organization.

One of the organizational themes chosen was 'curriculum balance'. The current position indicated that the core subjects were occupying, on average, about 40 per cent of the taught time. Information had been gathered by analyzing individual timetables and requiring teachers to carry out a curriculum inventory. Whilst there was agreement that this was disproportionate in terms of what needed to be covered in other foundation subjects, the concern centred around what should be left out if time allocation for core subjects was to be cut. The dilemma was further confused by national guidance on time allocation and teachers were left wondering how they could fit it all in.

It was decided to identify elements within core curriculum areas which could be taught through cross-curricular work and establish a more reasonable balance of time allocation. It was necessary, therefore, to consider how this might be addressed and attention was concentrated on project work as a vehicle for achieving this goal. Topic webs which have a reasonably balanced content can be drawn up and matched against the attainment targets and the programmes of study for National Curriculum subjects. This method of planning from activity to national curriculum will identify attainment targets and aspects of the programmes of study which do not fit into the web and must therefore be taught separately. Future plans would need to be modified to accommodate what is missing.

A second method which received consideration was to start with the National Curriculum Attainment Targets and Programmes of Study. Here, a single curriculum area could be the lead subject with other subjects, or parts of subjects, becoming involved where there was overlapping content or conceptual skills. It was recognized that several smaller topics would be necessary simultaneously to cover all the National Curriculum. Balance across a year would require the subject focus of the main topic being changed termly or half-termly.

Biennial Planning

Although both these approaches contained elements which were to prove helpful in planning for balance, it was the consideration of a third approach which offered some guidance on determining balance across a wider period of time than a single school year. This required the grouping of science attainment targets, together with the related programmes of study, to produce science-based topics that could be taught over a two-year period. Work in English and technology would service or complement the topic, with mathematics and other curriculum areas standing alone. Although it was felt that this method of 'adding on subjects' should not always have Science as its main focus, it directed our thinking towards planning in Key Stages as a whole school.

We decided, as a result of these deliberations, to plan topic/project work across a two-year period. Before this could be attempted it was considered necessary to assign levels of attainment to particular Key Stages and decide which attainment targets need to be aimed at each year and those that could be covered over a two-year period. A further requirement was to decide which curriculum area was to be the main focus of the topic. This was particularly important at that time as National Curriculum orders in technology, history and geography were about to be implemented.

They required an allocation of time which teachers were finding difficult to create. Figure 5.3 represents the outcome of planning topic work across years 3 and 4, and highlights the features of the agreed objectives. Biennial planning clearly creates a number of major benefits:

(i)   it offers the opportunity to develop a balanced diet for a significant period, with a variety of means of delivery and lead subjects;

(ii) it provides the confidence and comforts which come from sharing the task of development with others in the year group or Key Stage;

(iii) it establishes an easier review of what children have previously experienced.

The logistics of providing time and opportunity for the teachers of two age groups of teachers to meet and plan together was difficult and costly. They needed, first, to examine a summary of the previous year's work and note the gaps. Similarly, it was necessary to note which work had not been completed in year 3 before embarking on planning across years 3 and 4. The topic, 'Going into Europe', was to be a joint project. Release from teaching duties for half a day was clearly not sufficient and the exercise involved teachers attending several meetings. The outcome, however, was productive in that it presented opportunities for curriculum planning, with balance in mind, across a two-year cycle rather than the time limitations of one year. Further to this, it opened up the debate on the merits of staffing across a two-year cycle. Two major benefits of such a scheme emerged:

(i)   a team of four teachers could plan their work and establish breadth and balance across a longer and more reasonable period of time;

(ii) it reduced the points of transfer and exchange of information associated with them.

This alternative arrangement remains an option for future discussion.

So far, balance across the whole curriculum of a single year, or within a Key Stage, has been attempted during the planning process. A procedure to produce a curriculum inventory, a snap-shot of curriculum provision, is now established in the school. It requires year group leaders to present for each curriculum area the programmes of study from which the children in their year will be working. Using this information, the curriculum coordinators are able to prepare a balance sheet which identifies, within a single subject, duplication and where gaps need to be filled (see figure 5.4). A particular

Figure 5.3: Biennial planning

S: SCIENCE
H: HISTORY
G: GEOGRAPHY
L: LITERATURE

PLANNING

			COMPULSORY — EACH A.T. MUST BE DONE EACH YEAR			EACH A.T. MUST BE COVERED OVER 2 YEAR PERIOD — LIVING THINGS			
YEAR GROUPS	TOPIC		PROCESS SKILLS A.T. 1	MATERIALS A.T. 6	TECHNOLOGY A.T. 12	OURSELVES/ KEEPING HEALTHY A.T's 3 & 4	OTHERS PLANTS AND ANIMALS A.T's 2 & 4	ENERGY AND FORCES A.T's 10, 11, 13, 14, 15	EARTH ENVIRONMENT ATMOSPHERE SPACE A.T's 5, 9, 16
YEAR 3 TERM 1	LIGHT AND COLOUR		1					15	
	WEATHER	S	1					15	9, 15
YEAR 3 TERM 2	PINOCCHIO	L	1	6	12				
	ENTRY INTO EUROPE	G	1						
TERM 3	HEALTH AND SAFETY	S	1			3, 4		11, 13	
	INVADERS AND SETTLERS	H	1					10, 11	
YEAR 4 TERM 1	LITERATURE BASED CONSERVATION (animals, pets)	L G/S	1	6			2		5, 9
	MINI CHRISTMAS		1	6					
YEAR 4 TERM 2	TOYS	S	1	6	12			13	
	ENTRY INTO EUROPE	G	1						
TERM 3	HEALTH AND SAFETY	S	1			3, 4		13	
	HISTORY BASED	H	1						

Mike Ashton

Figure 5.4: Curriculum inventory

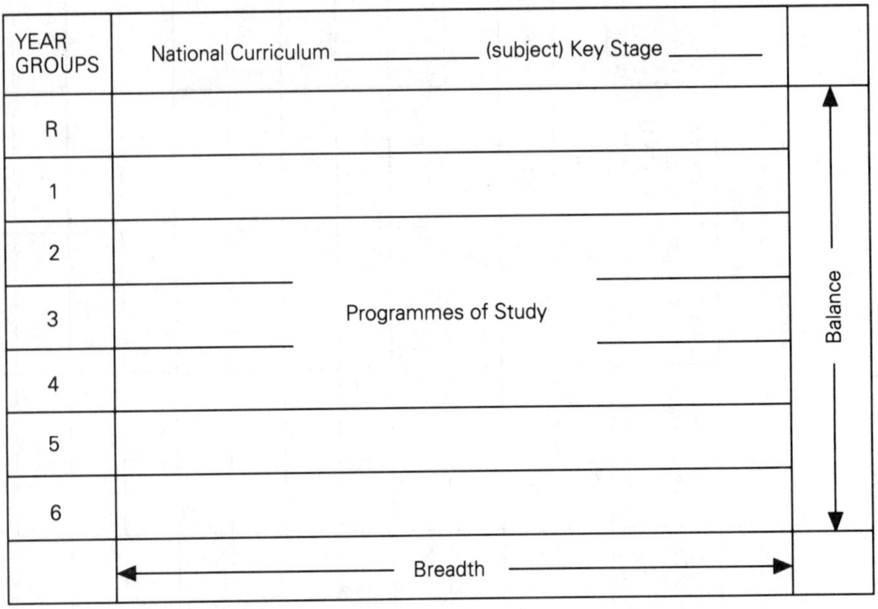

YEAR GROUPS	National Curriculum _____ (subject) Key Stage _____	
R		
1		
2		
3	Programmes of Study	
4		
5		
6		
	Breadth	

(Balance — vertical axis on right)

advantage of this instrument is that it feeds back useful information at the next stage of planning. Its limitations lie in the need to repeat the exercise for all National Curriculum areas. Having produced them, though, it presents opportunities to create a 'National Curriculum Map' from which the school Curriculum Development Plan can be directed. The large framework, very much like a wall mural, could be a useful instrument for considering balance in all curriculum areas and across the full primary phase. It offers at a glance curriculum continuity within each discipline over Key Stages 1 and 2.

Progression and Continuity

There is little doubt that the National Curriculum offers continuity and progression and a curricular language which all pupils and parents can share. It provides consistency through programmes of study and attainment targets which should enable children to move from class to class and from one area of the country to another.

A Framework for the Primary Curriculum (NCC, 1989) expressed the need for teachers to build on the work undertaken in previous years and Key Stages. It also called for assessment at the end of each Key Stage to influence decisions about work at the next stage. It rightly argued that continuity was no longer an optional issue in planning the curriculum, to be addressed at the point of transfer only.

To achieve continuity within our school we have engaged in a number of practical activities. The first is to plan for continuity through a variety of levels:

(i)   the whole school;
(ii) class and year groups;
(iii) individual and group.

These plans draw on the National Curriculum attainment targets and pro- grammes of study, together with the school's policy statements and schemes of work.

Delivery is through a variety of teaching approaches which include practical and theoretical, didactic and pupil-initiated, and individual, group and full-class teaching.

Whilst all year group teams of teachers plan, prepare and evaluate their work in similar fashion, methods of delivery are often quite different. The whole of the curriculum in Key Stage 1 is the responsibility of the class teacher who operates in the generalist mode. On the other hand, teachers working exclusively in Key Stage 2 share the expertise of colleagues in their teams to the advantage of all pupils in the age group. This form of organ- ization requires teachers, for some of the time, to work with different groups of children. It is seen as having the following advantages:

(i)   it reduces the amount of detailed preparation by individual teach- ers without losing any of the benefits of corporate planning;
(ii) it capitalizes on the individual strengths and expertise of its members;
(iii) it avoids the need for duplication of resources;
(iv) it requires a sharing of information on pupil progress and assess- ment;
(v)   it provides information on curriculum and pupil records for the next stage that reflect the opinions and observations of several teachers.

This last point refers to the second practical activity; the need to keep detailed records of pupils' achievements, together with evidence of work that shows development. We felt it necessary to have agreed systems of keeping records so that there is consistency and objectivity in the way that they are presented. The third activity is to communicate this information to the next stage. This may be between teachers in the same school or at meetings where teachers from different stages of education share a common goal.

Here, again, the National Curriculum offers the opportunity for the development of a programme for pupils from age 5 to 16. In this respect it coordinates details of the curriculum between one phase of education and another. Perhaps for the first time, it encourages teachers who are operating on either side of the primary/secondary divide, jointly to prepare programmes of work using common teaching approaches. No longer can one sector ignore what has previously taken place.

Indeed, the SEAC (1989) suggested that there were implications for the first three years of secondary education from the provision of National Assessment Information at the end of Key Stage 2. Our school has been engaged in link projects between secondary schools and their primary partners. Records of Achievement, which have gathered detailed information of the child throughout its life in primary school, are the vehicle for communicating evidence of these experiences. Teachers continue to meet with colleagues from similar and other phases of education to design and refine the transfer of documentation.

Accountability

Throughout this work, evidence gathered about our school has provided information on curriculum and the arrangements for school planning and development. It does not offer any measure of the quality, appropriateness and adequacy of these arrangements. Such judgments can be formed either by access to information now available as a result of legislation, or through a process of monitoring and evaluation.

Annual governors' meetings for parents, increased representation on governing bodies, the production of school prospectuses, and open enrolment are likely to persuade schools to take notice of the wishes of parents. In addition, the publication of assessment results will provide comparative data on the achievements of children on local schools and across the nation.

This increased awareness, however, need not intimidate schools but rather strengthen the relationship between teachers and parents. Curriculum workshops, parents' evenings and open days have traditionally featured in this partnership, and the legal requirement of schools to provide written reports on their pupils must be the outcome of continuous dialogue.

External monitoring, particularly through local education authority surveys, will go some way to providing accountability at that level and provide information which schools can use in their own development. Of greater importance is school self-review and development planning, the credibility of which may be validated by external review. Arrangements for self-review and planning are matters for governors, teachers and link inspectors.

DES (1991b) identified eight components for this procedure:

> Outline audit
> Priorities and timescales
> Action plans
> Budget statement
> Consultation with staff

Publication
Internal review
External review

In our school, at each stage of the procedure governors and link inspectors were asked to consider and approve results and recommendations.

Further opportunities for governors to consider and acknowledge arrangements for curriculum and school planning are at governor committees or specially-convened presentations by teachers with curriculum responsibility. Termly reports, which reflect the life and work, of the school, are presented to the governors and include contributions from every teacher.

Summary

This chapter has addressed two main issues throughout its analysis of a broad school balance sheet. It has considered:

(i)   time management in relation to core and foundation subjects;
(ii)   how the curriculum might be balanced within a school year and over longer periods of time.

Evidence from the real school situation has been used to illustrate how human and physical resources can influence curriculum plans.

It was not the intention of this chapter to offer practical guidance but a number of issues for practice have emerged from the evidence:

(i)   The construction of rigid timetables may not be desirable but curriculum time allocation cannot be ignored at the planning stage. What amount of time should be allocated to each area and how is this to be monitored?

(ii)   Does the balance of areas of study reflect the school's and national curriculum requirements?

(iii) To what extent does the curriculum offered within one area provide a broad experience of the defined subject?

(iv)   Planning for curriculum balance may be difficult to achieve in one year. What are the implications for management decisions on teacher deployment?

(v)   The determination of curriculum continuity and progression within the primary phase has implications for teaching methods. At what stage is subject specialism preferred to generalist teaching? How might this influence staff development and INSET arrangements?

(vi)   Whereas whole-school planning minimizes the possibilities of duplication and greatly enhances real continuity, it places the responsibility for planning and monitoring on the shoulders of curriculum

Mike Ashton

coordinators. Does this create some conflict between coordinators' management tasks and their duties as a classroom teacher?

References

AUDIT COMMISSION (1991) *Effective Resource Management in School*, London, HMSO.
CLEMSON, D. and CLEMSON, W. (1989) *The Really Practical Guide to National Curriculum, 5–11*, Bath, Bath Press.
DES (1985) *The Curriculum from 5 to 16: Curriculum Matters No. 2: An H.M.I. Series*, London, HMSO.
DES (1989b) *The Education (School Curriculum and Related Information) Regulations 1989*, London, HMSO.
DES (1989a) *The Implementation of the National Curriculum in Primary Schools*, London, HMSO.
DES (1991a) *Mathematics for Ages 5–16: Proposals of the Secretary of State for Education and Science and the Secretary of State for Wales*, London, HMSO.
DES (1991b) *Planning for School Development — Advice to Governors, Headteachers No. 2*, London, HMSO.
HARRISON, S. and THEAKER, K. (1989) *Curriculum Leadership and Coordination in Primary Schools: A Handbook for Teachers*, Whalley, Guild House Press.
LMS (1989) *The LMS Initiative: The Training Package, Level 1.*
NCC (1989) *A Framework for the Primary Curriculum*, York, National Curriculum Council.
SEAC (1989) *A Guide to Teachers Assessment*, London, HMSO.
SOUTHWORTH, G. (1989) 'Headteachers and collegiality' in GLATTER, R., PREEDY, M., RICHES, C. and MASTERSON, M. (Eds) in *Understanding School Management*, Milton Keynes, Open University Press.

Chapter 6

Balanced Thinking?
Curricular Tensions in a School Journey

Jennifer Nias

This chapter owes much to my personal contact with Alan Blyth. Firstly, it was he who, during the period that I was a lecturer in the University of Liverpool, first introduced me to the idea that the term 'curriculum' was both problematic and open to disciplined enquiry. I was fortunate in being in charge of the Primary/Middle PGCE course in the School of Education at the time when he and his associates were producing their pioneering work on the humanities curriculum. This not only influenced my work with my students in this area but also opened up for me new ways of thinking about the curriculum. In particular, it persuaded me that the primary curriculum was itself a fit subject for critical enquiry; up to that point I had tacitly believed that what children learnt from teachers' pedagogy was more important than the content to which they were exposed. It is no coincidence that the next post to which I moved was that of Tutor in Curriculum Studies, 3–13.

Secondly, Alan Blyth gave me gentle and timely help in the tentative research into teachers' work and lives which I began while he was my Head of Department. When this research, based on extended longitudinal interviews, was published as a book (1989), I was aware that its genesis fifteen years earlier owed much to Alan's belief and profession that in research into primary teaching respect for teachers' perceptions must go hand in hand with scholarship.

Thirdly, as external examiner at the Cambridge Institute of Education and editor of *Informal Education Today: Essays and Studies* (1989) he encouraged me to listen to teachers as they talked not only about their work but also about the curriculum, and to tease out from their accounts the beliefs and assumption which underpinned their practice.

In this chapter I have therefore chosen to bring together a study of teachers' experience of curricular tensions, and in particular of those associated with 'balance', through the words and thoughts of teachers themselves. However, on this occasion, I am one of those teachers and I use my own experience, documented in fieldnotes and a diary, as a main source of data and analysis, referring only occasionally to evidence supplied through interview by other participants. I make no apology for this subjectivity. In the first place, it draws attention to the valuable but often underestimated part which introversion may play in understanding teachers' worlds. In the second, it highlights some of the strengths and weaknesses of research undertaken by practitioners. Moreover, since research by teachers themselves is increasing in quantity and importance, I see value in sharing a small piece of it with a wider audience in a way which recognizes, but is not ashamed of, its imperfections. This stance is in itself a tribute to Alan Blyth's belief in the practitioner's capacity for continuing professional development.

Although this account relies heavily on my own interpretation of events in which I was a participant, all the data used appear in a case study of a primary school which has been read and validated by all its staff. This case study was part of a two-year research project (ESRC Ref No R000231069) into whole school curriculum development in primary schools during which my co-researchers, Penelope Campbell and Geoff Southworth, and I worked for a year as part-time teachers. Full details of our methodology are given in Nias, Southworth and Campbell (1992). Briefly, during our year's fieldwork we used ethnographic methods, particularly participant observation, interviews and documentary analysis. Using these data, we wrote case studies of the schools in which we had worked (in my case, this was one school). These were validated by participants and we then derived common themes and insights from all five case studies.

As part of my work as a teacher during the year, I was one of four adults accompanying a school journey for thirty 10- and 11-year-olds. This journey took place in the summer term, lasted five days, involved a coach trip of approximately six hours in each direction and residential accommodation at an out-of-season hotel.

The time was 1988/89, just as the National Curriculum was beginning to be introduced. However, though the National Curriculum was affecting teachers' planning, discussion and activity within the school, it had, as far as I was aware, very little impact upon the school journey. The events, conversations and personal reflections of that week seem rather to illustrate tensions within the primary school curriculum which transcend specific time-related considerations.

The school in which I worked and researched was Upper Norton (C of E Controlled) Primary School, a five-teacher village school for 4–11-year-olds. Full details of it are given in Nias, Southworth and Campbell (1992). Salient facts in this context are: The head of the school, Dorothy, had been in post for two years. During that time she had sought to liberate the talents and interests of her staff, particularly through the use of praise and encouragement. She had also sought to promote a broad curriculum and to increase the amount of practical activity, problem solving, group work and discussion which went on in classrooms. The adults on the journey were Katherine, Nancy, Norman and myself. Katherine, the Deputy, had been in the school for twenty-four years, for fourteen of these as Deputy. She taught twenty-seven children from years 4 and 5. She was used to a more book-bound and teacher-led curriculum than that encouraged by Dorothy. In addition there was a long history of mutual suspicion and misunderstanding between herself and Nancy. Nancy had been at the school for thirteen years, and had introduced the school journey some years previously. By her own account, she had blossomed personally and professionally under Dorothy's influence, taking on new challenges, interests and professional perspectives. She taught twenty-nine mixed-age children (years 5 and 6). Norman was a work experience student of 16 who joined the school one day a week throughout the year. He was a welcome addition to the school and was highly valued by staff and children alike for his maturity, reliability, initiative and good humour. I am a qualified primary teacher whose pedagogic skills are rusty, though I thoroughly enjoyed my year of working with children in the classrooms. It was twenty-five years since I had last participated in a school journey. I was invited by Dorothy, at Nancy's instance, to join the group and was happy to do so.

The catchment area of this 150-year-old school included both local families, often working in agriculture or allied industries, and a new generation of white collar commuters. The children included a high proportion of boisterous and headstrong boys and some children of both sexes who exhibited frequent signs of emotional disturbance. The journey was offered to all children in years 5 and 6 and about five out of six chose, or could afford, to come on it. The remainder stayed in school where special provision was made for them, in both social and curricular terms.

The school was a stimulating and friendly place in which to work. Like many primary schools, it had a tradition of staff isolation and individualism, but during the year, under Dorothy's leadership, a great deal of curricular discussion took place and staff worked increasingly together, inside and outside their classrooms. Children and staff were used to the presence of adults other than their classteachers and related easily to them.

I have highlighted four issues which aggravated the inevitable physical tensions of a residential journey. The first of these, relating to accountability, responsibility and control, underpins the next two. Both of these reflect the difficulties teachers experience in achieving curricular balance, on the one hand between different areas of experience and on the other between teachers' and pupils' conceptions of knowledge. The fourth concerns unscheduled disruptions and their impact on professional debate. All reflect unresolved tensions in the teachers' experience of the curriculum that they taught in school.

The first set of tensions derives from teachers' understanding of 'curriculum' as a complex, many-faceted, interrelated notion which is the servant of, and the vehicle for, their intention to educate individual children. Nias, Southworth and Campbell (1992) argue that the key to this comprehensive view lies in teachers' dual sense of accountability to and for their pupils (Elliott *et al*, 1981). They feel formally accountable to those (for example, headteachers, governors) to whom they have legal or bureaucratic obligations, but whom they often perceive as being distant or remote from their practice. They also, and much more powerfully, feel morally accountable for their pupils and through them to the latter's parents. This sense of moral accountability arises through, and is inseparable from, interpersonal contact and knowledge. The better they know their pupils, the more likely they are to feel morally committed to their progress and in many cases to their overall well-being. In Nias (1989), I made a similar claim. I argued, in the words of the teachers themselves, that to 'feel like a teacher' is to experience concern, responsibility and a desire to control, and that these feelings are interlinked. In particular, the felt-need to control is inseparable from concern and responsibility, particularly in the tense, crowded, swiftly-changing conditions of primary classrooms. Moreover, since many primary practitioners are socialized into a curricular tradition which stresses the importance of educating the individual and the 'whole child', they tend to feel responsible for children's development and learning across a vast, undivided curricular field. In turn, this sense of responsibility leads them to feel that they must exercise control over all aspects of the curriculum, if they are to meet their perceived obligation to educate each 'whole child' in their classes.

Furthermore, the isolated and individualistic conditions under which in the past much primary teaching has taken place has encouraged practitioners to invest a great deal of their sense of personal identity in the job (Nias, 1989). There is a widespread assumption that much of what individuals say and do should, indeed must, come from within themselves. The urge to control the curriculum which springs from concern and a deep moral sense of responsibility are compounded by the individual teacher's felt-need for self-reliance and self-expression.

In Upper Norton, as in all the case study schools, the close connection between accountability, responsibility and control was reflected in a general principle which seemed under almost all circumstances to guide the relationship between teachers and all other adults who were working with them, when children were present: One teacher, normally the classteacher, was in ultimate control of the others. Part-time teachers, students, welfare assistants, volunteers, parents, even supply teachers and the Head working alongside a colleague were all expected to operate under the guidance or direction of the children's main teacher. Similarly, when a teacher other than the classteacher had formal responsibility for part of the curriculum (for example, visiting specialists and advisory teachers), roles were reversed and the classteachers carried out the instructions they were given. 'Controllers' and 'helpers' both seemed happy with this situation.

However, as I worked in the school, I found that circumstances did not always make it easy for me to follow this tacit rule. Sometimes I encountered difficulties in fitting into a classroom because the extent of the responsibility which I was expected to assume had not been made explicit. At other times, my difficulties arose from the fact that the directions I was given took for granted a level of expertise which I felt I did not have (for example, in mathematics). This was particularly troubling because I felt accountable to the teachers in whose classrooms I worked, and did not want either to cut across their authority or to fail to fulfil their goals.

Although the circumstances of the school journey were different, I found that the tensions relating to responsibility and control were similar. During the week, the organization of the children into two classes for whom different teachers were responsible was suspended. Instead, Nancy assumed responsibility, as she had done in previous years, for all the children who came on the journey and Dorothy became the temporary, ex-officio 'class teacher' for those children from year 5 and year 6 who remained in the school.

That Nancy was in sole charge of the curricular and administrative arrangements for the journey was made very clear. In a summarized fieldnote during the spring term, I wrote:

Nancy has begun the preliminary arrangements. She asked me to go to an evening meeting with parents, 'so they can see you're a mature and responsible person'. This I did. I was impressed by Nancy's talk to them. It was lucid, friendly, detailed and uncompromising in its statements about what would count as unacceptable behaviour, and how this would be treated. Katherine (the Deputy) and Dorothy (the Head) were also present, but took a back seat. It was clearly Nancy's evening.

Katherine reported:

We didn't discuss a great deal what we were going to do. That is something that Nancy has always taken under her wing. We talked about some things, because I had been there, which places did I think we ought to visit . . . So a bit of discussion, but not a great deal. Nancy really did take that on herself.

During the follow-up period, when I worked in Nancy's classroom with my group, I noted:

Despite the arrangements I'd made two days before, I noticed when I came in that Nancy had done large folders for each group and had specific instructions for them, to carry them forward. Nancy obviously wants to control what is going on and I am quite happy that she should. It would make working in the same boat very difficult, if everyone wanted to steer.

Yet on the journey, the extent of the responsibility and authority which had been delegated was sometimes unclear. From the start, control of the children's social behaviour tacitly appeared to be a shared responsibility, especially on the coach, during mealtimes and the long evening and night hours. For example I noted in my diary:

> From about 10.00. pm. onwards followed a confused period in which we were all trying with various shades of bad temper, exasperation or amusement to settle particular children down. Everyone took a turn and in between times we sat in the bar, chatting and swapping stories from our past lives.

Norman later said:

> I did feel that as a staff group of four it ran quite smoothly. We all got on, we seemed to be able to cope with anything that came up without any problem at all.

I was also very confused about the extent of my responsibility for the curricular outcomes of the week. In my diary and in fieldnotes made during the follow-up period, I several times remarked that Nancy seemed to have a sharp picture in her mind of her learning aims for the journey and where these related to the curriculum already experienced by her own class. Afterwards she said:

> I would have said there were several aims relating to the work which both classes have done. Mine (related to) historical decisions, evidence of habitation, castles and defence and environmental choices of that sort. And some careful artwork in relation to what we were doing. Also reported facts and the response of their feelings to the various places.

However, the other adults did not share her clarity. During the preparation period, I noted:

> All of the staff have got a folder with the same information that all the children have got, but nothing very much else at the moment. The actual timetable for the day will be worked out daily according to the weather. Nancy clearly knows very well the background to the places we shall visit and seems to expect that the rest of us will pick it up as we go along.

and,

> Nancy spoke to both classes at the end of the afternoon. She told them that she was abandoning worksheets ... She went on, 'I've learnt the error of my ways. I've learnt that there are better ways to

do it.' She told them that they were going on the journey as reporters and they had got to observe, note, listen, draw and take photographs and that they were going to make a group newspaper. More details anon, she promised. Well, I certainly hope so because I'm still pretty cloudy about what is actually expected of me as a group leader . . .

During the journey I wrote:

The learning maps seem to exist very largely in Nancy's head. Does she not share them with us because she doesn't know how to, because she doesn't think it needs doing, or because her previous experience of working with other adults on school journeys has been that it's a waste of time?

Norman later said:

I don't think I really knew what I was supposed to be doing. I seemed to play it by ear for the majority of the week, taking it very much as it came. Obviously I knew which places we were going to, which days, various times of room inspections, what time they had to get up, what time they had to leave breakfast. But the rest of it I just played by ear . . . I felt that it was up to me with my group to point out various different things, to help with their learning, and then, once we had returned to the school, to continue that learning in their write-up and reports (but) if there was any, if you like weakness, it was that I didn't really know what the final outcome was going to be, therefore I didn't really know what the children were expected to do. That was why I asked you sometimes, as you seemed to know what was going on slightly more than me.

JN: Like you, I was making it up as I went along. Did anyone explain what the aims of the journey were to you?

No, they didn't. That possibly was also a handicap for me, not knowing what the aims were, so I could know what I, as a teacher, was expected to provide for the children.

A different problem arose in relation to the groups of children for whom, before the journey, each adult was given explicit responsibility — to work closely with them before and during particular visits and to monitor and evaluate their follow up work. In this instance our responsibility was clear, but it was difficult to discharge it effectively. There seemed to be two main reasons for this. First, it was extremely hard to keep the children together in their groups without destroying their incipient interest in, for example, Roman mosaics, the defences of mediaeval castles, different rock types. Within each group individuals moved, literally and intellectually, at different speeds and in varied directions. Some also wanted to rejoin the friends from whom for social reasons they had been divided or to abandon unpopular children with whom they had been placed. On no visit was I successful in keeping my group together for the whole of the allotted time and observation suggested that this was true of the other adults too. Occasionally this was my choice:

> After lunch, Nancy organized a rota for going round the mill. My group followed hers, so we were in the first room together. She was about to move on, but I couldn't bear to see all that basic technology being wasted. So I intervened, and began to talk and ask questions about the machinery. That was it for the next one-and-a-half hours. I found myself moving slowly round the mill with a flexible group of children (mostly, but not all, boys) who began to share my fascination with energy-transfer. I lost the rest of my group and just hoped someone else had an eye on them.

At other times I gave in to the diverse and exuberant interests of the children themselves and abandoned, not without qualms, what I knew was my responsibility for the behaviour and the learning of my group:

> We set off round the curtain walls ... By dint of constantly calling the runners back I was able to get most of them fairly, and some of them very interested in questions of attack and defence ... but once we were in the museum my group fragmented completely, and I found myself sharing particular exhibits with children from other groups too.

There was a second reason why I found it difficult to fulfil my responsibility for the learning of my group. On some occasions, particularly those which were tacitly, but not explicitly, viewed as times of general relaxation, children were not expected to keep to their groups. Instead they followed particular interests with different adults. For example:

> Once we got on the beach we divided naturally into four groups. Norman went running with some of the boys, Katherine got some children involved in collecting varieties of seaweed and Nancy had set up a competition for sand sculptures. I accompanied the 'explorers' out to the rocks at the far end.

So, all in all, I experienced a conflict between the expectations that I brought to the journey about accountability and therefore about my role as a 'helper', and the reality of the experience. I knew that Nancy was in charge of this journey, that she had done a great deal of work in preparation for it and that she had her own curricular goals for it. Furthermore, I had a great deal of respect and affection for her both as a colleague and as a practitioner. In my diary I wrote:

> I admire the work Nancy does with the children immensely and her relationship with them, which is warm, honest, tender, forthright and absolutely caring.

However, I was given little indication of her curricular goals. Moreover, circumstances did not allow me to substitute my own aims with my group or to carry these out in the ways in which I wanted. Furthermore, as a teacher, I could not bear to see particular learning opportunities lost to the children and occasionally therefore took control of a situation even when Nancy had made alternative suggestions or when to do so meant working with children other than those for whom I had explicit responsibility. Finally, some, but not all of the children's social education and behaviour was overtly seen as a responsibility which we all shared and in which everyone participated.

All in all, my unfeigned enjoyment of the week was marred by a perpetual sense of uncertainty as to whether, in relation to control, I was acting in normatively acceptable ways; by guilt when I felt that I was not; and by professional frustration because, though given partial responsibility for some children's learning, I could not guide it in the ways or directions in which I would have chosen if I had felt that I was fully responsible for it.

The second major set of tensions of which I was aware was a more clearly curricular one. It arose from uncertainty about the relative balance between the social, moral and 'academic' aims of the journey. The Head and staff of Upper Norton were agreed in placing a good deal of emphasis upon the social and moral education of their pupils. This was made explicit in the school brochure and constantly reaffirmed in interactions between the Head and individual pupils, in assemblies, and in day-to-day staff preoccupations and activities. Moreover, a good deal of time and energy were directed to those aspects of the explicit and hidden curriculum which were concerned with the children's moral, social and health education.

Not surprisingly therefore all the staff attached considerable importance to the social and moral aspects of the school journey and to its hidden curriculum. A number of factors made this clear. At the briefing evening in the spring term, the parents were given unambiguous information about the physical and moral care which would be taken of their children and of the social and moral standards which would be expected of them. They received no information of which I was aware about the teachers' aims or expectations in relation to other curricular areas or of the relationship between children's academic learning in school and during their week away. The children too were given clear guidance about the way in which they were expected to behave towards one another, and in public. I did not however witness or hear of any briefing about the places we were to visit, except in very general terms.

Similarly, Nancy's briefing to Katherine, Norman and myself covered only administrative and social matters.

Furthermore, the way in which the journey was conducted emphasized its social aims. The shortened diary extract below describes a typical occasion when, without discussion but with unanimous accord, the staff gave these priority over the environmental studies which they had earlier planned:

When we got within reach of our planned destination none of the roads were accessible for coaches and we ended up somewhere quite other ... By this time we had all been in the hot coach for about three-quarters of an hour and with one accord decided that we would not take anything with us on the beach at all ... Fairly soon the children wanted to know if they could paddle. Katherine suggested that they might take their trousers off and go in their underclothes. Soon almost everybody was cavorting with glorious spontaneity in the waves. E, for example, came racing back at one point and said, 'Can we get *really* wet?', took off his glasses, thrust them at Nancy and went plunging into the sea like a rather plump puppy ... So there we were, after a good half-hour, left with thirty children, all of them soaked from the waist down, many of them, especially the girls, with T-shirts soaked as well. So we set to, getting them to take their wet underpants off and putting them into their relatively dry trousers, wringing out T-shirts and getting them to run races up and down the sand, drying off. It had family feel to it and we all joined in ...

(Eventually) I let the winning racers run down the beach. We did a bit of casual geology on the way back but it seemed a shame to be didactic when they were so much enjoying the exercise. When we got back it was to find that friendship groups had split up over a stretch of sand and pools. Some had been making sand castles, including an attempt to model the castle we'd visited. A lot of them had been fishing in tidal pools and finding crabs of all sorts and one lot had been making a dam. A group of boys had embarked on an extensive piece of tunnelling and river direction. Nancy and Katherine had stayed still and children were running backwards and forwards show-ing them things and they were talking, naturally, about them. I looked at the crabs and admired them and then went off with one group to fulfil a promise going back two evenings, that we would make a sand castle that the sea could destroy ... M was unique in being ostenta-tiously bored. Nancy set her to work doing a large face of Medusa — at one point I went along and helped to find teeth and snaky hair for that ... In the end, our time ran out and then we all wandered in small groups back along the beach looking at seaweed and the sun on the sea. We had an absolutely wonderful afternoon. The children seemed ecstatic, the adults too were manifestly relaxed and happy.

The journey also presented many opportunities for the staff to emphasize its moral aims, and in particular to show that however tiresome or antisocial particular children might sometimes be, they cared about them and respected their individuality. One evening, I recalled in my diary:

> Meanwhile, R (whose behaviour in school was frequently very disruptive) had lost a very precious shirt given him by his mother especially for the journey. Nancy had exhausted herself looking for it. I asked if I could help. She said would I come and finish the search through suitcases and bedding . . . As luck would have it, (my conversation with R) triggered off a memory of where he had put it. We were able to take it downstairs, where everyone shared his pleasure.

The journey also put teachers under pressure to act as surrogate parents, a challenge which they willingly accepted. A typical incident occurred on the third night away:

> There was a bit of tearfulness and homesickness and, among the group of girls for whom I was responsible, a lot of carry-on because T had diarrhoea . . . By 11.00 they had all got something wrong with them and needed a cuddle to settle them down . . . Nancy too went along to see them. She, Katherine and I later stood for quite a long time on the stairs discussing the fact that when she went in to see them, they'd said, 'Mrs R, can we ask you some questions?' and then proceeded to ask her a number of questions which, as she said, she felt they should be asking their mothers, but 'Mrs R, we couldn't talk to them about that'. They had asked a number of very frank questions about sexual matters and were given equally frank responses. We talked about the trust that she must have established with them to make these kinds of questions and answers possible. We also talked about the ways in which the sexuality of the 11-year-olds begins to assert itself and how evident the interest of some of the boys is in sex, and in girls.

Indeed, the easy, unforced way in which adults and children related to one another on occasions such as these, and the unquestioning manner in which the adults attended to the latter's physical and emotional needs, helped to create an atmosphere throughout the journey which more closely ressembled that of a large, boisterous, extended family than a school.

That the teachers expected the journey to contribute to the social and moral education of the children was also evident from our discussion of their behaviour and of the ways in which they related to one another. In my diary I noted, towards the end of the week:

> Our talk about the children is always in terms of manners, sensitivity, maturity, those sorts of things, and also what we have learnt about

the 'whole child'. I haven't so far heard any discussions about what they might be learning or the kind of academic standards we should set or expect from them.

Further, we made our values obvious to the children through selective use of praise and reproof as we observed and intervened in their dealings with one another. The way in which the staff tried to behave towards one another was also consistent with the moral emphasis of the journey. We had not come together as an adult group out of friendship or agreed educational values. Yet I was frequently conscious that each one of us was making an effort to overcome our differences, to work constructively together and to get to know and appreciate one another as people. In particular Nancy and Katherine who in school often irritated and misunderstood one another, and sometimes openly disagreed, coexisted relatively harmoniously for a week in the enforced intimacy of a shared bedroom and during the day worked productively together as a team. One later said in interview:

> Sharing journeys has been very important. We've found that we can get on together professionally without being close friends . . . And we know a great deal about each other at a very personal level . . . I think I am much fairer to her now than I was.

Norman too — the only male, a student, many years younger than the rest of us — later said that one of the pleasures for him had been the way in which we had all worked together as a team. I shared this feeling and was conscious, as he was, that it had been a deliberate, though unspoken, choice on the part of us all.

However, clear though the importance of the journey's hidden curriculum was, the week was also conceived and planned as a set of learning experiences which spanned many other aspects of the school's curriculum, particularly English, art, history and geography. In school the staff talked about it as an 'educational visit' and referred to it in these terms to parents. The Head corrected children and their parents if they spoke of it as a 'holiday'. It took place in school time, and did not include a weekend. Further, Nancy selected the itinerary with a view to the learning potential of particular places and daily follow-up activities and periods of quiet, sustained 'homework' were planned, even if they did not always take place.

Yet, as a staff group, we gave no collective attention to the activities that we might ask children to engage in or to the learning which might result. Nancy later pointed out to me that she could not make the latter too explicit lest the journey itself be defined as part of the curriculum and the school, under the DES's funding regulations, be held responsible for it for all children. Be that as it may, opportunities for guided learning and for follow-up were frequently crowded out by administrative mishaps and social interaction. A typical diary entry reads:

Originally we'd planned that we'd settle down to work at the bay for an hour before we went down to the boat. But their berserk behaviour over lunch made this impossible. We planned instead a long work session after dinner. By this time we were all feeling in need of an occasion when we could settle down in concentration with our groups. Unfortunately dinner took two hours and it was after eight o'clock by the time we got out of the dining room. We knew we couldn't do more than half an hour then ... Half of them were late starting, N was so tired he had gone beyond reason and was distracting everybody all the time, and V and NK were very slow to settle ... We were constantly disrupted by some of Norman's group coming in and out, by the fact that one of his group had lost a watch on the beach and that an outsider wanted to use the bar where we were working.

Under these circumstances, I experienced two sets of tensions in relation to the curriculum of the journey. First, there was the *de facto* imbalance between its social and curricular aims. Second, my own priorities as a teacher were disturbed by the fact that we neither acknowledged nor addressed this disequilibrium. I see the social, emotional and moral development of children as a necessary but not a sufficient purpose for my work as a teacher. To be sure, it was clear from the work that Nancy and Katherine undertook with their classes in school that they too were concerned with the children's cognitive and aesthetic development even though on the journey their priorities sometimes seemed to be different from my own. Indeed, when, later on, I talked to Nancy about the week, she herself was aware of the difficulties of achieving a balance between the journey's academic and its other purposes.

What you never think of beforehand is the absolute exhaustion of yourself and the children within the day. You work all day and most of the night, but the children aren't working all the time. (You forget) that they will subvert academic work all the time with very great skill and energy and that the overriding factor of safety takes a lot of time away from the work ... That they are happy is equally important too or you'll get no work out of them at all. Then (there's) all the other social factors about behaviour and relationships with other people which make the work sort of a poor fourth really. Yet you find that some children are learning a very great deal and getting a great deal of pleasure out of it.

Moreover, as I have earlier described, I did not feel entirely free to pursue my own goals because I was unsure of the extent of my responsibility and therefore of my control. One ambiguity therefore amplified the effects of the other.

Both were increased by observing and listening to the children. They

were not troubled by adult anxieties about the curriculum. For them, learning
was an indivisible process. After the unscheduled and 'ecstatic' afternoon on
the beach, I reflected in my diary:

> I certainly don't think they would have learned more in conventional
> 'academic' terms if we'd tried to constrain them and direct their
> learning, because they were not ready to be confined and it would
> have been a physical impossibility anyway. Also the beach and water
> and pools offer so many natural opportunities for trial and error
> learning . . . This afternoon did demonstrate two things abut learning.
> The first is the importance of motivation . . . It is how you capitalize
> on that experience without killing it that is important. The second is
> that learning can be made a natural thing, something that happens
> when children and adults spontaneously do things or explore to-
> gether and when this activity is set within a framework where chil-
> dren's physical needs and desire for enjoyment are taken into account.

The third main set of tensions that I experienced was epistemological and,
by extension, pedagogical. It too reflected ambiguities which already existed
within the school about the extent to which adults should attempt to structure children's learning or could trust the latter to construct their own knowledge and meaning in collaboration with their teachers. At Upper Norton, as
in the other case study schools, a great deal of emphasis was placed upon
achievement and 'hard work' (a favourite staff phrase). Moreover, no one
deemed it appropriate to leave individual pupils in control of the substance
or manner of their own learning. That said, the staff differed from one another in the extent to which they felt that learning, especially in relation to
the basic skills and concepts of language and mathematics, could arise incidentally from children's own interests or should be planned and taught in
accordance with pre-determined adult structures. Nancy, in particular, had
begun to move in the previous two or three years towards the former view
and away from the reliance on the external sequencing provided by 'schemes'
and workcards which Katherine seemed to value. Increasingly Nancy felt that
she could teach children what she felt they needed to know through their
own interests and that she could help individuals to construct their own sense
of purpose, direction and progress. Talking about her classroom work she
said:

> I would say over the last two years I have assimilated the ideas that
> I have been looking at for the previous two. Dorothy was anxious for
> the children to use books in a real sense, not as a reading scheme,
> and anxious that their writing should not be related just to the book
> they were reading, but come out of their real experiences. Or if they
> were writing about a book, it was to share the experience of the book
> and then encourage other people to read it. I had been anxious to do

this for several years and had been very pleased to have . . . a scheme like 'Targets' which gave good reasons for looking things up (and I still use those for some things). But I suddenly realized I didn't need the prop. Really, all the children require the (basic) skills. So I said to individuals, 'What are you looking for, what are you doing?' And the more practical the work, the easier it was for them to say, 'If I need to make something, I've got to look at how to make it'. . . . I haven't used any formal textbooks hardly at all this year, maybe a little for slower children . . . it just came together as a coherent whole, I think. I might use some formal work again to give myself a bit more space, to keep one week at a time quieter, but I still think it would be very rare. I would rather relate it to the task in hand . . . It takes a level of courage and confidence. I've been teaching twenty-four years. You have bouts of confidence and bouts of panic.

For my part, at the start of the year I was uncertain of where I stood on this matter. In particular, I had carried with me from my previous classroom experience a feeling that children make greater sense of new learning if they are given a framework within which to assimilate it. I did not know how far one could help them to achieve such a structure retrospectively.

The school journey deepened my uncertainty. I began the week by attempting before the visits to share with my group my sense of the structure of history as a body of adult knowledge. For example, having made largely unsuccessful attempts to guide their observations as they moved through a Roman villa on the first day, I decided to take a firmer line on our next architectural visit.

> We went to the castle . . . I sat my group down in a quiet piece of the grounds and told them I didn't want questions or comments, then talked to them for about ten minutes about the development of the castle.

Throughout the week, I continued to search for opportunities to transmit my understanding of 'knowledge' to the children. For example,

> We arrived at different times on the beach with no clear direction as to what the children were to look at while we waited . . . I stayed with the throwers and soon found myself being shown different stones, so I began to look with them at sedimentation and at the properties of flints.

Yet many of my attempts to provide the children with my epistemological structure were manifestly unsuccessful. Paradoxically, this seemed sometimes to be because I was insufficiently didactic or controlling. Typically:

This evening, when we talked about our period of group work, I asked Katherine what her group had been doing, because when I had passed the room earlier on, they had seemed absorbed and settled, whereas mine had not. She told me she had directed very closely how they were to organize what they were writing, so that the task was very straightforward.

By contrast, Nancy seemed to give the children a fairly free rein in their learning. She had developed as a teacher to the point where she trusted the children to create their own meanings within the very flexible curricular framework that she provided. She also seemed confident that once they had returned to school she would be able to help individuals to make sense in their own terms of their multitudinous experiences. She said:

> I have an idea each year. There's a broad educational pattern before you go, but that is just a theory when you get there. By the time you've been, you've got a greater idea of what you have covered and what can be achieved. You never get it right in advance because the possibilities that open out when you've been are enormous. You see all sorts of patterns of work and of learning coming out afterwards.

This is not to suggest that she did not guide or intervene. Rather, she did so in response to individual reactions, instead of attempting, as I was doing, to direct the children in advance. For example, after our visit to an open-air museum I commented:

> I noticed how often Nancy would say 'You know how in the class-room we have to knead the clay and squeeze it', or, 'Well done, yes, we did see one of those in Northumbria last year.' Having the long-term, shared experience with the class makes building concepts a good deal easier.

As the week went on, events progressively challenged my thinking. I continued to try to pre-focus the children's attention. However, at the same time, I began to notice that individuals were creating their own cognitive structures, almost irrespective of what we did or did not do to guide them. In my diary, I wrote:

> We (the staff) ... have not talked about the aims for each visit or had information about the sites we are going to. Nor shared any suggestions for suitable work while we are there, nor for follow up ... But when you talk to the children they surprise you by making connections between the things they have seen and remembering details and ideas from one day to another.

On another occasion, I noted:

> On the way back, we saw a working mill and it was very good to see them making comparisons with the still one that we had seen the day before. I was also able to help a small group find fresh ways of transferring energy from a horizontal to a vertical plane, using angle irons and joints.

Later, Nancy said:

> You get more than you think. Less written down at the time but more afterwards. It has happened to me every time that somebody will refer back the following year and say, you know, 'Remember we saw the energy transfer from the horizontal to the vertical, didn't we'? There's this overlap or growing knowledge all the time and the pleasure in being able to refer back and say, 'do you remember'?

Reflections

I found that on the journey, as in school, I was conscious of two apparently conflicting imperatives and that productive choice between them was inhibited by uncertainty about the extent of my curricular responsibility. One set of pressures, from inside myself and from the children, was moving me towards tighter control over their learning. Another, coming mainly from my observation of the children's reactions to their experiences, led me towards a more responsive and individualized approach.

Indeed, I still puzzle over this dilemma and over possible solutions to it. Yet, although I find the uncertainty that this questioning raises is uncomfortable and sometimes frustrating, I am certain that it is professionally productive. The fact that neither I nor teachers like Nancy can achieve a final sense of balance in these matters creates a strong likelihood that our thinking will not stagnate.

The three sets of curricular tensions that I encountered on this journey were compounded by a fourth which is a familiar one to primary teachers. It is also one which repeatedly emerged in different contexts during my year at Upper Norton (see Nias, Southworth and Campbell, 1992). Over and over again on the journey, our plans and our management of time were so frustrated by unforeseen events that it became almost impossible to manage the curriculum in an orderly fashion. Even if we had all felt that it was desirable to have agreed aims and a clear framework within which to direct the children's learning, it would have been difficult to achieve them, because the timing and sequence of planned activities were so often disrupted by events which were beyond our control.

Such disruptions also indirectly aggravated the tensions which I have described. Questions of accountability, responsibility and control, of curricular aims and emphases, of epistemology and pedagogy can seldom be resolved without prolonged debate. To be sure, the kind of shared experience which this school journey richly provided also plays a part in the forging of common understandings, not least because it can be a starting point for informed professional discussion. But to be effective such discussion must be sustained, over time, if not at one time. This is particularly difficult to achieve when schedules have constantly to be revised.

In any case, even when everything runs smoothly, the adults on a residential school journey have little time to talk to one another, especially about profound professional matters. In this respect too, our experience on the journey echoed that which I frequently encountered in school. Although during the year the staff tried hard to find time to talk to one another about important and pressing issues, on many occasions their attempts fell victim to changes imposed upon them from outside, particularly those related to the introduction of the National Curriculum or to training for it. The stressful and arbitrary context in which teachers currently work creates severe obstacles to productive debate on curricular differences.

That said, there is nothing new in the claim that primary teaching is an occupation full of tension. Indeed in Nias (1989) I argued that when I first talked to my interviewees in 1974–76, they reported stress as a painful and debilitating part of their lives. To be sure the pressures upon them have greatly increased following the 1988 Education Act, but many of the findings of recent research by, for example, Campbell and his colleagues (Campbell and Neill, 1990; Campbell *et al*, 1991) show differences in degree, rather than in kind, from earlier studies of teaching.

However, simply to accept that very high levels of tension and fatigue are endemic in teaching is defeatist. Teachers could do a good deal to ameliorate their own working conditions, if they could distinguish between those tension-inducing aspects of their professional identities and lives over which they can exercise control and those which they cannot alter.

It is in this context in particular that I have found useful this study of one school's residential journey. Before, during, and immediately after the journey, I perceived it as separate, physically, socially and in curricular terms, from the daily life of the classroom and the institution. Indeed on my return I wrote:

> Dorothy was in the playground to give us a warm welcome. But it's extremely odd to feel that the whole of the rest of the school has been living a separate life for a week while the four of us and the children have been caught up in our own set of intense experiences.

However, this sense of separation was misleading. It initially blinded me to the ways in which, as teachers, we carried with us our attitudes to work, our occupational culture and the culture of the school itself. When I first began this analysis, I looked for differences. Yet the richest insights have come from identifying similarities, as I slowly realized that the four main sets of professional tensions which I experienced on the journey also existed in Upper Norton School during the rest of the year. Neither in school nor on the journey were responsibilities always clearly delineated, with the result that the focus and nature of control over children's behaviour and learning were sometimes also uncertain. Similarly, in school it was left to individual teachers to discover through trial and error how to balance their social and moral with their other curricular goals. Nor was there any agreement about whether and, if so how, to attempt to reconcile adults' sense of epistemological structure with children's capacity to construct their own meanings. Finally, we found neither time nor opportunity collectively to address or resolve these issues.

To be sure, this was possibly in part because they had not been identified, as I had not identified them until I undertook this analysis. It is also likely that the staff as a whole had not pinpointed them, though individuals raised them with me in interview, because there were other more pressing matters demanding their collective attention during 1988/89. It may also be that these areas had been left unexamined because the Head, reflecting the silent weight of the school's history, felt that discussion of them might open up unbridgeable differences. Finally, however, it is possible that the teachers had become so inured to working in a stressful environment and to accepting ambiguity as part of their curricular context that it did not occur to them to see remediation of these conditions as lying within their control.

Yet, with hindsight, I feel that two of these areas of tension would have been fairly easily amenable to resolution. As a newcomer, I could have asked for, and would have been willingly given, clarification of roles and responsibilities. Similarly, it would not, I think, have been unduly difficult or time-consuming for all the adults involved in the journey to have agreed in advance the optimum balance between its curricular aims and to have discussed the main strategies that could be used in pursuit of it. By contrast, the epistemological questions which I have raised come much closer to dilemmas (Berlak and Berlak, 1981) and, as such, are not open to long-term resolution. It is however possible that discussion of them would have productively fed into the continuous development process which was one of the school's hallmarks. Only the fourth set of tensions, that created by external events, was, then, completely beyond the teachers' control.

I have one final point to make. Even if I had never attempted to understand the curricular issues that confronted us during this journey, I would still have been shaped as a teacher by the experience. As I wrote at the time:

> It's been a rich and intense week and I wouldn't have missed it for anything. Nor I think would the children. They'll remember some of the things we did and saw for the rest of their lives. And so shall I.

For that I am deeply in the debt of Nancy and her colleagues.

Jennifer Nias

References

BERLAK, A. and BERLAK, H. (1981) *The Dilemmas of Schooling*, London, Routledge.

Blyth W.A.L. (1989) *Informal Education Today: Essays and Studies*, Lewes, Falmer Press.

CAMPBELL, R.J., EVANS, L., NEILL, S. and PACKWOOD, A. (1991) *Workloads, Achievement and Stress*, London, Assistant Masters and Mistresses Association.

CAMPBELL, R.J. and NEILL, S. (1990) *1330 Days: Teacher time in Key Stage 1*, London, Assistant Masters and Mistresses Association.

ELLIOTT, J., BRIDGES, D., EBBUTT, D., GIBSON, R. and NIAS, J. (1981) *School Accountability*, Oxford, Blackwell.

NIAS, J. (1989) *Primary Teachers Talking: A Study of Teaching as Work*, London, Routledge.

NIAS, J., SOUTHWORTH, G. and CAMPBELL, P. (1992) *Whole School Curriculum Development in the Primary School*, London, Falmer Press.

Part 3

The Social Subjects

Chapter 7

Place, Time and Society, and the Schools Council 8–13: Breadth of View and Balance of Interests

Ray Derricott

Alan Blyth's work has shown, over a generation, a consistent interest in the middle years. In 1971 he became Director of the Schools Council Project History, Geography and Social Science in the Middle Years of Schooling (HGSS). The Project, based at the University of Liverpool, was run by a six-strong team which was given the task of reassessing the teaching of history and geography and exploring the potential of the social sciences in the education of children 8 to 13. The Project was the result of four or five years of negotiation between and within the complex committee structure of the Schools Council. A middle years project had to be steered successfully through both the primary and secondary committees and in this specific case through the subject committees of history, geography and social science, as well as through the Programme Committee.

The initial move towards a major national project had seen the setting up of a working party to consider social studies, 8–13. A small research group, headed by Denis Lawton, was given the task of surveying the field, assessing teachers' needs and the need for supporting materials and for producing some recommendations. The group produced Working Paper 39, *Social Studies 8–13* (Lawton *et al*, 1971). The Working Paper identified some outstanding, but sporadic, examples of 'good practice' in using the social sciences with young children and indicated that there was a lack of appropriate support materials for teachers. The major recommendation of Working Paper 39 was to establish the need for a major national project on the teaching of history, geography and social science in the middle years of schooling.

In the late 1960s and early 1970s a major project from the Schools Council required the allocation of over £100,000 for three years. The separate subject committees of history, geography and social science knew that alone they had no chance of attracting such a resource allocation. In coalition, they could do so. Plaskow (1985), in his later analysis of the workings of the Schools Council, indicated that a major weakness in the organization was the Council's

inability to establish a policy and a priority for its programme of development. Alan Blyth, at the time, referred to the practice within the Council of
'Buggin's turn' in the allocation of funding. Whatever the reason, the History, Geography and Social Science Project was funded.

The natural home for the Project would seem to have been the London
Institute of Education with Lawton as the Director. However, once more,
extraneous events interfered with the Schools Council's decision-making.
The level of overheads to be charged for a London base was thought to be
too high. Alan Blyth, who had been Chairman of the Social Studies 8–13
Working Party, was offered the Project. Liverpool was cheaper than London.

A major challenge faced by Alan Blyth in directing the HGSS Project
was how to control and limit its breadth and scope and how to maintain a
balance amongst what appeared to be competing disciplines. His recognition
of these issues and the way in which he began to tackle them can be seen in
the appointments he made to the six-strong team in the spring and summer
of 1971. As Director, Alan Blyth was initially seconded full-time from his
University duties. He was both a geographer and a historian; his major academic research and writing had been on primary education and were in the
area of the sociology of education, although he has never used the term
'sociology' to categorize his work. His team consisted of a Deputy Director,
three Senior Research Officers — a historian, a geographer and a sociologist
— and an Evaluator (who was also a teacher of history and a philosopher).
The team was well qualified in history, geography, sociology, economics and
political science. All had substantial teaching experience in the middle years
and some had teacher education experience. The team reflected both breadth
and balance.

The Schools Council provided each of its projects with a brief for the
guidance of the directors and, if necessary, to act as a kind of 'contract' in
what was usually a rather loose and 'soft-centred' form of accountability.
Rather surprisingly, in the first year of the Project's life, the team came into
conflict with its Project Officer who was a senior civil servant seconded from
the Department of Education and Science. What was in question was the
team's attempts to walk the fine line between materials production and teacher
development. The Project brief was clear that a major outcome of the activities
would be materials for both teachers and pupils. The Project in its first year
took the line that was later immortalized by Lawrence Stenhouse (1975), that
there could be no curriculum development without teacher development. We
had been putting our emphasis strongly on the uniqueness of each situation
in which the key variables were the child, the teacher, the school and the
environment. Our workshops concentrated clearly upon the *process* not the
product of curriculum development (see Derricott, 1975). The Project Officer,
backed by the then Joint Secretary of the Schools Council, called a meeting
in August 1972, with the Chairman of our Consultative Committee and the
Project team. We were reminded that the prevailing orthodoxy of the Schools
Council was to increase the options of teachers by providing materials; the

Council at that time had not taken on a major role in in-service, although with the James Report and the White Paper (DES, 1972) as contemporary issues, a change in this orthodoxy might have been anticipated.

Alan Blyth, as Project Director, led the team's negotiations which resulted in a balanced compromise. The team would produce exemplar materials which would illustrate the process of teacher-centred curriculum development. These materials would include those which could be used directly with children in classrooms such as *Rivers in Flood* or *Life in the Thirties* and handbooks for teachers as exemplified by *Curriculum Planning in History, Geography and Social Science, Themes in Outline* and *Teaching for Concepts.*[1] We stuck to this plan and were helped in our focus on teacher development by a change of Joint Secretary, the influence of the discussions on INSET begun by the James Report and a quite clear shift in emphasis within the Schools Council's committees. The substantive ideas of the HGSS Project also reflected the theme of breadth of view and balance of interests. The basic value position of the HGSS Project cannot be better expressed than it is in *Curriculum Planning*, (Blyth, *et al*, 1976):

> Two values emerged as basic to the Project's thinking and intentions. The first of these was that each person and culture has its own claims to legitimate existence and that, therefore, education ought not to be based on the assumptions that some persons and some cultures are superior to others. Instead, it should enable children to develop their own ways of looking at individuals and cultures and their own criteria for deciding which, if any, are preferable in their eyes. This implies in turn the second basic value, namely that children should be actively initiated into the discussion of problems and issues in society rather than being shielded from problems, or being taught about problems as though there were always 'right' answers, like the answers to be found at the back of traditional textbooks in mathematics. (p. 23)

This liberal-democratic view of learning *from* and *about* society was shared by members of the team and returned to time and again when reviewing our work with both children and teachers.

In microcosm, the project team represented a breadth of view and a challenge to maintaining a balance of interests. The Project brief charged the team with maintaining the integrity of the subjects of history, geography and social science and with exploring their use with children in the middle years 'separately or in combination'. Within the team, members fought hard to maintain the influence of their subjects upon the Project's main ideas and sought ways of combining or interrelating the subjects without sacrificing the validity, principles and integrity they each valued as specialists.

The solution was to use a framework for planning which advocated that *objectives* be used alongside *key concepts*. Within this framework subjects were to be used as a resource in curriculum planning. The decision to use objectives and key concepts together enabled the Project team to maintain a breadth of view of the area of the curriculum most closely linked with social learning. One of the early problems the HGSS Project faced (and some would say never satisfactorily overcame) was the existence and use in schools of a multiplicity of labels to describe this broad curriculum area. In use were social studies, which gave off signals as a weak, soft-centred low status approach to learning; humanities which gave off similar signals and was often, in practice, associated with a different coalition of subjects including religious education and sometimes literature; environmental studies which, in the view of the team, was too much associated with the physical environment and 'things' in the environment rather than people; and integrated studies which, if anything, had too much breadth and immediately placed a project using this label into the middle of a philosophical debate about the nature of curriculum integration which was current at the time (for example, Pring, 1973). There were, of course, concurrent initiatives being supported by the Schools Council in the early 1970s — namely the Humanities Curriculum Project, the Keele Integrated Studies Project and Environmental Studies, all of which were 'competing' to establish an image in the market for curricular innovations. In trying to maintain a distinctive position, the HGSS project borrowed from the Scottish system the term — the social subjects curriculum — to describe the broad area of their activities.

The decision to use objectives alongside key concepts also confronted some of the major issues of the time. Lawrence Stenhouse (1971) had just produced his well-known paper on some of the limitations in using objectives in curriculum research and planning and Sockett (1971) and Pring (1971) had fuelled the debate which was engaging the minds of those working in the (then) growth industry of curriculum studies. The Project team of HGSS had discussed the use of objectives with Stenhouse at a Project seminar — one of a series organized by Alan Blyth in order to test, refine and sharpen our ideas in debate with leading thinkers. The Project team went further, by organizing a conference at Homerton College in which all our theoretical ideas about curriculum development were exposed to an invited group of around fifty leading academics, scholars and teachers. The conference membership list read like a Who's Who of Education at the time. This negotiation and refining of the project's ideas was led deliberately and boldly from the front by Alan Blyth.

In using objectives, we were not advocating them as strictly defined behavioural goals, but in Hilda Taba's (1962) sense as 'roads to travel'. The framework of objectives could be interpreted as lists of intellectual, personal and social skills and qualities to be encouraged during a pedagogic process and not as objectives to be ultimately achieved. For example, 'the ability to evaluate information' is an ability which is never finally achieved but which can be worked towards. It must also be remembered that the groups having to make sense of such a list of objectives were teachers — with whom we had to communicate and, at that time, teachers were not familiar with, and were often resistant to, the idea of objectives. Teachers of young children, in particular, often saw objectives as imposing adult structures, purposes and thinking upon developing young minds. Our approach to objectives was therefore 'user-friendly' and had to be exemplified with illustrative vignettes of teaching and learning in an attempt to raise levels of acceptability.

If objectives, even in the form we used them, came from the Chicago school of Bloom, the use of key concepts owed much to the influence of Hilda Taba's programme for social studies. The influence of the Taba team was a direct one as Tony McNaughton (who had evaluated the Taba project) spent three months working with us in Liverpool during the early formative period of project training.

The seven key concepts — communication, power, values and beliefs, conflict/consensus, similarity/difference, continuity/change and causes and consequences — represented high levels of abstraction and were intended to aid teachers in the process of selection, organization and sequencing of content. They had to be acceptable to historians, geographers and social scientists as representing both breadth and balance between the subjects. It was understood that subject specialists, coming together to plan a national project or a social subjects curriculum for a single school, would need to make compromises in order to use the key concepts effectively. The three Senior Research Officers debated and negotiated intensely over a period of several weeks before agreeing on the seven. The alternative to the use of a small cluster of key concepts was the generation and advocacy of long lists of subordinate or lower level concepts — some shared by all three subjects, some with specific significance to two subjects and some representing a view from within a single subject.

The Project team was learning the nuances and potentialities of the use of key concepts in planning a social subjects curriculum at the same time as having to encourage teachers to experiment in their use. It is not surprising that the Project's message about the use of key concepts was unclear and probably remained so for many teachers during most of the 1970s. Certainly, in the early years of the HGSS Project, the geography and history inspectorate remained unconvinced and even agnostic towards the value of key concepts. This did change with significant changes of personnel in the Inspectorate in the mid-seventies.

Perhaps the least understood element of the work of the HGSS Project was social science. It was often misunderstood as 'social studies' or misread as social sciences. The singular version 'social science' reflected the subject committee that sponsored the Project within the Schools Council, that is the Social Science Committee. Misunderstandings arising from the label 'social science' were many. Social science interpreted as social studies suggested to some groups that the HGSS Project was about integrated studies which did not appeal to subject specialists especially those who taught in secondary schools. Another group of sceptics perceived the Project as introducing ideas from the social sciences — from anthropology, economics, psychology through to sociology — in a spurious and over-academic way to young children who were not ready for them. A reflection on our value position as quoted above indicates that the Project team thought that there were many social experiences which young children came across every day at home, in school, and in the neighbourhood which should not be ignored, but which could be used as a basis for social learning. Thus, rules and authority at school, relationships between individuals and groups within the community should not be ignored as having no importance to young children and no significant meaning for them. The Project's work in classrooms produced scores of examples of how sensitive social issues could result in reflective social thinking and learning in young children, if the teacher-pupil relationship in which these ideas were being introduced was secure and supportive.

The Project's work in social science uncovered the greatest need for accompanying in-service training and professional development. This training need in turn revealed a need for a teacher development project in its own right to increase teachers' potential for delivering the social science ideas contained in the HGSS Project. In the 1970s this potential was not there in middle years teachers, and it is doubtful whether it is present in teachers of children 8–13 in the 1990s.

In common with most other Schools Council projects, HGSS had the task of developing processes for curriculum planning, developing and trialling ideas and materials, refining these materials for publication and finally disseminating both processes and products within the schools system. This all sounds neat, orderly, sequential and rational. In practice many of these phases within the Project's life overlapped and interfered with each other. For example, the production of carefully designed, commercially viable teaching materials requires concentrated effort, time to research sources, to reflect, to test for readability and to edit. This does not sit easily alongside the need of Project team members to be 'on the road' meeting the demands of the dissemination programme. There was a period between 1974 and 1975 when neither of these tasks could be given sufficient time to be fully effective. A balance was very difficult to maintain.

The period of funding for HGSS was extended initially from three to four years and then after a gap of over a year, a limited funding was provided for further development and dissemination between 1977 and 1979. The funding enabled Fred Thompson to be appointed as National Development Officer under my direction.

The dissemination of the HGSS Project was a difficult and challenging process. The breadth of vision encompassed by the Project was a strength but also a weakness. The breadth of the Project's ideas produced a complex message about curriculum planning. The work of Fullan (1982) indicates that the more complex the message of an innovation, the lower the degree of implementation. The adoption of a logo which described the Project as the study of man in *Place, Time and Society* was an attempt to produce a more distinct image and to summarize the message as succinctly as possible.

Nevertheless, in the market place for innovation, middle years projects were dismissed as *middle school* projects by both primary and secondary teachers. Projects spanning 8–13 were often seen as primary projects by secondary teachers and viceversa. A project which mentioned *subjects* was thought to be a secondary project by primary teachers. One that mentioned two or three subjects was seen as an integrated project by subject specialists. In effect, the breadth of the Project made it difficult to market.

Even in local authority advisory services it was not clear which adviser or advisers should take ownership of the Project. At this stage, the Project was well supported by primary advisers but support from specialist history, geography or humanities advisers was more sporadic. The social subjects area was also a low priority area for development.

More significantly, the Project's message was about fundamentally re-viewing and developing structures and practice. The ideas and products of the Project did not lend themselves to limited sampling. Being as much about process as product the Project demanded teachers' time and the support of a trained mediator from either within or outside a school. The Project was about curriculum building but provided little advice about how this might be done. Three examples of a four-year curriculum, indicating principles upon which progression in the learning of skills and concepts might be applied, were provided in *Curriculum Planning* (Blyth *et al*, 1976). However, one of the central messages of the Project indicated that each situation was unique and therefore such guidance required relatively sophisticated knowledge of curriculum building for this guidance to be translated into practice.

A dilemma faced by any Schools Council project, and particularly by HGSS, was that it could not be prescriptive but could only give advice. There was no legitimation from the educational establishment. This did not come until the publication of *Primary Education in England* (DES, 1978) and the surveys of combined and middle schools in the early 1980s (DES, 1983 and 1985a). All of these reports made the same point. History and geography were being badly planned and not well taught, and there was a need for systematic treatment of this area of the curriculum.

In 1972 the HGSS Project had described the social subjects curriculum as being *random, repetitive* and *risk-free*. By this it was meant that children's experiences consisted of a series of projects on random topics, often repeated from year to year and not addressing sensitive social issues. *Primary Education in England* (DES, 1978) repeated the message about randomness and repetitiveness but avoided the judgment about the 'risk-free' nature of children's experiences. From this point, HGSS became a history and geography project and *Place, Time and Society* emphasized the contexts of place and time. This was perhaps the beginnings of a process which saw sociology dubbed as the government's least favourite social science in the 1980s. The establishment view was that social science was not for young children.

The legitimation by HMI of the need to reassess and systematize the teaching of history and geography in the primary and middle years increased the demand for dissemination workshops and, until the funds ran out at the beginning of 1980, the National Development Officer was kept very busy.

What traces of the HGSS Project remained throughout the 1980s and into the 1990s? This is a difficult question to answer because the breadth and scope of the Project laid down many possible trails. In history, for example, the ideas of HGSS and the History 13–16 Project, especially on the use of evidence, became intermingled and eventually indistinguishable. The two HMI discussion document entitled *Geography from 5 to 16* and *History from 5 to 16* (DES, 1986 and 1988), show traces of the influence of HGSS. Both documents use objectives, and in both objectives become more specific as a progression (often implied rather than explicit), is plotted from early primary through later primary to secondary years. In the early primary years geography is seen to be 'more likely to be organized around activities and topics than in the form of subjects'. In the later primary years 'most pupils undertake studies that are more clearly recognizable as geographical'. Such approaches echo the view of the HGSS Project that subjects, and the more formal ways in which knowledge is organized, have to begin to be discovered in the middle years. The traces of the Schools Council project are much clearer in the *History 5 to 16* document. The section on the development of skills (p. 8) correlates highly with the skill objectives of *Place, Time and Society*. Whereas the geography document identifies specific geographical concepts such as location, the history document parallels the use by HGSS of change and continuity and sequence and causation. In general, it can be said that the establishment view as represented by HMI rejected almost entirely the ideas about teaching the social sciences to young children which were central to the HGSS Project. The geography establishment expressed ideas which were not in major conflict with those of the Project, although usually expressed in more precise geographical terms. On the other hand, the history establishment proposed a framework which could have been written by members of the Project team. This acceptance of the historical ideas of the Project by HMI was even more clearly expressed in another of their reports, *History in the Primary and Secondary Years* (DES, 1985b), which not only reproduces the objectives and key concepts planning framework of HGSS, but also exemplifies its use with suggested curricula and ways to develop work in historical concepts. The emphasis on history and evidence and the notion of empathy also permeates this document.

Do these traces of the Schools Council project extend to the Statutory Instruments for History and Geography in the National Curriculum? Using one's imagination it is possible to see influences but the realistic answer must be negative. Except at Key Stage 1, where both National Curriculum documents retain an element of child-centredness, the Programmes of Study assert the separate claims of both subjects for separate treatment. Both documents appear to allow scope for teachers to plan and build their own studies, but the demands of the programmes in general upon teachers' time make this very unlikely to occur. Space does not allow for a more detailed analysis but the orders for both National Curriculum subjects seem to encourage a return to prescribed topics and themes reminiscent of long used and well tried schools texts. Perhaps the geography document is less prone than the history one to do this, but even the former begs questions about how teachers might interpret, for example, *the local area* or *the home region*.

The critical perspective quoted in the central value position of the HGSS Project that the social subjects curriculum 'should enable children to develop their own ways of looking at individuals and cultures and their own criteria for deciding . . .', and that 'children should be actively initiated in the discussion of problems and issues in society . . .' seems to have been rejected. The National Curriculum in history and geography is expert/politician designed and is meant to be controlled by teachers. Children's thinking and social learning, their attempts to make sense of complex and problematic social arrangements seem to have been left behind.

If there is a gesture towards the treatment of potentially sensitive social issues with children of 5–16, it is in the elaboration of the cross-curricular themes of environmental education, education for economic and industrial understanding and citizenship (NCC, 1990a, 1990b and 1990c). Each of these documents is full of good intentions. Each has the potential for introducing sensitive issues into the curriculum. For example: 'Education for citizenship involves discussing controversial issues upon which there is no clear consensus . . . Where political issues are brought to the attention of pupils, there is also a duty to ensure that they are offered a balanced presentation of opposing views' (p. 14). Members of the HGSS Project could say 'Amen' to this, but it must be remembered that the cross-curricular themes, like the social science of HGSS, have to fight for a place in the curriculum and are not to be assessed and reported upon. Their status is, quite clearly, relatively low. (See Ross in this volume)

This attempt to reflect on the influence, under Alan Blyth's direction, of the HGSS Project on current thinking about the status and teaching of the social subjects, shows that the massive scope and breadth of vision expressed in the ideas of the Project and attempts to balance all the interests involved, were bound to result in partial and intermittent effect. The successes of the Project can only be judged in broad terms. Like many innovations, it was perhaps before its time. In 1971, the educational system and the state of thinking about the curriculum was not ready for a sophisticated and complex approach to planning. What the Project did do was to keep an acceptable form of the objectives model, alongside a use of concepts, on the agenda for debate throughout the 1970s and 1980s. Whichever document produced during these two decades is consulted, it takes an attitude either positive or negative towards objectives and concepts. The concern over sensitive issues and young children was perhaps better handled by being taken up by groups focussing on anti-racist and multi-ethnic education. The ideas about the development of political and economic literacy were perhaps best taken up by the Schools Curriculum Industry Project and the Hansard Society.

Ray Derricott

One constant remains, that is Alan Blyth's persistent concern that the social subjects, or humanities (which is the label he has favoured recently), should not be ignored, neglected when resources are allocated, or left on the sidelines in important educational debates. Crucial to this is the role he ascribes to teachers and their professionality. He sees them as central in the delivery of the curriculum and to the monitoring and assessment of children's progress. He ends his latest book by expressing this position clearly (Blyth, 1990):

> First, teachers as a profession have to accept their claim to be able to monitor, sensitively, the development of every child in the perspectives of humanities. . . . Second, in doing so, they have to Make the Grade for Humanities in the primary curriculum as a whole. (p. 157)

To Alan Blyth, teachers and a confidence in the uniqueness of professional judgement have always been the central factor in the effective, sensitive education of children.

Note

1   All the materials of the HGSS Project were published by Collins/ESL Bristol between 1976 and 1978.

References

BLYTH, A. (1990) *Making the Grade for Primary Humanities*, Buckingham, Open University Press.

BLYTH, W.A.L., COOPER, K.R., DERRICOTT, R., ELLIOTT, G., SUMNER, H. and WAPLINGTON, A. (1976) *Curriculum Planning in History, Geography and Social Science*, London, Collins.

DERRICOTT, R. (1975) *Working with Teachers* HGSS, Working Paper No. 1, University of Liverpool.

DES (1972) *Education: A Framework for Expansion* (The James Report) Cmnd. 5174, London, HMSO.

DES (1978) *Primary Education in England: A Survey by HMI Inspectors of Schools*, London, HMSO.

DES (1983) *9–13 Middle Schools: An Illustrative Survey*, London, HMSO.

DES (1985a) *Education 8–12 in Combined and Middle Schools*, London, HMSO.

DES (1985b) *History in the Primary and Secondary Years*, London, HMSO.

DES (1986) *Geography from 5–16*, Curriculum Matters 7, London, HMSO.

DES (1988) *History from 5–16*, Curriculum Matters 11, London, HMSO.

FULLAN, M. (1982) *The Meaning of Educational Change*, Ontario, OISE.

LAWTON, D., CAMPBELL, R.J. and BURKITT, V. (1971) *Social Studies 8–13*, Schools Council Working Paper No. 39, London, Evans/Methuen.

NCC (1990a) *Curriculum Guidance 4: Education for Economic and Industrial Understanding*, York, NCC.

NCC (1990b) *Curriculum Guidance 7: Environmental Education*, York, NCC.

NCC (1990c) *Curriculum Guidance 8: Education for Citizenship*, York, NCC.

PLASKOW, M. (Ed) (1985) *Life and Death of the Schools Council*, Lewes, Falmer Press.

PRING, R. (1971) 'Bloom's taxonomy: A philosophical critique', 2, *Cambridge Journal of Education*, 2, pp. 83–91.

PRING, R. (1973) 'Curriculum integration' in PETERS, R.S. (Ed) *The Philosophy of Education*, London, Oxford University Press.

SOCKETT, H. (1971) 'Bloom's taxonomy: A philosophical critique', 1, *Cambridge Journal of Education*, 1, pp. 16–25.

STENHOUSE, L. (1971) 'Some limitations on the use of objectives in curriculum research and planning', *Paedagogica Europaea*, 6, pp. 73–83.

STENHOUSE, L. (1975) *An Introduction to Curriculum Research and Development*, London, Heinemann Educational.

TABA, H. (1962) *Curriculum Development: Theory and Practice*, New York, Harcourt, Brace and World.

Chapter 8

Breadth, Balance and Connection in the Primary Curriculum: Bridge-Building, Past and Present

Bill Marsden

... in every case the teaching, whether elementary or advanced ... should not fail to represent the subject justly as a mode of creative activity, and an aspect of the essential spirit of civilization. (Nunn, 1940)

We too readily accept that educationally we are always on the horns of a dilemma, preferring the disjunctive 'or' to the conjunctive 'and'. (Entwistle, 1970)

Collection and Connection

That achieving *breadth* is an aim of overriding importance in 'whole curriculum planning' has long been part of the conventional wisdom, and is now statutory. The focus of the current argument is not so much about the general principle as about its implementation. The strategy adopted in the National Curriculum, namely of a range of core and foundation subjects plus religious education, with the gaps left plugged by cross-curricular dimensions and themes, manifestly represents a particular conceptualization of breadth which, heavily biased as it is towards the 'traditional' subjects, has predictably been contested.

Balance is a kindred concept, in that the 'whole' is too large and complex to accommodate in the curriculum. So for overall planning purposes we think in terms of a balanced 'selection from the culture'. There are other dimensions in the concept of balance, of course. It needs to be qualitative as well as quantitative. The idea that the selection offered by the National Curriculum is genuinely well-balanced can thus be questioned on the grounds of its consecutive and implicitly hierarchical mode of delivery, strongly weighted in favour of the core subjects, offering a lower priority to the creative arts and cross-curricular work, with subjects like history in between.

Another element of 'balance' needs considering. In an earlier article (Marsden, 1991) I argued that there was need, in all phases, for a balance between the pedagogic, content and social contexts of curriculum planning, at whatever phase, and that in the grammar school tradition the content factor was overemphasized and, in the progressive primary tradition, the pedagogic. It is an inconvenient fact that address to one of these principles may be at the expense of, rather than complementary to, another. Thus the necessary pedagogic simplification of historical material for younger children may result in bad history and negative social stereotyping. There are endemic tensions between subject-centred approaches, child-centred approaches, and society-centred approaches, of course. A major objective of this chapter is, however, to demonstrate that while these principles are indeed in tension, they are not of necessity incompatible, and that balance in this sense can be achieved.

The chapter is therefore based on the premise that breadth and balance are necessary but not sufficient attributes of curriculum planning. A curriculum that is a mere *collection* of material can have breadth and balance. There has long been criticism, for example, of conventional progressive topic-based approaches in the primary school on the grounds of their promoting mere loose accumulations of curriculum material. Thus Warwick (1973) illustrates the point by an example of a topic on 'The Sea', commended by its compilers as 'remarkable for the variety of material we had managed to accumulate', and culminating in 'an exhibition of the things associated with the sea'. The exhibition obviously had breadth and could well have had balance, but seems hardly to have been distinguished by any conceptual coherence.

A further essential attribute of good practice in curriculum planning must then be *connection*. An initial act of brainstorming and the penning in of a network of threads in a topic web diagram does not of itself produce conceptual coherence. The connections come not from the shifting sands of the theme's surface, but the deeper structures beneath. From this it follows that a resolution of the tensions, between the abstractions that these structures imply, and child-centred principles, needs to be achieved.

Such tensions are not resolved by dichotomization, however, in which the situation is presented as one of opposing approaches (in some cases inflated into belief systems) from which one has perforce to choose one or the other. In the event, the choices offered are not logically the extremes of one particular thought spectrum. The polarities indicated below are false.

Subject-centred - - - - - - versus - - - - Integrated
Society-centred - - - - - - versus - - - - Child-centred
Secondary practice - - - - versus - - - - Primary practice

They suggest that a curriculum cannot have a high degree of child-centredness and society-centredness, for they are opposites. But as these are not on the same logical spectrum, it is both a matter of principle and, I would argue, of good practice, that curricula must achieve a balance between child-centredness *and* society-centredness. The balance to be achieved should be the outcome of refined judgments as to the degree of importance the different elements in a complex of complementary pedagogical, content and social education factors should enjoy in particular circumstances. It is therefore argued that a triple economy that enshrines good pedagogy, good content and good social education is necessary.

Commonly agreed elements of good primary practice include that it should be:

> Experience-based
> Activity-based
> Enquiry-based
> Issues-based
> Learner-centred
> Success-centred

For those dedicated to dichotomization, these would be placed in one column, and associated with integrated, child-centred practice. In fact, progressive protagonists for subjects whether in the primary or secondary phase, would think their subjects only justified in the curriculum if their implementation embodied such elements of good practice.

Over the last twenty-five years, the polarization process has intensified far beyond the pedagogic issue. One reason for this has been the backlash against progressivism triggered by the Black Papers (Cox and Dyson, 1969a, 1969b and 1970; Cox and Boyson, 1975 and 1977). The attitudinal gulfs resulting have by no means been the sole responsibility of right-wing pressure groups, however. Among professional educators over the same period there has been a similar tendency to add novel and divisive layers to the debate through, for example, the unearthing of conspiracies which have allegedly been used by traditional subject lobbies to repel more integrationist intruders. Under the face-value statements micropoliticians of the curriculum have discerned subversion, practised by curiously labelled bodies: 'competing coalitions', 'monolithic epistemic communities', 'subject hegemonies' and, more legibly, 'vested interest groups', responsible for 'territorial disputes' and the 'invention of traditions'. These have reinforced the notion that there are two undifferentiated approaches to attach allegiance to: primary practice (good, even though rarely unpacked as a concept); and subject practice (bad, for the primary phase in particular).

This is in no sense to deny the presence of an underlying politics of the curriculum. As Goodson (1988) has more than once pointed out, geography is a particularly interesting example of a subject which, from a low status base, as a result of shrewd political campaigning and, conceivably, having a good case to make, has established itself firmly in secondary as well as primary curricula over the last one hundred years or so (Marsden, 1986). The 'coalitions' within geography have in recent years only too effectively demonstrated political skills in maintaining their subject in the National Curriculum at a time of threat, finding it conspicuous by its absence in official DES statements of the early 1980s (Bailey and Binns, 1987). This is not to accept the conspiracy theory, merely to indicate a more successful example of the same type of lobbying undertaken by, say, protagonists for economic awareness as a foundation subject. The fact that a case was accepted, even by a reactionary set of political masters, is not *prima facie* evidence that the case was a reactionary one. But it may have been. Let us look therefore at the case which has been made, and continues to be made, for geography, as a 'selection from the culture' which, properly used, offers breadth, balance and connection to the curriculum: a bridge-building subject, in fact.

The Case for Geography

The case for geography is here deliberately not made from the claims of geographers, but from the arguments of leading progressive educators. Part of the ammunition used by those who oppose the introduction of subjects into the primary curriculum, has been the selective citation of major progressive figures of the past; an appeal to 'authority' to justify denial of the value of the contribution of subjects to the primary school curriculum. The evidence selected frequently represents a false charting of curriculum history (Marsden, 1991). Counter-evidence is offered below to demonstrate that pioneering progressive voices, as distinct from those of some of their disciples, categorically did not authorize any polarization of the issues, notwithstanding their devotion to child-centred education. Indeed, they offered a sophisticated and a multi-faceted approach to the structuring of the primary curriculum. As one distinguished American educationist tellingly pointed out, the problem with Dewey was that his ideas produced too many who quoted him instead of doing more of what he did (Rugg, 1960).

To start with an early HMI, Moseley, well versed in the progressive thinking of his time. As early as 1845 he was stressing the importance of direct observation, the appreciation of relationships and development of intelligence and imagination. The besetting limitation of the elementary curriculum at this stage was its superficiality, a blind concentration on facts and their recall. In its 'capes and bays' mode, geography was a major culprit. But as Moseley (1845) observed, it had much wider potential.

Geography acquires its full value as a branch of education only when it loses the character of an accumulation of facts, undigested by the child's mind, but heaped up in his memory, linked by no association with the world of thought and action which immediately surrounds it, or with that which is within.

By the time of Arnold, the official educational codes had enshrined 'capes and bays' teaching in the subject. Arnold, following Moseley, distinguished between the pursuit of true geography and the need to hit the mechanical requirements of the code.

> The ridiculous results obtained by teaching geography . . . under these conditions, may be imagined. A child who has never heard of Paris or Edinburgh, will tell you measurements of England in length and breadth, and square mileages, till his tongue is tired. (Arnold, 1869)

Similarly we know well that that arch-evangelist of English progressivism, Edmond Holmes, was contemptuous of the rigid educational codes and their associated passive learning methods. What is less well publicized is that he did not associate arid memorization with genuine subject teaching. He revealed rather a nuanced concept of 'knowledge', which for him was clearly something beyond mere factual recall:

> Information as to the names and positions of capes and bays, as to areas and populations, and other geographical facts, is easily converted into knowledge of those facts, but it is not easily converted into knowledge of geography . . . in the absence of . . . the geographical sense, the possession of . . . geographical information cannot be converted into knowledge of . . . geography. (1911)

Perhaps the most frequently used historical missile launched by progressive thinkers against those supporting subject specialisms in the primary school is the celebrated maxim in the Hadow Report (1931) that

> the curriculum is to be thought of in terms of activity and experience rather than of knowledge to be acquired and facts to be stored.

It is again less often realized that Hadow offered an extensive appendix on the teaching of various branches of the curriculum, which covered a range of subjects, including geography. Work in geography, Hadow argued, *as in other subjects* had to be thought of in terms of activity and experience. There was no suggestion of an innate incompatibility between this broad principle and subject teaching. There was a clear acceptance of the importance of subject content, as in the advocacy of the teaching of the geography of distant places through topics interesting to the children which, when complete, would 'together build up a conception of the world as a whole'.

Meanwhile, in the United States, there had also been long-standing support for the presence of geography and history in the primary curriculum. Thus in a contribution to the journal of the National Herbart Society, Spencer Trotter (1898) noted geography, correctly interpreted, as 'one of the great social and moral forces in education'.

The end in view is to develop a *social intelligence* and, consequently, *a social disposition*; to break down *local prejudice* and to produce a broader spirit of sympathy and a tendency toward a more efficient cooperation.

More probingly, Charles McMurry (1899), a prominent Herbartarian, teased out relationships between geography as a subject and the pedagogic frame into which it should be inserted. He conceived this in terms of *type studies* (not essentially different from the *locality studies* promoted by the National Curriculum Geography Working Group nearly 100 years later).

... with children, these type studies must be capable of graphic, picturesque treatment. They should be rich in instructive and interesting particulars, not abstract, formal and barren. Our type studies, therefore, must combine two great merits: they must involve representative ideas of wide-reaching meaning in geography, and they must, at the same time, be concrete, attractive, and realistic.

The bridging function of the subject was also noted, again in terms anticipating current justifications in making the case for geography, in arguing for what was in essence a *rapprochement* between a subject and an integrated topic approach, but giving the latter a particular focus.

A topic in geography is never strictly identical with one in natural science, however they may overlap ... A geographical topic is, generally a geographical unit, which involves incidentally a variety of facts from natural science and history.

In order to secure and establish the independent right of geography in the sisterhood of studies, it is necessary to make out a series of important type-subjects, in each of which a characteristic central thought is so distinctly geographical that no other standpoint of natural science or history is able to dislodge the teacher from his geographical stronghold.

The type-studies were, in fact, place studies. Examples offered included a Californian gold mine, Minneapolis, Lake Superior, the Andes Mountains, and the Rhine River, each centred in 'a geographical idea that is a natural stronghold'.

The most revered of American progressives, John Dewey, was equally positive about the contributions of geography (and history), properly conceived. More misinformation about Dewey's ideas has been passed down than about most of the other pioneers of educational progress. His approach to child-centredness was, for example, more cautions and shaded than that of many of his disciples to come, not least in Britain.

It will do harm if child-study leave in the popular mind the impression that a child of a given age has a positive equipment of purposes and interests to be cultivated just as they stand. Interests in reality are but attitudes toward possible experiences; they are not achievements; their worth is in the leverage they afford, not in the accomplishment they represent ...

How, then, stands the case of Child vs. Curriculum? ... The radical fallacy in the original pleadings with which we set out is the supposition that we have no choice save either to leave the child to his own unguided spontaneity or to inspire direction upon him from without ... the value of the formulated wealth of knowledge that makes up the course of study is that it may enable the educator to *determine the environment of the child*, and thus by indirection to direct. Its primary value ... is for the teacher, not for the child. Such and such are the capacities, the fulfilments, in truth and beauty and behaviour, open to these children ... (Dewey, 1902)

Geography to Dewey was a unifying subject. 'The unity of all the sciences is found in geography' (Dewey, 1900). Geography and history were the information studies *par excellence*, the nature of 'information', however, being scrupulously defined.

... the difference between penetration of this information into living experience and its mere piling up in isolated heaps depends on whether these studies are faithful to the interdependence of man and nature which affords these studies their justification.

The function of historical and geographical subject matter ... is to enrich and liberate the more direct and personal contacts of life by furnishing their context, their background and outlook ... The classic definition of geography as an account of the earth as the home of man expresses the educational reality ...

When the ties are broken, geography presents itself as that hodgepodge of unrelated fragments too often found ... a veritable ragbag of intellectual odds and ends: the height of a mountain here, the course of a river there, the quantity of shingles produced in this town, the tonnage of shipping in that, the boundary of a county, the capital of a state.

Geography and history are the two great school resources for bringing about the enlargement of the significance of direct experience. Unless they are taught for external reasons or as mere modes of skill their chief educational value is that they provide the most direct and interesting roads out into the larger world of meaning. (Dewey, 1916)

The American paradox was that while the espousal of geography, culminating in the 32nd Yearbook of the National Society for the Study of

Education on *The Teaching of Geography*, (1933) was more sophisticated, certainly in terms of a formal curriculum theory, than most similar British offerings of that time, the subject did not take root in the schools. One of the reasons would seem undoubtedly to have been the intellectual and political power of Harold Rugg and his peer professors of education, whose influence in the inter-war era in the United States was prodigious. The success of the integrationist and educationist lobby could here too be interpreted in conspiratorial terms: it may also be it made a better case.

Unlike Dewey and other progressives, Rugg translated his theoretical ideas into school texts, a large-scale social studies series, ranging from elementary to advanced grades. While framed under a social science umbrella, Rugg ensured that the quality of the resource drawn from the subject disciplines was high. He sought a synthesis between (a) the findings of specialists at the frontiers of knowledge; (b) an integrative curriculum framework based on over-arching concepts; and (c) research into children's thinking.

Somewhat unlike McMurry, who sought 'type-studies' of a distinctively geographical nature, Rugg required an overarching framework of key or 'theme concepts' which the scholars of the time 'were then forging'.

> The sources of our documented description of the social order are found in the works of persons I have chosen to call 'frontier thinkers'. The materials of civilization and culture are being studied in this generation by indefatigable workers on the frontiers of economic, political and social life. (Rugg, 1931)

Rugg was no supporter of either/ors. He sought to conflate the ideas and the ideals of the frontier researcher and the pedagogue. The cardinal aim was to achieve the two great ends of education: 'tolerant understanding' and 'critical questioning'. He demanded a curriculum which

> deals in a rich vivid manner with the modes of living of people all over the earth; which is full of throbbing anecdotes of human life . . . which is built round a core of pupils' activities — studies of their home community, special reading and original investigation, a constantly growing stream of opportunities for discussion, debate and exchange of ideas . . . which is constructed on a problem-solving organisation, providing continuous practice in choosing between alternatives, in making decisions, in drawing generalisations, which so makes use of dramatic episodic materials illustrating great humanitarian themes, that by constant contact with it children grow in wise insights and attitudes and, constructively but critically, will be influenced to put their ideas into action. (Rugg, 1926)

While subjects such as geography were seen in the first place as means to child-centred *and* social reconstructionist ends, Rugg was clear that there had also to be a rigorous subject base. The child-centred needs were to be catered for in the aesthetic side of the curriculum, in which self-directed activities and creative self-expression would dominate, while the development of conceptual thinking had to be teacher-controlled and systematically pre-structured.

While American educators as a whole opted for integrated social studies at both primary and secondary levels, there was none the less strong advocacy from geography lobbyists for their subject to occupy as of right a slot in the school timetable. Most of the contributors to the 32nd Yearbook of the National Society of the Study of Education on *The Teaching of Geography* took this view, though not, as they pointed out, in any isolationist spirit. There was interest in the relative merits of what were termed 'fusion theory' and 'subject theory'. In one Harvard PhD thesis cited in the Yearbook, an exploration of the two approaches came to the fairly pragmatic conclusion that the differences identified between the two were not sufficient to rule either out of consideration. Advantages of subjects lay in historical development rather than in logic, and also in the practical considerations of teacher preparation. Fusion theory was more of service to social science teachers, and was useful as a variant, in emphasizing general educational concepts frequently forgotten, and 'as a balance against undue conservatism and a prod to action' (Wilson, 1931).

The vital connecting link between this enormously productive era of curriculum-making in the United States and the latter-day emergence of 'rational curriculum planning' in Britain was provided by the Tyler-Taba axis. Like Rugg, Tyler was more interested in promoting a rapprochement between different ideologies, and gave each due weight in his approach to curriculum planning. Like Rugg, the subject fields were not ends in themselves, but essential resources:

> ... we must keep in mind that the role of the separate subject fields in education (is) to act as resources which can be used to equip the student with ways of thinking, feeling and acting which can help him to live more effectively and with greater dignity and satisfaction. For us to use each subject in this way we need to understand what the subject really is, at its best, so that we can avoid prostituting it in a caricature for school children. This kind of understanding can be obtained only from serious scholars who are actively involved in the subject. (Tyler, 1963)

Tyler's co-worker, Hilda Taba, similarly supported a balanced approach to curriculum planning.

> Child-centered, society-centered and subject-centered curricula are vying with each other as the exclusive approaches to the entire curriculum. An emphasis on a single basis, such as the content, the needs

of society, or the needs of the learner, have produced an unnecessary *versus* thinking with its unfortunate juxtaposition of considerations that should be combined into one comprehensive curriculum theory: interest *vs* subject matter; life-centeredness *vs* subject-centeredness; method *vs* content . . .; basic skills *vs* the growth of the whole child, and so on. (Taba, 1962)

At the same time Taba was highly critical of what she termed 'traditional subject organization' seeing *subjects alone* as wanting as a basis for integrating *disciplined knowledge* into curriculum organization as a whole. In the event, Taba used the characteristic American social studies approach, arranged in a concentric framework, moving out from the local area, as a basis for permeating into the curriculum place content as well as other social content.

Formal curriculum thinking of any significant scope belatedly leapt the Atlantic in the 1960s. Wheeler, a research student of Taba, produced an influential book entitled *Curriculum Process* (1967) in which now familiar notions such as rational curriculum planning, criteria for selecting content, key ideas, conceptual frameworks, evaluation and the like were introduced. While to many educational pundits there was suspicion over the application of 'scientific' approaches to curriculum planning, perhaps more critical was the fact that to the politician and interested lay-person curriculum theory merely added to the profusion and confusion of the educational plant life in the secret garden. 'Rational' though it was, the new curriculum thinking probably helped indirectly further to polarize the debate.

At about the same time that 'rational' curriculum planning was implanted in this country, the Plowden Report (1967) was published and from the first proved one of the more contentious documents of English educational history. To its supporters it served as an apogee of progressive primary thinking. To its critics it represented an assault on academic standards and an over-correction of the earlier authoritarian and instrumental approaches associated with the elementary tradition.

The Report quickly became a quarry for material with which to defend or attack a particular educational cause or belief. The debate which followed was a harbinger of a growing propensity in British educational circles less to differentiate discussion and, more defensively, to ascend quickly a piece of moral high ground and preach to the converted. Thus Peters (1969) began the 'libel by label' campaign in presenting Plowden as mere ideology. Other educationists actively supported the Black Paper movement. Much elitist play was made with the famous quotation which characterized the school as something more than a 'teaching shop', and stressed children should first and foremost learn to live as children and not as future adults. Following Hadow, the curriculum should lay emphasis on discovery and firsthand experience and on opportunities for creative work. In fact the Plowden Report was careful to qualify what it meant by discovery, acknowledging that what was discovered might be trivial, and that the method might be inefficient and an over-consumer of time. While the Report made it crystal clear that young children's learning styles did not fit in with formal subject categories, it accepted at the same time that towards the top of the junior school the conventional subjects became more relevant. There were more than four pages of densely packed advice on how geography might be introduced. While Plowden did not produce one of the seminal contributions to the history of geographical education, most of its advice was sound, and was particularly approving of the use of 'sample studies' which 'carry much of the authenticity of local geography and permit comparisons to be made with the home region', helping to lead outwards from local studies to the investigation of areas that could not be visited. The Report did not restrict primary practice to dealing solely with what could be covered by direct experience. In sum, it was a more balanced and differentiated report both in general and in its particulars than either its subsequent critics or uncritical supporters were to acknowledge.

From the late 1960s also, another body destined for controversy, the Schools Council, sponsored projects which set out among other things to apply the new ferment of theoretical ideas about the curriculum to practical planning of programmes of study. Secondary projects were subject-based, while primary tended to reflect an integrated approach. One that bridged the gap was the Liverpool *History, Geography and Social Science 8–13* project, directed by Alan Blyth (1976). This was one of relatively few ventures of its time to reflect 'and' rather than 'or' thinking, and indeed a continuity of thinking with earlier progressive statements. The Project separated notions of 'subjects' and 'disciplines', seeing the former as expendable as timetable labels, but the latter as critical *resources*, which should be used in *interrelation*.

This was too well balanced an approach for its time, however. The angry reaction against continuing *Black Paper* attacks on education reinforced the slide towards the abyss of polarized thinking. The greater weight of opinion in the educational literature was against subject divisions, though this may well have been more evident in the theory than the practice. Just a few writers argued for more flexible approaches. Entwistle (1970) regarded Peter's concept of 'cognitive overspill' as a possible means of exploiting the potential of the cross-curricular links of different disciplines, resolving tensions rather than heightening confrontation. He pointed also to the paradox in the primary school of subjects like history and geography being penned in integrated topic approaches while mathematics was often delivered as a discrete and tightly structured subject in the timetable. He concluded with a warning about the perils of the cultural parochialism he perceived in extremist child-centred approaches.

Like Entwistle, Alexander (1984) later highlighted some of the contradictions in progressive primary school practice in England and Wales. While supporting the great merits of the primary school ethos at its best, he also identified deep-rooted weaknesses in curriculum planning and pedagogy, weaknesses also publicized in HMI surveys of primary school practice (for example, DES, 1978 and 1989). Alexander referred critically to the 'unnecessary dichotomies' exemplified in undifferentiated child-centred versus society-centred debates and quoted projects such as Bruner's *Man: a Course of Study* and the Liverpool Schools' Council project as effecting sensible reconciliations.

HMI documents, reflecting increased central intervention in the curriculum following Callaghan's Ruskin College speech of 1976, in general steered a middle course, albeit shifting in the 1980s from a short-lived preference for an 'areas of experience' mode of organization (DES, 1985) to a more subject-based format. What were valuably identified, though in practice subsequently relegated to the status of being non-statutory, were cross-curricular dimensions, skills and themes, to be woven in with the statutory subjects, in a kind of 'cognitive overspill' framework.

Summary

In focussing on the long-standing debate over subject and integrated approaches to curriculum planning, and in taking the case of geography, as seen through the eyes of progressive non-specialist individuals or committees, to illustrate the issues, it is hoped that the idea that the stronger infusion of subject emphases will inevitably reduce qualities of breadth and balance has been countered, in one general area of the curriculum at least.

A potentially valuable feature of the work of the National Curriculum working groups and the National Curriculum Council has been in identifying overlaps and complementarity of offerings. In the achievement of balance, important areas of knowledge have inevitably been excluded as statutory elements. Whether the curriculum should include political science rather than history, and economics and sociology rather than geography has been decided, with inevitably differing views as to reasons for the decision. Primary teachers are left, rather than to permeate the skills and conceptual frameworks of disciplines into an integrated approach, something previously done, if done at all, very asymmetrically and unsystematically, to adjust to a different emphasis. It should be stressed, however, that there is nothing in the statutory orders which demands an organization of the timetable in terms of traditional subject boundaries. We need to distinguish, as Rugg, Blyth *et al* and Alexander have variously argued, between subjects in the timetable and the contributions of the disciplines of knowledge, as selections from the culture.

Thus the traditional brainstorming topic-web, which in its blunderbuss way inevitably made some real connections but was also riddled with pseudo-connections, has now to be audited more carefully. It will be found that traditional broad-ranging primary topics will have to bridge a series of attainment targets, while subjects like geography, history, literature and science, providers of essential concepts for explaining society and the environment, in themselves also provide potential bridges for constructing, for example, more illuminative and interesting approaches to language, number and a range of aesthetic activity.

While there is a theoretical opportunity for capitalizing on this shift from 'or' to 'and' approaches, there remain grave causes for concern. One is the continuing and almost pathological tendency of many in government, the media and in right-wing educational think-tanks (though using a language of contamination more characteristic of thought police operations), to ulcerate the debate, more intensely perhaps than at any time since the Revised Code of the 1860s. In no period since then has government so openly incited popular contempt for the professional educator. This has been reinforced by the growing politicization of educational matters again more unremitting than at any time since the religious issue which split educational opinion for over 100 years.

Another serious anxiety relates to the crazily rushed and sequential system of curriculum planning which from the start introduced an unfortunate hierarchical ordering: starting with the (hard) — core subjects; followed by the 'soft-core' foundation subjects (in themselves ranked in a chain of being: technology; geography, history, modern languages; with art, music and physical education coming up behind), and ending with the essentially non-statutory cross-curricular activities. At the same time, the Secretary of State cannot prevent these being given some priority if schools choose to do so. Official rhetoric tells us these are important, therefore we should take sustenance from and build on the rhetoric. The fear nevertheless is that primary schools will take the system at face value and revert to subject divisions, on the grounds that this is how reporting to parents will take place, and therefore will be how parents expect arrangements to be made. There is already evidence that primary schools have structured their post-National Curriculum topic work to the requirements of the science attainment targets, in the hope that the subsequent targets of history, geography and other subjects will fit in. Thus any complementary planning exercise is necessarily delayed, and an enormous waste of effort has already resulted.

In forging anew principles of breadth, balance and connection into the primary curriculum, any optimism must be based on the fact that the nature of the National Curriculum positively incites teachers to talk to each other and become aware of overlaps, complementarities and general possibilities for cooperating in meeting the onerous demands of the legislation. My centrist proposal is that in general an integrative approach to primary timetabling should be retained, and that the rather tighter structuring of topic work, which is both necessary and overdue, can positively be helped by a subject such as geography which, in its long-standing function as a bridge between the humanities and the sciences, can contribute valuably to the desired breadth, balance and connection in the primary curriculum, if properly used. In arguing that it and other subjects can be permeated without tissue-rejection into a topic-based structure, while acknowledging the complexities of auditing and recording that the more negative parts of the National Curriculum demand, it may be appropriate to draw attention again to the quote from the Hadow Report (1931) that usually is left buried:

Work in the primary school *in geography*, as in other subjects, must 'be thought of in terms of activity and experience rather than of knowledge to be acquired and facts to be stored'.

References

ALEXANDER, R.J. (1984) *Primary Teaching*, London, Holt, Rinehart and Winston.

ARNOLD, M. (1869) *Reports on Elementary Schools 1852–1881*, London, HMSO (1908).

BAILEY, P. and BINNS, T. (1987) *A Case for Geography*, Sheffield, Geographical Association.

BLYTH, W.A.L. *et al* (1976) *Place, Time and Society 8–13: Curriculum Planning in History, Geography and Social Science*, Glasgow and Bristol, Collins/ESL Bristol.

COX, C.B. and BOYSON, R. (Eds) (1975) *Black Paper 1975*, London, Dear.

COX, C.B. and BOYSON, R. (Eds) (1977) *Black Paper 1977*, London, Temple Smith.

COX, C.B. and DYSON A.E. (Eds) (1969a, 1969b and 1970) *Black Papers No 1, 2 and 3*, London, Critical Quarterly Society.

DES (1978) *Primary Education in England: a survey by HM Inspectorate*, London, HMSO.

DES (1985) *The Curriculum from 5 to 16: Curriculum Matters 2 — An HMI Document*, London, HMSO.

DEWEY, J. (1900) *The School and Society*, Chicago, Phoenix Books, University of Chicago Press reprint (nd).

DEWEY, J. (1902) *The Child and the Curriculum*, Chicago, Phoenix Books, University of Chicago Press reprint (nd).

DEWEY, J. (1916) *Democracy and Education: An Introduction to the Philosophy of Education*, New York, The Free Press.

ENTWISTLE, H. (1970) *Child-centred Education*, London, Methuen.

GOODSON, I.F. (1988) *The Making of Curriculum: Collected Essays*, Lewes, Falmer Press.

HADOW REPORT (1931) *Report of the Consultative Committee on the Primary School*, London, HMSO.

HOLMES, E. (1911) *What Is and What Might Be: a Study of Education in General and Elementary Education in Particular*, London, Constable.

McMURRY, C.A. (1899) 'A course of study in geography for the grades of the common school', *Fourth Yearbook of the National Herbart Society for 1898, Supplement*, Chicago, IL, University of Chicago Press.

MARSDEN, W.E. (1986) 'The Royal Geographical Society and geography in secondary education' in PRICE, M.H. (Ed) *The Development of the Secondary Curriculum*, London, Croom Helm.

MARSDEN, W.E. (1989) 'Primary school geography: The question of balance' in CAMPBELL, J. and LITTLE, V. (Eds) *Humanities in the Primary School*, Lewes, Falmer Press.

MARSDEN, W.E. (1991) 'The structure of omission: British curriculum predicaments and false charts of American experience', *Compare*, 21, pp. 5–25.

MOSELEY, REV. H. (1845) 'Report on the Midland District' in *Minutes of the Committee of Council on Education*, London, HMSO.

NUNN, SIR P. (1940) *Education: Its Data and First Principles*, London, Edward Arnold.

Bill Marsden

PETERS, R. (Ed) (1969) *Perspectives on Plowden*, London, Routledge & Kegan Paul.

PLOWDEN REPORT (1967) *Children and their Primary Schools, Vol. 1*, London, HMSO.

RUGG, H. (1926) 'The school curriculum and the drama of American life' in WHIPPLE, G.M. (Ed) *The Foundations and Technique of Curriculum Construction: 26th Yearbook of the National Society for the Study of Education*, Bloomington, IL, Public School Publishing Company.

RUGG, H. (1931) *Culture and Education in America*, New York, Harcourt Brace & Company.

RUGG, H. (1960) 'Dewey and his contemporaries: The frontiers of educational thought in the early 1900's', *Bulletin of the School of Education of Indiana University*, 36, pp. 1–14.

TABA, H. (1962) *Curriculum Development: Theory and Practice*, New York, Harcourt, Brace & World, Inc.

TROTTER, S. (1898) 'The social function of geography', *Fourth Yearbook of the National Herbart Society, 1898*, Chicago, IL, University of Chicago Press.

TYLER, R. (1963) Contribution to SOWARDS, G.W. (Ed) *The Social Studies: Curriculum Proposals for the Future*, papers presented at the 1963 Cubberley Conference, School of Education, Stanford University, Chicago, Scott, Forsman.

WARWICK, D. (Ed) (1973) *Integrated Studies in the Secondary School*, London, University of London Press.

WHEELER, D.K. (1967) *Curriculum Process*, London, University of London Press.

WHIPPLE, G.M. (Ed) (1926) *The Foundations and Technique of Curriculum Construction: 26th Yearbook of the National Society for the Study of Education*, Bloomington, IL, Public School Publishing Company.

WILSON, H.E. (1931) 'The fusion of social studies in the junior high school' in WHIPPLE, G.M. (Ed) (1933) *The Teaching of Geography: 32nd Yearbook of the National Society for the Study of Education*, Chicago, IL, University of Chicago Press.

Chapter 9

The Subjects that Dare Not Speak their Name

Alistair Ross

The purpose of this chapter is to examine the place of the social subjects within the primary curriculum of the 1990s. The term 'social subjects' rarely occurs in the current formulations of the National Curriculum or the whole curriculum: indeed, the very word 'society' is notable by its infrequency. This was not the case through the 1970s and early 1980s: there were then some lively and growing innovations, not yet in all schools, but growing. Has this work ceased with the implementation of the curricular provisions of the 1988 Education Reform Act? I will argue that while the social subjects are largely neglected in the *National* Curriculum, they have found a place, albeit in rather a covert manner, in the way in which the idea of the *whole* curriculum has become articulated. However, the pressures on teachers now are such that there will need to be a considerably stronger articulation of the social elements needed to create a broad and balanced curriculum, to give teachers the necessary direction, confidence and knowledge necessary to develop these areas. I will also argue that such an articulation may *lighten* the demands of the National and whole curricula, by providing some much needed elements of unity between the fragmented list of subjects in the legislation and National Curriculum Council (NCC) documentation.

Defining the curriculum for primary education has never been a straightforward matter. There have been advocates of subject-based approaches, of societal and skills-based approaches, and of child-centred approaches. Most definitions that have emerged from national bodies over the past fifteen years have used subject headings, of a sort, to pinpoint the activities that they expect to see happening in primary schools, though often qualifying them, presenting them as ingredients, rather than as a menu of distinct courses. Alan Blyth *et al* made the analogy of a well-balanced meal: the cook will use her/his knowledge of dietary needs and balance to prepare a meal that contains a necessary and appropriate range of nutrients, of which the person eating the meal does not necessarily need to be aware (Blyth *et al*, 1976, p. 33). In the same way, they argued, the primary teacher needs to have an understanding of the contributions of different disciplines to the overall learning of the child. Figure 9.1 compares some of the various ways in which the primary curriculum has been divided and described since the Plowden Committee reported. Each vertical column represents the classification or analysis used by one publication or series of publications. Similar or cognate areas have been aligned horizontally, so that shifts in emphasis or in nomenclature, or the arrival or departure of some elements, can be seen more readily. Some of the definitions of what is supposed to be covered in the primary school appear to have had a long and troubled background. One can note the differences between subject definitions, area definitions and the listing of skills. The organizational headings used by HMI in their decennial post-Plowden surveys (in columns 2, 6, 7 and 13) demonstrate this variety, especially when juxtaposed to their 1981 View of the Curriculum (column 3). But there are in many places remarkable consistency and stability of view, as was noted in *Primary Practice* (Schools Council, 1983, p. 27). Mathematics and science, religious education, music and physical education are only qualified in minor ways over the period. The area of language is clearly more difficult to define: HMI seem to prefer the term language and literacy, except in periods when they are under pressure from their political masters (HMI, 1980 and 1985a), when they use the DES-approved term of English.

But the principal areas of disagreement, on which this chapter will focus, are in the central and lower horizontal lines of the diagram: what would in Scotland be simply, and uncontroversially, known as the social subjects. Here we can see that there have been some important changes in nomenclature, as well as shifts in emphasis. In the 1978–83 period, terms such as 'social studies, including RE, history and geography' were used (HMI, 1978), or 'Learning about people' (HMI, 1982). History was linked to 'social studies' (HMI, 1980; Schools Council, 1981). History and geography were linked under the heading 'topic work' by the DES (1981), brought together again in a description of the middle school curriculum (HMI, 1983), and have recently been brought together again (HMI, 1990). In 1985 HMI were still referring to the importance of the 'human and social' area of learning and experience (HMI, 1985b), and the White Paper *Better Schools* (UK, 1985, para. 61) stated that the primary school curriculum should 'lay the foundation of understanding in religious education, history and geography, and the nature and values of British society'. Even as late as 1987, one can find examples of stubborn rearguard action by some HMI: 'good practice can be found whether the subjects are taught separately or subsumed under headings such as social studies' (HMI, 1987, p. 11).

But it was in 1984 that the Social Science Research Council was required, by the Secretary of State, to change its name to the Economic and Social Research Council, and the reason behind these changes in approved nomenclature, in both primary education and in research, might well have been revealed in the words of Margaret Thatcher in 1989: 'Society? There is no such thing as society — there are individuals and there are families' (*The Guardian*,

Figure 9.1: The division and description of the curriculum since Plowden

Children and their primary schools	Primary education in England	A view of the curriculum	The school curriculum	The practical curriculum		Education 5 to 9: First schools
1967	1978	1980	1981	1981 infants	juniors	1982
English	Language and literacy	English	English	English	English	Language and literacy
Mathematics	Mathematics	Mathematics	Mathematics	Mathematics	Mathematics	Mathematics
Science	Science	Science	Science	Nature study	Science	Learning about the physical world, about materials, plants and animals
Arts and crafts	Aesthetic and physical education: Art and craft	Graphic arts (1)	Art and craft and physical education	Art Craft	Art - from - Craft Design Technology, Home economics.	Art and craft
Physical education	Aesthetic and physical education: Physical education	PE including movement, dance and games	Art and craft and physical education	PE Games	PE Games	Physical education
Music	Aesthetic and physical education: Music	Music and drama (1)	Music	Music	Music	Music
Religious education	Social studies: Religious education	Religious education	Religious education	Religious education	Religious education	Religious and moral education
History	Social studies: History	History and social studies	Topic work: History	Environmental studies	- from - Social studies History Geography	Learning about people
Geography	Social studies: Geography	Geography	Topic work: Geography	Environmental studies	- from - Social studies History Geography	Learning about people
Foreign languages		(Foreign languages)	(French)			
Sex education						

Figure 9.1 continued

9–13 middle schools	Better schools	The curriculum from 5 to 16	Curriculum matters (series)	The National Curriculum (England)	The whole curriculum	Aspects of primary education (Series)
1983	1985	1985	1985–89	1988	1990	1989–91
Language and literacy	The use of language*	Linguistic and literary	English (1985)	English		Language and Literacy (1990)
Mathematics	Mathematics	Mathematical	Mathematics (1985)	Mathematics		Mathematics (1989)
Science	Science	Scientific	Craft, design and technology (1987) home economics (1985)	Science		Science (1989)
	Craft and practical work leading to design and technology	Technological		Technology		Design and technology (1991)
Home studies						
Arts and crafts	Arts	Aesthetic and creatives		Art		
Physical education	Physical education (1)	Physical	Physical education (1989)	Physical education		Physical education (1991)
Music		(Aesthetic and creative)	Music (1985) Drama (1989)	Music		Music (1991) Drama (1990)
History, geography and religious education	Religious education, history and geography, and nature and values of British society	Spiritual Human and social	History (1988) Geography (1986)	History Geography	Religious education	History and geography (1989)
Modern languages	* not normally foreign languages					
Health education	Health education (1)	Health education	Health education (1986)		Health education	
	Moral education (1)	Moral				
	How people earn their living	Economic understanding				Economic and industrial Understanding
	Nature and use of new technologies	Information technology	Information technology (1989)			
		Political education			Citizenship	
		Environmental education	Environmental education (1989)		Environmental education	
			Careers education and guidance (1988)		Careers education and guidance	
			Classics (1988)			
			PSE (1989)			

Notes on Figure 9.1

This has been compiled from a variety of sources, listed below. Most of them have been used as either a description, or a prescription, of the primary school curriculum, although in some cases the analysis was for both primary and secondary education. In some instances the analysis was explicit, in others it was implicit, being the chapter or section headings used in a description of the primary school curriculum. In two instances, the descriptions are taken from the titles used in series of pamphlets that describe the curriculum.

Specific sources are as follows:

Central Advisory Committee for Education (1967) *Children and Their Primary Schools: Volume 1* (The Plowden Report), HMSO (section headings used from chapter 17).

Her Majesty's Inspectorate (1978) *Primary Education in England: A survey by HM Inspectorate of Schools*, HMSO (section headings in chapter 5).

Her Majesty's Inspectorate (1980) *A View of the Curriculum, HMSO* (drawn from chapter 2, and listed in a broadly similar form in Schools Council (1983) *Primary Practice: A Sequel to 'The Practical Curriculum'* (Working Paper 75), Methuen, pp. 26–7).

Department of Education and Science/Welsh Office (1981) *The School Curriculum*, HMSO (drawn from paragraphs 33–8, and listed in a broadly similar form in Schools Council (1983) *Primary Practice: A Sequel to 'The Practical Curriculum'* (Working Paper 75), Methuen, pp. 26–7).

Schools Council (1981) *The Practical Curriculum* (Schools Council Working Paper 70), Methuen, pp. 38–9.

Her Majesty's Inspectorate (1982) *Education 5 to 9: An Illustrative Study of 80 First Schools in England*, HMSO (section headings, chapter 2).

Her Majesty's Inspectorate (1983) *9–13 Middle Schools*, HMSO (section headings, chapter 7).

United Kingdom (1985) *Better Schools*, Cmnd 9469, HMSO (paragraph 61: the content of the primary phase).

Her Majesty's Inspectorate (1985) *Curriculum Matters 2: The Curriculum from 5 to 16*, HMSO (areas of learning and experience for all schools in paragraph 33; and 'essential issues which are not necessarily contained in subjects but which need to be included in the curriculum' in paragraphs 26 to 29).

Her Majesty's Inspectorate (1984–89) *Curriculum Matters* (series), HMSO (this list includes all titles that specifically included reference to ages 5 to 11 in their title — thus including classics, but omitting modern languages. Note that the *Curriculum Matters* series did not include titles on science or religious education).

Department of Education and Science (1988) *The National Curriculum: England*, HMSO (the Core and other Foundation subjects included in the Education Reform Act, 1988).

National Curriculum Council (1990) *Curriculum Guidance 3: The Whole Curriculum*, NCC (religious education and the cross-curricular themes identified by the NCC as necessary components of the 'broad and balanced curriculum' required by the Educational Reform Act).

Her Majesty's Inspectorate (1989–91) *An Inspection Review: Aspects of Primary Education: The Teaching and Learning of . . .* (various titles as listed) (series), HMSO (column includes all titles published to date).

1989). *Better Schools*, the 1985 White Paper that reflected the government's thinking on the school curriculum in the mid-1980s, described one curriculum purpose as 'helping pupils to understand . . . the interdependence of individuals, groups and nations' (para. 44). No mention of societies there. One commentator — a Conservative MP *and* a social scientist — suggested that 'the initial reaction of Margaret Thatcher, Keith Joseph and others against the statist and corporatist assumptions of the 1960s and 1970s had led them to equate the social sciences with social engineering' (Foreman, 1991).

In teacher education there has been an increasing emphasis on linking primary education students' main subject area with particular areas of the primary school curriculum. In particular, applicants for PGCE courses are now required to have a first degree that is deemed relevant, and the Council for the Accreditation of Teacher Education (CATE) has applied this in practice to exclude graduates from the social sciences — sociology, economics, politics, psychology, etc. — unless the graduate can demonstrate that his or her particular course of undergraduate study included substantial elements of 'relevant' subjects (for example, of history). Similarly, main subject studies in undergraduate courses of initial teacher education have been scrutinized by CATE to exclude references to the social sciences, because, it is stated, these are not relevant to the primary school curriculum. (Curiously, such scrutiny is not applied to other main study subjects of first degrees. For example, the study of English literature is assumed always to be relevant to primary education, though such study may be predominantly of some aspect of literature such as middle English, the direct relevance of which to primary children is at least as questionable as are the social sciences.)

These, then, are 'the subjects that dare not speak their name': the social subjects that had begun to be developed within the primary curriculum in the late 1960s and 1970s. How did these areas come to develop in primary education?

The Plowden Report of 1967 did not refer to these social subjects. Vincent Rodgers, an American educator visiting Britain at the time and preparing a book entitled *The Social Studies in English Education* (1968), scoured the index of *Children and Their Primary Schools*, and reported he could find no reference to any social science. This lack of recognition did not last long: a post-Plowden conference on what might be a suitable curriculum for the middle schools that the Plowden Report had proposed received three separate papers on the social studies curriculum, from John Backhouse, John Hanson and Denis Lawton (Schools Council, 1969).

In his contribution, Lawton set out a series of aims for the social understanding to be achieved by the end of full-time education:

* the ability to access information about society;
* an awareness of the structure and complexity of society;
* the ability to distinguish between fact and opinion, opinion and theory, hypothesis and proof;

* the ability to distinguish different kinds of evidence and to evaluate them; and
* the ability to distinguish relevant from irrelevant facts.

These, he argued, were not over-ambitious aims for eleven years of full-time education, but were too much to be accomplished in a crash course in the final couple of years. Thus, he asserted,

> what we really need is a properly-planned integrated course, starting in the primary school with simple social concepts, concrete descriptive materials and simple experiences . . . It is not simply a matter of history and geography: there are many other disciplines which have an important part to play. (Lawton, 1969)

Lawton was subsequently asked by the Schools Council to survey and identify good practices in social studies teaching in the 8–13 age range. He reported (Lawton *et al*, 1971) on 'the tremendous difficulty experienced in locating examples of work incorporating concepts, materials and methods from the social sciences'. But they did find much evidence that primary aged children were capable of learning in these areas, and some arguments for why they should be taught in this area. He concluded that, although 'social studies is a curriculum area universally considered central to children's development as individuals and as members of society . . . (it is) generally neglected in curricular planning in schools'. He suggested a curriculum development project, that the Schools Council subsequently asked Alan Blyth and his team to develop at the University of Liverpool's School of Education from 1971 to 1975.

Part of the contribution of this project, *Place, Time and Society 8–13*, has been analyzed elsewhere in this volume (Derricott). The project's key document (Blyth *et al*, 1976) identified the social disciplines as history, geography, economics, sociology, social anthropology, social psychology and political science. It claimed that the contributions of these disciplines should be a necessary element of the curriculum: 'Is it possible to talk of someone as being educated if he has no conception of the past, no awareness of the world around him, and no understanding of human society? If such a conception is not possible, then we are clearly entitled, if not mandated, to include such study in our curriculum.' The idea of using academic disciplines as a resource for learning, rather than the discipline being taught as such, was an early example of viewing the curriculum as the development of cognitive processes, emphasizing the processes of learning rather than its outcomes. As such, it did not match either of the then current dominant curricular models in primary education identified by Eisner and Vallance (1974) and Alexander (1984): curriculum as self-actualization or consumatory experience (personal purpose, autonomy and growth) and curriculum for social reconstruction or relevance (education for societal goals, to produce individuals who will fit into current social structures and reflect dominant value systems).

The project led to a period of innovation, admittedly patchy, across the country. There were pockets of innovation and good practice, for example, in Oxfordshire, of clear curriculum guidance from local authorities, for example, in Merton (Merton/Schools Council, 1981; Harries, 1984) and Northamptonshire (Northamptonshire, 1982), and of materials development, for example, the ILEA *People Around Us* series (ILEA, 1978, 1979, 1980a and 1980b). National surveys by HMI detected these innovations only in pockets, as when the *Primary Education in England* survey noted that history work was superficial in four out of five classes, with only rare examples of children developing an understanding of historical change, cause, or the nature of evidence, and that work in geography was also superficial, with little evidence of progression (HMI, 1978). Similarly, the *Aspects of Primary Education* report (HMI, 1989) found that the vast majority of geography and history work was taught through topic or project work, and that this work was 'considered reasonably satisfactory in the majority of schools'. The work that was specifically historical and geographical was far less satisfactory. However, a more focussed study by the Social Science Committee of HM Inspectorate identified the need for 'a well-designed syllabus (in social sciences in primary schools) covering work done by all age groups and the relation of this syllabus to the schools' language and mathematics policies' (Anglesey and Hennessey, 1984). The schools they reported on did not have a clear social sciences policy as such, but 'rather, individual social sciences were tapped from time to time in social studies or environmental studies programmes. Economics were weak, and sociology tended to be empiricist and functionalist'. The priority, they suggested, was 'to escape from the thralldom of *ad hoc* topics and to move instead to a form of syllabus which sets out to answer the question "What should infant and junior school pupils know about the size, shape and workings of their own and other societies, and of the economies on which they depend?" '

But this encouragement and direction was set in an atmosphere of increasing misunderstanding, even of hostility, towards the social sciences in general. There seemed at times to be an outright suspicion that any attempt to identify and examine 'the social', at any level, and this became explicit, with the publication of *The National Curriculum 5–16: A Consultation Document* in July 1987 (DES, 1987). Although this made some claim to build upon the explicit references in *Better Schools* (UK, 1985) to insights into the adult world and to an understanding of society in references to pupils being 'equip (ped) for the responsibilities of citizenship and for the challenge of employment in tomorrow's world' (para. 4), the list of nine primary subjects was, with the exception of technology, a highly traditional and asocial congerie. Figure 9.2 represents the proposals in the document. There was an indication that there might be 'additional subjects or themes ... which can be taught through other subjects'. Health education and information technology were the examples given, but it was firmly asserted 'that such subjects or themes should be taught through the foundation subjects' (para. 18): as White (1988) put it, 'the wayward horse (was) soon reined in'. The emphasis was on the

Figure 9.2

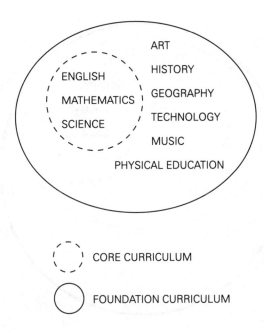

ART

HISTORY

ENGLISH

MATHEMATICS   GEOGRAPHY

SCIENCE   TECHNOLOGY

MUSIC

PHYSICAL EDUCATION

CORE CURRICULUM

FOUNDATION CURRICULUM

core curriculum of English, mathematics and science that are held to be essential to future economic growth. Any areas of the curriculum that might lead to children becoming critically aware of society, or disposed to question authority, were excluded. There was no reference in the consultation document to the 'balanced and broadly based curriculum', which phrase did not emerge until the Education Reform Bill was published the next year. The Act was significantly different from the proposals made in 1987, in offering an important point of entry into the curriculum for other areas or subjects. In its legislative passage, while the National Curriculum and its subjects were confirmed in their statutory position, Religious education was added (or perhaps more accurately, confirmed) as a statutory requirement. So what was now termed the 'basic curriculum' comprised two statutory elements, the National Curriculum and religious education. But this basic curriculum was not what schools were enjoined to provide: the Act gave them a statutory duty to provide a broad and balanced curriculum — the whole curriculum — that was, in some unspecified way, greater than the basic curriculum. Figure 9.3 shows this in diagrammatic form. Duncan Graham, the first chair of the NCC, subsequently noted this 'generosity' in the Act as 'perhaps surprising in something so prescriptive' (Graham, 1992). It is not clear yet precisely how this distinction between the whole and the basic arose: the notion of 'other subjects and themes' was present in the 1987 consultation document, but was not articulated in a way to create the space that the Act eventually allowed.

Figure 9.3

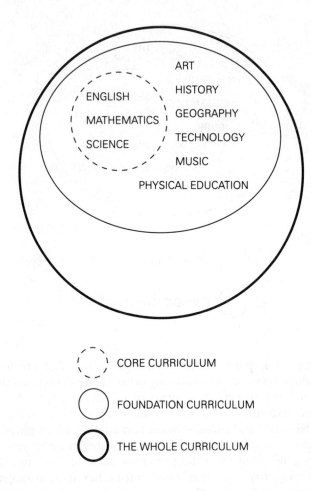

One possibility is that the notion of a whole or a broader curriculum emerged in the discussions about relationship between the core and the other foundation subjects. If the other foundation subjects had been diminished in importance in order to augment the status of the core, as the then Prime Minister was thought to favour, then the description of a whole curriculum might have been included in drafts of the Bill as an indication of the areas beyond the core. When the other foundation subjects retained their position in the version of the Bill that was published, the 'balanced and broadly based' reference to the whole curriculum was left in. Whatever the process, the distinction between the two definitions left a very obvious gap. It was left to the National Curriculum Council to consider what guidance should be offered to schools on what might fill this space between the basic and the whole. The position was curious: state-maintained schools were statutorily obliged to offer something greater than, but containing the National Curriculum, but only the National Curriculum elements were to be defined by statutory instruments. Religious education had to form part of the broad and balanced curriculum, but the definition of this was left to statutorily-established Standing Advisory Councils on Religious Education (SACRES). But the Act required a whole curriculum greater than this to be offered. The NCC were later to assert 'the basic curriculum as prescribed in law is not intended to be the whole curriculum' (NCC, 1989). Figure 9.4 shows one way of representing this situation. The Council established a working party ('The National Curriculum Interim Whole Curriculum Committee'), chaired by Malcolm Brigg, to consider the potential components of the whole curriculum. There was no shortage of claimants for inclusion. Many curriculum initiatives, from LEAs, from the Schools Council, and from the Schools Curriculum Development Council, had found no ready place in the proposed new framework. For example, the Education for Economic Awareness programme had been established by the Schools Curriculum Development Council in 1986 as a result of a direct request by the Secretary of State (see Ross, 1990, for details). The government had committed itself to pursuing policies of gender and ethnic equality in education. Considerable resources had been given to promoting information technology awareness and capability across the school curriculum, and not merely in the potential enclave of the National Curriculum's subject of technology. Major curriculum projects had been devised in health education, and there was a particular concern emerging in the late 1980s about developing an awareness of AIDs in the school population. There were also special interest groups, of careers teachers, for example. All these areas seemed to have been excluded, or at best marginalized, by the rigidity of the National Curriculum. The NCC Whole Curriculum working party took account of the various curriculum initiatives and educational issues that had arisen in the 70s and 80s in their considerations of what should be included within the whole.

The Brigg group's draft report was completed in early 1989: various curriculum planning groups (for example, a Schools Curriculum Industry Partnership conference of primary schools at Stoke Rochford in April) were informally told of the main proposals. However, there was a considerable delay before the report was eventually published, in March 1990, as *Curriculum Guidance 3: The Whole Curriculum* (NCC, 1990a). Through the summer of 1989 there were reports of disagreements between the DES and the NCC over whether schools should be given any direction over the nature of the whole curriculum. DES approval seems to have been necessary for the publication of substantial documents such as those in the *Curriculum Guidance* series. Graham reports his recognition, at this point, that 'what was really wanted was a narrow "basics" diet, minimally at risk of dilution' (Graham, 1992). In October 1989 the NCC were able to publish a simple four-page circular, *The National Curriculum and Whole Curriculum Planning: Preliminary Guidance (Circular No 6)* (NCC, 1989). This effectively preempted publication of the

Figure 9.4

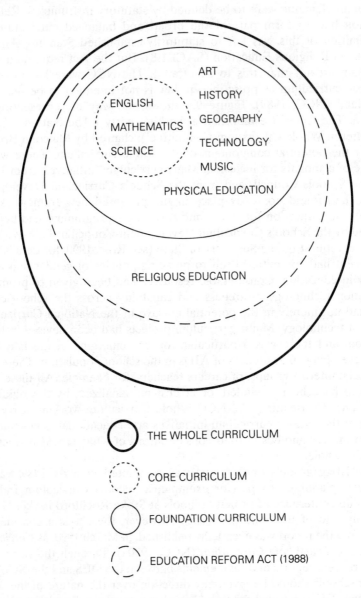

ART
HISTORY
ENGLISH
GEOGRAPHY
MATHEMATICS
TECHNOLOGY
SCIENCE
MUSIC
PHYSICAL EDUCATION

RELIGIOUS EDUCATION

THE WHOLE CURRICULUM

CORE CURRICULUM

FOUNDATION CURRICULUM

EDUCATION REFORM ACT (1988)

full report, identifying the (what it termed) dimensions, skills and themes that it claimed, in a rather strained metaphor, would bind together the bricks of the programmes of study and attainment targets of the Foundation subjects (*ibid*, para. 19). 'This', wrote Graham of the publication, 'was the National Curriculum Council's finest hour. It fought resolutely for the whole curriculum and won' (Graham, 1992).

Curriculum Guidance 3 offers a reappraisal of the curriculum, from a position that recognizes the constraints and the partialities of the National Curriculum. The vacuum created between the National and the Whole Curriculum had been effectively filled, as figure 9.5 indicates. The social subjects had, through this definition of the whole curriculum, been readmitted into the potential entitlement of the primary school child. The various dimensions, skills and themes can be analyzed to show their heavy reliance on the social sciences and social subjects. It can also be argued that, since the whole curriculum and the Curriculum Guidance documents 4 to 8 that described the themes in greater detail (NCC, 1990b, 1990c, 1990d, 1990e and 1990f) were explicitly directed to cover all four Key Stages, that these subjects were now for the first time clearly part of the primary school agenda. Hitherto, the various references to the social subjects and to social studies had been merely enabling: the NCC was now arguing that all children had a legal entitlement to a broad and balanced curriculum which schools were required to provide.

Examining the various additional parts of the whole curriculum described in *Curriculum Guidance 3*, a number of 'social' elements can be identified, both within the cross-curricular elements (dimensions, skills and themes) and in other elements (such as personal and social education). The dimensions and skills are identified in a relatively brief form. Dimensions were seen at first as concerning 'the intentional promotion of personal and social development' (NCC, 1989, para. 9). The only dimensions that are indicated clearly in the final report are in the phrase 'a commitment to providing equal opportunities for all pupils, and a recognition that preparation for life in a multicultural society is relevant to all pupils' (NCC, 1990a). Equal opportunities are further elaborated to cover sex, social, cultural and linguistic factors. Such opportunities must go beyond merely ensuring equality of access, but must 'challenge attitudes present in society', and schools must 'foster a climate ... in which positive attitudes to gender equality, cultural diversity and special needs of all kinds are actively promoted'. This is not quite as powerful an analysis as that offered by the ILEA in their documents on race, sex and class earlier in the decade, which spoke of having identified 'institutional sexism and unconscious sexist attitudes as the twin barriers to equal opportunities between the sexes' (ILEA, 1985), and of educational 'measures to unlearn and dismantle racism' (ILEA, 1983).

Cross-curricular skills receive rather less attention in *Curriculum Guidance 3* — a slight 161 words, within which it manages to list the six identified skills twice, but with the promise of further guidance on, for example, personal and social skills.

But while the dimensions offer a social framework within which the teacher and the school need to be aware that they are operating, and the skills represent a set of competencies, the five cross-curricular themes — 'more structured and less pervasive aspects than other cross-curricular provision' (NCC, 1989, para. 16) — represent an important and significant toe-hold for

Figure 9.5

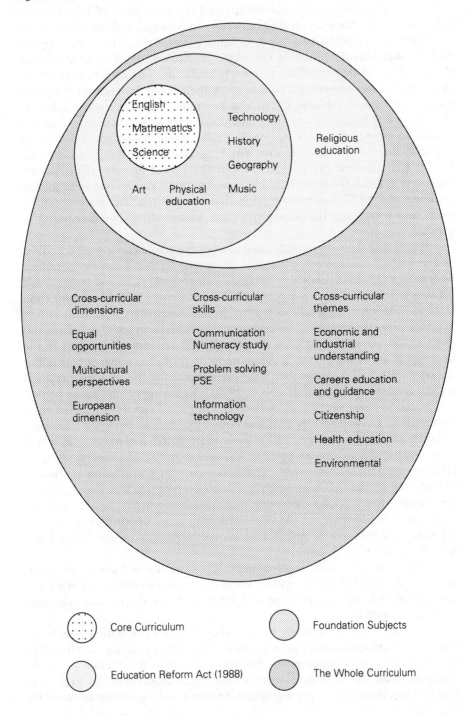

English
Mathematics
Science

Technology
History
Geography

Religious education

Art   Physical   Music
        education

Cross-curricular
dimensions

Cross-curricular
skills

Cross-curricular
themes

Equal
opportunities

Communication
Numeracy study

Economic and
industrial
understanding

Multicultural
perspectives

Problem solving
PSE

Careers education
and guidance

European
dimension

Information
technology

Citizenship

Health education

Environmental

Core Curriculum   Foundation Subjects

Education Reform Act (1988)   The Whole Curriculum

the social sciences. Economics, the Conservative-preferred social science of the 1980s, had the pre-eminence of being named in the title of one of the themes, economic and industrial understanding. Alan Blyth elsewhere explores the at times uneasy coalition of industry — 'a field of economic and social behaviour' — with the subject of economics (Blyth, 1992, in press). Political science, in an applied form, appears in education for citizenship, another particular and individualistic construction of the government, but nevertheless a theme which will permit children space for critical reflection and analysis. Sociology, unsurprisingly, is not so clearly favoured, but there are distinct niches for sociological study in the 'industrial' part of economic and industrial awareness, in large elements of citizenship, and also in aspects of environmental and health education. Anthropology, however, is not discernible in the themes.

What is the status of these cross-curricular themes? There is some understandable ambivalence on the part of the National Curriculum Council on this. From being 'important issues which schools might consider' (NCC, 1990a, foreword), they slip towards stating that 'the National Curriculum alone will not provide the necessary balance' to meet schools 'statutory responsibility . . . to provide a broad and balanced curriculum" required by the Act. Schools will meet this responsibility by '*augmenting* the basic curriculum (foundation subjects and religious education)' with 'an accepted range of cross curricular elements' (*ibid*, p. 1, emphasis added). 'Augmenting' is an important shift from the original conception that cross-curricularity could be achieved simply by combining elements of the existing basic curriculum: the themes are an addition to the basic. But when the first theme was published, it was stressed by Graham in his foreword that education for economic and industrial understanding 'is not an additional subject. Most aspects can be developed through the foundation subjects . . . especially in the earlier key stages' (NCC, 1990b, foreword). By the time that the education for citizenship document was published seven months later, this health warning had been modified: this theme 'is not a "subject" as such. *Elements of it* can and must be taught through the subjects of the National Curriculum . . .' (NCC, 1990f, emphasis added). Clearly, other elements could not so be taught. The authors of the economic and industrial understanding document were not as cautious as Graham: the theme 'is clearly required if schools are to provide a curriculum which promotes the aims defined in the . . . Act', and it would need to be taught 'through foundation subjects *and other areas* of the school curriculum' (NCC, 1990b, p. 1, emphasis added). The overall impression given by these various presentations is that the National Curriculum Council:

* would like the cross-curricular themes to be statutory;
* believes that they are essential if a broad and balanced curriculum is to be provided;
* is aware that their belief on its own does not make the provision statutory, but;

       *   wants to remind schools that they are responsible for providing a depth and a balance that the National Curriculum plus religious education alone does not do, and that this deficiency is acknowledged in the Education Reform Act (1988).

It is also interesting to note that the NCC moves from a simple list of five 'themes identified in NCC Circular 6' (NCC, 1990b) to noting in the final Curriculum Guidance that this concerns *'one of the . . . themes* on which it is giving *initial* guidance' (NCC, 1990f, emphasis added). More themes may follow.

    What has been the effect of these cross-curricular themes in practice? A limited number of copies were sent to each primary school when they were first published. Some anecdotal evidence suggests that some headteachers assumed, from the titles, that they had been sent in error and were intended for secondary school distribution. The economic and industrial awareness document in particular was seen by the Department of Trade and Industry to be yet another way that they might influence the school curriculum, and a sum of around one million pounds was made available by the DTI for the NCC to provide INSET materials to support *Curriculum Guidance 4*. As well as foundation subject INSET suggestions for Key Stages 3 and 4, it was at one stage in 1991 intended to provide video and print based INSET materials for primary schools INSET: tenders were invited in June (NCC, 1991a), but this was later dropped: only materials for middle and secondary schools were to be published (NCC, 1991b).

    Students preparing to become primary teachers may be more aware of the economic and industrial understanding theme than serving teachers, if the activities of the EATE agency are effective. This group, with a remit to promote enterprise, industrial and economic awareness in initial teacher education courses, was funded first by the DTI, and later by the Employment Department. But they have a major task to accomplish. A survey of students beginning their primary teaching courses in 1990/91 (by the present author and colleagues) asked students to rank the five cross-curricular themes in order: the results are revealing:

	Percentage of student teachers ranking particular cross-curricular theme as most important
Health education	41
Environmental education	35
Citizenship	17
Careers education and guidance	5
Economic and industrial understanding	2

(*Source*: Ross, Ahier and Hutchings, 1991)

This ranking of the clearest 'social' cross-curricular themes, showing less than 20 per cent in aggregate, is rather depressing. Students, and probably serving teachers, given any degree of optionality or choice, prefer to select the safer, less controversial and non-social areas of the curriculum (Carrington and Troyna, 1988). The social subjects may not be merely ones that dare not speak their name: they may also be perceived as areas of children's learning that many teachers do not even wish to articulate.

When one puts this probable low perception by teachers of the social subjects in primary education, as articulated in the cross-curricular themes, alongside the high levels of response now being demanded to the foundation subjects of the curriculum, and the need to assess these at the ages of 7 and 11, the outlook is not encouraging. If the social subjects can indeed be delivered through the existing foundation subjects, then a much greater degree of articulation and explicitness will be required in the way in which the foundation subjects are expressed. If the social subjects require some additional form of delivery, beyond the foundation subjects (as is implied in some of the forewords to the *Curriculum Guidance* documents), then some reformulation of the Education Reform Act will be necessary, to give clear and unambiguous weight to the constitution of 'a broad and balanced curriculum' — and perhaps to supplement this with some form of reported assessment.

The former course of action seems more likely than the latter: a clear set of principles, methods and resources that highlight the social elements within the existing documentation, would at least provide the possibility of progress. Such a statement would presumably centre on the foundation subjects of history and geography, though they would also be able to draw in a perhaps surprisingly considerable way from technology. The formula used by the History Working Party to create the History Study Units stressed the social foundations of history: each unit had, in the final report, a political, economic, social and cultural strand (DES, 1990). This, coupled with the human and economic geography elements in the geography curriculum, might perhaps provide a suitable core for the social science-based cross-curricular themes. Without some such impetus, the social subjects will remain fragmented across elements of some foundation subjects and sections of the cross-curricular themes: without a sense of unity, these parts will always remain less than the potential of the whole.

Most primary teachers have an intuitive, rather than a well-articulated, view of the social in the curriculum. Only a minority of them have the energy, the analysis, or indeed the courage, to weld a social studies curriculum out of the jigsaw of the National Curriculum's foundation subjects and the whole curriculum's themes. To many, the concept of moving towards breadth in the curriculum implies something wider, something more than is already there. To suggest a balanced curriculum means adding yet more weight to make up the shortfall. A successful broadening and balancing of the curriculum will entail this majority being convinced that a well-constructed whole curriculum will be simpler and less complicated to deliver, as well as more meaningful for children.

The social subjects are an essential part of that whole curriculum. That they 'dare not speak their name' is a result of three principal factors:

* the social sciences, particularly at the level of compulsory education, have been effectively driven into hiding by politicians who do not understand them or are frightened by them;
* the social subjects necessarily deal with controversial matters, and are therefore avoided by many teachers;
* if the social areas of the curriculum become articulated as 'subjects', this implies that space must be found for them in an already over-cluttered timetable of subjects.

Nevertheless, not only are the social subjects a necessary part of the whole curriculum, they are already available, in piecemeal form within the existing skeleton of the National and whole curricula. The only way of making them sufficiently explicit, and thus achievable, will be to draw the disparate parts together, and offer this as something not only greater than its parts, but also simpler than its parts.

References

ALEXANDER, R.J. (1984) *Primary Teaching*, London, Holt Rinehart & Winston.

ANGLESEY, K.J. and HENNESSEY, R.A.S. (1984) 'Social sciences in primary schools', *The Social Science Teacher*, 13, 3.

BACKHOUSE, J. (1969) 'Social studies' in Schools Council *The Middle Years of Schooling from 8 to 13* (Working Paper No 22), London, HMSO.

BLYTH, W.A.L., COOPER, K. and DERRICOTT, R. *et al* (1976) *Place, Time and Society 8–13: Curriculum Planning in History, Geography and Social Science*, Bristol, Collins/ESL.

BLYTH, W.A.L. (1992) 'The place of economic and industrial understanding in a different primary curriculum', *Journal of Education and Work*, 5.

CARRINGTON, B. and TROYNA, B. (1988) *Children and Controversial Issues: Strategies for the Early and Middle Years of Schooling*, Lewes, Falmer Press.

CENTRAL ADVISORY COMMITTEE FOR EDUCATION (1967) *Children and their Primary Schools: Volume 1* (The Plowden Report), London, HMSO.

DEPARTMENT OF EDUCATION AND SCIENCE/WELSH OFFICE (1981) *The School Curriculum*, London, HMSO.

DEPARTMENT OF EDUCATION AND SCIENCE (1987) *The National Curriculum: 5–16: A Consultation Document*, London, HMSO.

DEPARTMENT OF EDUCATION AND SCIENCE (1990) *The National Curriculum History Working Party: Final Report*, London, HMSO

EISNER, E.W. and VALLANCE, E. (Eds) (1974) *Competing Conceptions of the Curriculum*, Berkely, CA, McCutchan.

FOREMAN, N. (1991) 'Viewpoint' in *Social Sciences: News from the Economic and Social Research Council*, 12 (November), Swindon, ESRC.

GRAHAM, D. (1992) 'Beware hasty changes', *Times Educational Supplement*, 3 January, p. 10.

Guardian, The (1989) report 6 September.

HANSON, J. (1969) 'Social studies 11–13 in Schools Council *The Middle Years of Schooling from 8 to 13* (Working Paper No 22), London, HMSO.

HARRIES, E. (1984) 'Social sciences 7–13: The view and role of the local authority', *The Social Science Teacher*, 13, 3.

HER MAJESTY'S INSPECTORATE (1978) *Primary Education in England: A Survey by HM Inspectorate of Schools*, London HMSO.

HER MAJESTY'S INSPECTORATE (1980) *A View of the Curriculum*, London, HMSO.

HER MAJESTY'S INSPECTORATE (1982) *Education 5 to 9: An Illustrative Study of 80 First Schools in England*, London, HMSO.

HER MAJESTY'S INSPECTORATE (1983) *9–13 Middle Schools*, London, HMSO.

HER MAJESTY'S INSPECTORATE (1985a) *Curriculum Matters 3: English from 5 to 16*, London, HMSO.

HER MAJESTY'S INSPECTORATE (1985b) *Curriculum Matters 2: The Curriculum from 5 to 16*, London, HMSO.

HER MAJESTY'S INSPECTORATE (1984–89) *Curriculum Matters* (series), London HMSO.

HER MAJESTY'S INSPECTORATE (1989–91) *An Inspection Review: Aspects of Primary Education: The Teaching and Learning of . . .* (various titles) (series), London, HMSO.

ILEA (1978) *People Around Us: Unit 1: Families*, London, ILEA Learning Materials Service.

ILEA (1979) *People Around Us: Unit 2: Friends*, London, ILEA Learning Materials Service.

ILEA (1980a) *People Around Us: Unit 3: Work*, London, ILEA Learning Materials Service.

ILEA (1980b) *Social Studies in the Primary School* (ILEA Curriculum Guidelines), London, ILEA Learning Materials Service.

ILEA (1983) *Race, Sex and Class: 3 — A Policy for Equality: Race*, London, ILEA.

ILEA (1985) *Race, Sex and Class: 6 — A Policy for Equality: Sex*, London, ILEA.

LAWTON, D. (1969) 'Social studies' in Schools Council *The Middle Years of Schooling from 8 to 13* (Working Paper No 22), London, HMSO.

LAWTON, D., CAMPBELL, J. and BURKITT, V. (1971) *Social Studies 8–13* (Schools Council Working Paper 39), London, Evans/Methuen Educational.

MERTON/SCHOOLS COUNCIL (1981) *The New Approach to the Social Studies: Continuity and Development in Children's Learning through First, Middle and High Schools*, London, Schools Council.

National Curriculum Council (1989) *The National Curriculum and Whole Curriculum Planning: Preliminary Guidance* (NCC Circular No 6), York, NCC.

NATIONAL CURRICULUM COUNCIL (1990a) *Curriculum Guidance 3: The Whole Curriculum*, York, NCC.

NATIONAL CURRICULUM COUNCIL (1990b) *Curriculum Guidance 4: Education for Economic and Industrial Understanding*, York, NCC.

NATIONAL CURRICULUM COUNCIL (1990c) *Curriculum Guidance 5: Health Education*, York, NCC.

NATIONAL CURRICULUM COUNCIL (1990d) *Curriculum Guidance 6: Careers Education and Guidance,* York, NCC.

NATIONAL CURRICULUM COUNCIL (1990e) *Curriculum Guidance 7: Environmental Education,* York, NCC.

NATIONAL CURRICULUM COUNCIL (1990f) *Curriculum Guidance 8: Education for Citizenship,* York, NCC.

NATIONAL CURRICULUM COUNCIL (1991a) *Economic and Industrial Understanding: Invitation to Tender for INSET/Distance learning package for Primary Teachers* (Tender 000707) (June) York, NCC.

NATIONAL CURRICULUM COUNCIL (1991b) *Publications Programme on Economic and Industrial Understanding* (November, pamphlet) York, NCC.

NORTHAMPTONSHIRE EDUCATION AUTHORITY (1982) *Humanities: Curriculum Guidelines for the Middle Years (8–14),* Northampton, Northamptonshire Education Authority.

RODGERS, V. (1968) *The Social Subjects in English Education,* London, Heinemann.

ROSS, A. (Ed) (1990) *Economic and Industrial Awareness in the Primary School,* London, PNL Press/SCIP.

ROSS, A., AHIER, J. and HUTCHINGS, M. (1991) *Student Primary Teachers — Their Economic and Industrial Background, Understanding and Attitudes: An Investigation* (EATE Research Report No 1), Bath, EATE.

SCHOOLS COUNCIL (1981) *The Practical Curriculum* (Schools Council Working Paper 70), London, Methuen.

SCHOOLS COUNCIL (1983) *Primary Practice: A Sequel to 'The Practical Curriculum'* (Working Paper 75) London, Methuen.

UNITED KINGDOM (1985) *Better Schools,* Cmnd 9469, London, HMSO.

WHITE, J. (1988) 'An unconstitutional National Curriculum' in LAWTON, D. and CHITTY, C. (Eds) *The National Curriculum, Bedford Way Papers 33,* London, Institute of Education.

Part 4

A Comparative Perspective

Chapter 10

Balance and Diversity in the Primary Curriculum: Lessons from Europe

Maurice Galton

The last two decades have seen a vigorous, if largely polemic, debate about the nature of primary education in England and Wales. Starting with the Black Papers of the early seventies (Cox and Dyson, 1969a and 1969b), followed by the then Prime Minister, James Callaghan's (1976) initiation of the 'great debate', the HMI paper on the Curriculum 5 to 16 (DES, 1985) came forward with a recommendation for the use of curriculum consultants and increased subject specialization in the junior phase. This recommendation, translated finally into the National Curriculum, was implemented through the Council for the Accreditation of Teacher Education (CATE) which has required teacher training programmes to emphasize subject competence rather than pedagogy. There is now once more, both among government ministers and the media, increasing calls to abandon 'progressive practices' and return to what are termed 'traditional methods' (*TES*, 15 November 1991).

In arriving at a position which seems very similar to that pertaining in the early 1970s, research is once again used selectively to bolster up this thesis. In the seventies it was the Bennett (1976) study which was often cited whereas now it is what has come to be known as the Alexander Report (Alexander, 1991). The target of much government criticism now appears to be the use of group teaching — an ambiguous term which can cover anything from differentiated seating arrangements, to cooperative activities in mixed ability groups. While research over these two decades can properly claim to have established the need to strike a more reasonable balance between the use of whole class teaching and individualized working, such class teaching embodies the notion of 'direct instruction' (Rosenshine, 1987). This is somewhat removed from the over simplified media view that sitting children in rows rather than groups and talking *at* them rather than *with* them is the means by which we can raise the standards of basic numeracy and literacy in our primary schools.

A disinterested continental observer would surely be surprised at the insularity of this public debate. Rarely, apart from a few visits to continental schools by HMI (DES, 1986 and 1987) have these discussions been illuminated by any comparisons with primary practice within the schools of our European neighbours. How different it was a century ago. As Alan Blyth, in whose honour this chapter is offered, notes in the introduction to the *Handbook of Primary Education in Europe*,

> ... it is a strange reversal of the situation in the previous century, when the ideas of Pestalozzi, Froebel and Herbart, were eagerly espoused and developed. (Galton and Blyth, 1989, p. 5)

There are a number of explanations for this sense of British isolation, many of them mirrored in current political debates about the closer integration of the United Kingdom within the European Community. The thin line which can exist between education and indoctrination has meant that all countries have sought to exclude matters of schooling from majority decision-making within the European community. Moreover, there would appear to exist among both the leading members of the teaching profession and educational administrators a belief that the best primary practice is British and that we, as a nation, have little to learn from colleagues in other countries.

One striking example of this attitude was reflected in the British contribution to the Council of Europe's Project No 8, *Innovation in Primary Education in Europe*. Council of Europe projects invariably consist of a mixture of research workshops, conferences and case studies of school practice. The arrangements for these activities are such that costs are shared between the Council of Europe and the host country. During Project No 8 the smallest countries, such as Liechtenstein and Luxembourg, each hosted one workshop and one conference. In most cases the main objective of these occasions was to share expertise among member states so that national contributions were interspersed with presentations from visiting experts.

The United Kingdom was a reluctant participant in such activities, agreeing after much pressure to host a workshop on teaching science in the primary school in Cambridge in the summer of 1986 (DECS/EGT [86] 59). However, the workshop consisted, in its entirety, of presentations by HMI on recent developments in teaching science within the United Kingdom, including the testing procedures of the Assessment and Performance Unit. Participants were lectured, received demonstrations and then were invited to engage in practical activities related to the science curriculum. No external presentations were included, notwithstanding the excellent work reported by Elstgeest (1985) from Holland. Certainly the perception of participants from other member states of the Council was that they had gathered in Cambridge to receive instruction about 'best practice' rather than to debate issues and solve problems connected with teaching science at this age range.

Such attitudes have over the last two decades lulled us into a sense of complacency whereby those who should have known better have done little to help change existing practice, thereby making it possible for the resulting 'backlash' by the media and for the criticisms of 'lobbyists' such as the Hillgate Group (1987) to acquire public credibility. During the eighties it became fashionable among some academics to dismiss the research findings from studies of primary classrooms as constituting a 'deficit' theory which served only to further demoralize teachers at a time when they were under increasing attack from the media and government who claimed to represent parents' views. Instead these academics argued that it was better to celebrate teaching excellence, even if the evidence for much of this excellence was anecdotal and could not be presented in operational terms. Using such outstanding teachers as mentors was seen as the major way of improving practice, as if by some process of osmosis the skills of one practitioner could be transferred to another. As the eighties decade progressed there was increasing criticism of empirical studies and theories derived from educational disciplines such as psychology. Such theories it was argued only constituted 'technical' knowledge as opposed to 'craft knowledge' which resulted from practices which teachers developed through some intuitive understanding of when they were performing effectively (Elliott, 1989).

Much of this 'craft knowledge', although clearly one element in a consensus concerning effective practice, might have been regarded with some circumspection if primary practice in the United Kingdom had been viewed within a European tradition rather than considered in isolation. Thus the futility of teaching a second language to children in the junior classroom would need to be considered against the common practice in most other European countries of teaching English alongside the mother tongue. Indeed a small country such as Iceland, where schools only operate between the months of September and May and where children only attend during a morning or an afternoon session, can still manage to teach English and Danish, as well as the mother tongue, to a large proportion of primary aged children (DECS/EGT [86] 36). Debates about reading methods and reading standards should surely take into account the remarkable achievements of a country such as Denmark which has the highest proportion of book buyers in Europe and where standards of functional literacy have twice been redefined more rigorously over the past two decades (Jansen *et al*, 1978; Jansen, 1989). Everyday experience does not suggest that the majority of continental Europe's citizens are any less well educated than their British counterparts. Yet in many of these countries children receive less formal schooling, entering primary school at 6 and, in some cases, at 7.

Examining primary education within a European, rather than strictly national, dimension does not mean that individual contexts should be ignored. For example, when teaching English as a second language, there is enormous motivational impetus within many European countries because a considerable part of the 'pop culture' is conducted in the medium of English. Similarly the performance of Icelandic children must be set against the fact that class sizes are, on average, approximately half those in the typical English primary school although this in turn raises the interesting issue of whether it is better to be in a small class for half the time or in a class twice the size for twice the time. Whatever these contextual differences, however, there do exist patterns and trends which should be considered within our own primary education system and which might move the debate away from the narrow confines of progressivism versus traditionalism.

In the next section, therefore, consideration will be given to some of the common themes which have emerged across Europe within the primary phase. Much of the evidence summarized within this chapter is reported in the *Handbook of Primary Education* (Galton and Blyth, 1989) and it is therefore appropriate, before reviewing the data, to say something about the methods used to collect the evidence and assess its value.

The Council of Europe and Project No 8

The Council of Europe's activities concerning education and culture are run by the Council for Cultural Cooperation (CDCC). The aims of the CDCC are to bring the new ideas, techniques and achievements of each of its members to the notice of other states, to increase the contacts and cooperation between European educators, to take up questions of importance identified by European Ministers of Education and Culture, to develop mutual aid among member states and to make the people of Europe aware of their common heritage. At the time that Project No 8 began there were twenty-three member states. The decision to launch a project on primary education was taken at a meeting of the Education Ministers of member states early in 1981 and arose partly because of an awareness of common problems relating to changes in demography and the nature of employment likely to be available to citizens in the last part of the twentieth century and the first part of the twenty-first. For example, most member states had sparsely populated rural areas resulting from internal migration to urban areas. At the same time migration across national boundaries was increasing. Not all of these movements were the result of a shift from southern to northern Europe by migrant workers looking to take up less attractive jobs in more prosperous countries. Considerable migration also resulted from decolonization giving rise to a substantial movement of populations from former colonies. Whatever the reasons, however, these shifts in population produced considerable problems for schools requiring additional support for mother tongue teaching in pursuit of a policy of integration. Other significant social trends arose from the declining birth rate and the increase in one parent families. These were common experiences in most countries within the CDCC.

The growth of new technologies also presented common challenges. Science and computing became part of 'the new basics' to be added to literacy and numeracy so schools could produce an educated workforce to match the needs of a 'service' rather than a manufacturing society. At the same time another growing trend was recognized whereby increasingly Europe's citizens were calling for greater participation in the decision-making processes on matters which related directly to their quality of life. For the primary school this meant greater power sharing between the teachers and the local community with parents having more say in curriculum decisions including the use of appropriate teaching methods.

Having established these commonalities it was decided by the ministerial conference to set up a project which would redefine the aims of primary education for the 1990s such that they met the challenges posed by these demographic, social and technological changes. An inaugural conference was therefore held in 1982 at Vadus, Liechtenstein, under the title of *Primary Education in Western Europe: Aims, Problems and Trends* (DECS/EGT [83] 64). The conference produced a report which was then used as a working paper for the project whose task was to identify examples in member states where these various aims had been implemented successfully and to interpret these successes in ways which could then be of use as models to other member states. In addition to representatives from each of the CDCC member states, four consultants, from France, Italy, Norway and the United Kingdom, were appointed.

At its inaugural meeting at Strasbourg in November 1982 the project group decided to depart from previous practice within the CDCC in two very important ways. The first of these departures related to the way in which case studies were to be conducted. In the past, such studies consisted of a report by those responsible within the member state of the particular example of innovation under consideration. Thus, if a country claimed that a particular form of reading was successful in helping children of migrant workers then those responsible for the innovation would write an account of their work and submit it to the project group. This system clearly provided questionable data in that those responsible for the innovation had a vested interest in presenting the cases studied in the best possible light. Accordingly, the project group decided that all case studies would be conducted by a person with expertise in the particular area but from another member state. The main limitations on the choice of a particular expert was that he/she was able to speak the language of the host country in those cases where English or French (the working languages of the CDCC) was not widely used.

The second major change in working methods was to establish a set of twelve schools as a supportive network. The purpose of these *contact* schools was to act as examples of successful innovation and practice and also to act as a 'sounding board' for ideas generated by the project group. Towards the end of the project they were also asked to review the recommendations and to comment on the evidence on which these recommendations were based.

Thus, in summary, four sources of evidence were taken into consideration in arriving at recommendations.

(i) Reports of practice within each Member State submitted by individual Governments. The data within these reports were unchecked although countries were asked to update these statements towards the end of the project.

(ii)   Evidence from experts from different countries in the form of contributions to seminars and workshops including summaries of research findings on specific topics relating to the primary school.

(iii) Case studies carried out by individual 'neutral' experts into key areas of primary practice.

(iv)   Exchanges between teachers in a network of twelve contact schools which also acted as a referent in checking data collected from other sources.

Within a year, following its successful inaugural meeting, the project group decided that the original brief was far too wide. All member states reported that the problems did not lie in establishing common aims nor in devising suitable programmes for translating these aims into practice. Rather it was the implementation of such programmes within the school that was found to be the most difficult task, irrespective of country of origin. Accordingly, the project group decided to focus more narrowly on the question of innovation itself and to use particular examples of innovation relating to the various agreed aims of primary education as a means of studying the innovation process. The project therefore changed its title to that of *Innovation in Primary Education*.

What was to emerge from the project provides an interesting paradox. Just as policy makers in the United Kingdom were attempting to establish a greater degree of uniformity on the system, not only by the introduction of the National Curriculum but also through a programme of standard assessment tasks, educators within continental Europe were beginning to turn away from such models. Instead they sought to strengthen in their schools a capacity for flexibility to deal with the likelihood of continuous change. This policy accords with Vandenberghe's (1989) view which perceives change as a continuing process in which all schools, at any one time, will not be at the same stage of development. School diversity is therefore one of the biggest obstacles for policy makers, whether they be national governments or local authorities, wishing to educate pupils in accordance with national needs. Vandenberghe (1989) also warns governments, and this is surely timely within the current debate taking place in the United Kingdom, that they should not seek to judge the extent of the change solely in terms of easily identifiable outcomes. Such approaches generally result in what Vandenberghe (1989) describes as *additive* policies of school development rather than *long term* policies (p. 15). Only the latter type of policy brings about improved teacher effectiveness.

Central to this view is a realization that any proposed change, no matter how remote it might seem from classroom practice, will ultimately have an effect on the teacher-pupil relationship and thereby on the pupil's learning. The success of a policy designed to meet the new technological challenge by introducing computers to the primary school, for example, might be evaluated at government level in terms of the take-up of computers, the demand for software and the extent to which schools expand the range of computer facilities through fund-raising by parents. But from the initial government decision, through the local authority's formulation of a policy for the schools, to the final implementation within the classroom, decisions have to be made at every stage which ultimately affect the opportunities for pupils to learn. At local authority level it may have to do with the purchasing scheme, at school level with the organization of the computers to maximize their use. The most fundamental impact, however, will be at classroom level where the introduction of a computer brings a whole range of problems concerning the ways that pupils should work together and the cognitive demands made on both the teacher and the pupils. Unless, therefore, the culture of the school is geared to frequent change it is unlikely that teachers will give serious consideration to these pedagogic issues. Instead the computer will be seen as another additional demand which has to be fitted into the existing curriculum and teachers will cope with these demands by attempting to absorb innovations into their existing practice. Certainly that is what appears to have happened in the Leeds PRINDEP project (Alexander *et al*, 1989) and also within the ESG Curriculum Enhancement Programme for small schools recently evaluated by Galton *et al* (1991). In this latter study no teacher claimed to have done more than 'bolted' onto their existing practice the new initiatives in computing, design and technology, art and craft, which the ESG programme was designed to introduce. Thus the key to the debate concerning continuity and coherence within primary education in most European counties centres round not so much '*what is to be taught*' but '*how it is to be taught*'. Continuity of teaching methods rather than continuity of subject matter has become the prime concern.

Greater importance is also given to the nature of relationships between staff, including the role of the headteacher, once it is accepted that schools are places where change has to be accommodated. Accepting that all change involves a challenge to one's values and is therefore a situation of potential conflict, staff development programmes which help schools cope with difficult decision-making are considered to be of prime importance. Furthermore the need to communicate these decisions to parents, given the emphasis on greater community participation in all countries, must also be given high priority because during periods of change teachers need to be in continuous dialogue with their clients about the way in which the curriculum develops. If it is possible to sum up the main purpose of all these developments it is to provide teachers with '*freedom within a curriculum framework*' whereby policymakers set guidelines and schools are expected to be responsible for deciding how they should meet these specifications.

Different countries adopt different practices to ensure that schools act responsibly. In some, such as Germany, it is the assessment procedures which are used to evaluate a school's progress (DES, 1986) whereas in The Netherlands (DES, 1987) schools submit a schools plan to the authority every two years and only receive their grant in full when their school plan has been accepted. In all European countries, therefore, to a lesser or greater degree, there is a move away from highly centralized control of the curriculum although in some countries, such as Denmark, where schools have enjoyed considerable freedom, some retrenchment has taken place. The main reason for their shift of policy has been the need to produce schools which are more adaptable. Another reason has been the experience of some countries that when schools are given more responsibility within a secure framework they also become more flexible in the use of resources. Thus instead of every new proposed innovation being accompanied by claims from schools for increased sums of money to meet the costs of introducing the new components of the curriculum, schools and teachers are more prepared to look for ways in which existing resources can be adapted and transferred to other uses. This lesson was clearly brought home in the case studies carried out for the CDCC's Project No 8 on the use of computers. In the case of France, the development of computing in the region of Bar-le-duc (DECS/EGT [85] 44) floundered once the support team was withdrawn. The teachers refused to continue with the programme unless the level of resourcing was maintained and since the responsibility of the teachers was primarily to their employers (the state rather than the school) there was little that the local headteachers could do to reverse this decision.

Before, however, considering particular cases demonstrating the way that these principles were put into practice a general summary of the common trends reflected in the pattern of primary education throughout Europe will be provided by way of context.

General Aims of Primary Education

Thomas (1989) defines a country's educational aims as 'statements about the directions in which one wishes to go'. Thomas identifies four common Western European themes. The first of these is the emphasis on the uniqueness and rights of individuals. This has led to stress upon the importance of a curriculum which takes into account the interests of children. In some Scandinavian countries (Norway and Denmark), for example, children have some say in their activities. Self-assessment is also seen as important because it helps children make informed choices.

Interestingly, Thomas points out that while many countries embody in their aims a notion that children, through primary education, should be able to develop to the *full*, this word can refer either to the provision of a wide range of activities from which the child can make a choice or to a structure which enables each pupil to realize their maximum potential, even if that potential is in a specialist area of the curriculum (p. 9). Within the first interpretation, most Western European countries consider that primary schooling should cover the full range of children's intellectual, social, moral and spiritual, emotional and physical development. While different countries place a different emphasis on these aspects of child development there is broad agreement that the primary curriculum should extend beyond the traditional subject areas and be concerned with the development of the imagination and of aesthetic and artistic appreciation.

The second use of *full* refers to a pupil's progress. There exists a general consensus among European educators that today's pupils mature more quickly than those of previous generations, partly because of the wider range of experiences to which children are now exposed. For example, unlike earlier generations, many more children have experienced travel to different countries and all these developments present teachers with more difficult choices in both selecting appropriate content and, at the same time, attempting to maintain the widest possible curriculum coverage which allows pupils maximum opportunity of choice at the secondary stage of education. Some countries, notably Denmark, attempt to compromise by having a compulsory National Curriculum with an equal amount of time devoted to options which reflect community differences. Other countries, notably Austria and the Federal Republic of Germany, favour allowing children to enter schools at different ages and also either to move up into a higher age class or to repeat a year, although this practice appears to be diminishing. In concluding his analysis, Thomas issues a timely warning to policy makers in thinking that balance can be achieved by defining different aspects of the curriculum and in believing that if each is dealt with in its own periods the separate parts will then add up to the whole (*ibid*, p. 26). He warns that,

> Where the timetable is used to define the curriculum, proper recognition and prominence are seldom given to teaching children the broader lessons to be drawn from the social changes experienced on entering school. The processes of social adjustment seem to get in the way of learning rather than being an opportunity for learning. (*ibid*)

The Content of the Curriculum

As Blyth (1989) reports, considerable consistency exists in what is offered within the primary curriculum among the various member states of the Council of Europe. While all countries place the emphasis on mother tongue teaching, all member states express a concern for the preservation of minority languages. As referred to earlier, most other countries offer a second language, usually English, although the age in which this second language is introduced varies. Turkey, along with the United Kingdom (apart from the Celtic fringes where Welsh and Gallic is taught) are the main exceptions. The emphasis given to science varies considerably although increasingly this is changing. There is also a wide variation in the humanities. Geography and

Maurice Galton

history are sometimes combined within topic work whereas in other countries the emphasis is on civics (Norway), environmental studies (Greece), while the social aspects are stressed in Sweden. All countries offer some form of art and crafts but not always music.

As might be expected, given the history of Christianity within Europe following the reformation, there is considerable diversity in the provision of religious instruction. Some countries (such as Norway and Portugal) offer compulsory instruction while other countries (such as France) are more concerned with teaching ethics and bringing about socialization (what in the United Kingdom is called personal and social education). In summary, therefore, although the patterns of curriculum, across different European countries are very similar, the balance varies. There is a shift from countries such as France, where all schools are given precise definitions of what should be taught (although this is now also changing) to countries where a statutory element is provided but a certain proportion of time is allowed for optional choices by children or for subjects which arise out of the needs of local communities. In general, the trend has been for those countries which accorded schools greater freedom gradually to restrict this over the last decade whereas countries where, initially, more rigid central control was exercised, have gradually begun to loosen these bonds. Denmark provides an example of the first category. There more structured approaches to curriculum organization have been put in place, accompanied, as in the United Kingdom, by a switch from an Advisory Service to an Inspectorate. In the second category is France although, as studies have shown, (Moon, 1986) the commonly supposed notion that on any day of the week at any hour it is possible to know what is being taught in French primary schools is open to challenge.

Diversity Within European Schooling

As observed briefly earlier, when citing the case of Iceland, a distinguishing feature of European primary education is the wide variation in the amounts of schooling available in different countries, particularly the starting age and the length of the school day. Some of these differences reflect the legacy of an elementary system of schooling based upon Herbart's theory of 'culture epochs' where each new generation of children trace in their own development the experiences of their forebears in the correct chronological sequence. Thus the kindergarten stage emphasized motor development and social skill training which was characteristic of the primitive stage of civilization when humans first began to cope with the natural environment and to organize themselves into groups for protection. Elementary schooling marked the transition from the primitive stage to one where groups began to communicate with each other through symbols. This transition was said to occur around the age of 7 and in many European countries this age still marks the entry point to primary schooling when instruction in the basic language skills

168

of reading and writing begins. For this reason responsibility for the kindergarten often rests with the Department of Health rather than Education.

This division of responsibility is further reinforced because of concerns expressed by primary teachers that their status could be eroded by allowing nursery staff to carry out pedagogic functions within the kindergarten. Thus in Sweden (DECS/EGT [87] 33) delegates visiting a kindergarten, during the course of the workshop, saw children write letters on the blackboard which were back to front. The nursery 'teacher' did not correct this mistake because, as she explained, 'Her task was to make certain that the children were able to write on the blackboard in a legible way in letters of a reasonable size. It was not to teach them their letters.' However, in most countries, the educational provision for children below the age of 7 is now being re-examined (Gather-Thurler, 1989) since it is recognized that the increasing demands of the curriculum require children to have more time in primary school. Countries such as The Netherlands and Switzerland now have an integrated school system covering the age range 4–12. Other countries (Norway) are lowering the age of entry to primary school from 7 to 6 years.

Mention has already been made of the variation in the hours that children attend the primary school during each day. In some countries children attend school on Saturday mornings (Austria) whereas in others (Luxembourg) they attend for less than the customary five days. Such data, however, can be misleading because the length of the school day also varies enormously as does the length of the school year. It can, however, be said that there are wide variations in the number of hours of schooling which children in different European countries receive. Given the findings from the United States (Denham and Lieberman, 1989) concerning the links between school attendance and pupil progress there are clearly areas for further research, since a general consensus would not indicate that there are wide variations in attainment across the more industrially developed European states where some of these time variations are greatest. The inference must be that countries which allocate some of the largest amounts of time to primary schooling do not always use this time effectively.

Another area where wide variations in practice exist between European countries and where attempts are being made to move to a greater degree of standardization is the training of primary teachers (Neave, 1987). After 1992 greater teacher mobility will become possible across member states. Teachers from countries where salaries are low may be expected to move elsewhere in search of greater rewards. The need for greater compatibility in the length of the training course will therefore become important. At present some countries have a pattern which extends over five years (Malta) and includes a period where the novice teacher acts as a worker-student, whereas Turkey offers a very general training of only two years duration. The normal pattern is three years but in many countries considerable tension exists between primary teachers with this three years general training and colleagues in the secondary phase, some of whom can go straight into teaching after the completion of a university degree while still enjoying higher salaries and status. In Blyth's (1989) report teacher education was cited as a problem in over 50 per cent of the countries represented in the survey. The next greatest concern was length of schooling, followed by the need to reappraise the relationships between central government and local authorities.

Implementing Change in the Primary Schools

In giving further consideration to what has become an important theme of European primary education, the creation of a 'culture of flexibility' within schools such that they can readily respond to change, the role of the contact schools in the Council of Europe Project No 8, proved particularly illuminating. Twelve schools took part in the contact plan from Austria, Cyprus, Denmark, Finland, Germany, Greece, Italy, The Netherlands, Norway, Sweden, Switzerland and the United Kingdom. The schools chosen were felt to represent aspects of development in primary education from northern, central and southern European member states of the CDCC. In Italy, for example, in the Civitavecchia experimental school the aim of the innovation was to integrate two types of establishment, the nursery (3–5 years) and the primary school (6–11) into a single integrated school. The aim of the most northern school, Linnala school, in Imatra, Finland, was to develop greater cooperation between the school and parents. Each contact school was visited regularly by a small team of observers led by Dr. Dook Kopmels, the Director of the Regional Pedagogic Centre (Regional Pedagogisch Centrum) of Zeeland in The Netherlands. As a result of these case studies, Kopmels (1989) developed the 'five zones model'. Each zone needs to be reviewed continually during the process of innovation. The zones thus delineate the key areas where school improvement needs to take place. Changing elements in any one zone has effects on the others so that for an innovation to be carried out successfully changes in all five zones must be carefully planned and integrated.

The first zone is concerned with *aims and principles* which guide the work of the teaching staff and most importantly, as Kopmels stresses, it must deal with pedagogy as well as questions to do with *what* is to be taught. Zone two is concerned with the *organization* of education and deals with matters such as class size and composition, the allocation of children to groups and the reporting system. Zone three concerns the *subject matter* and involves the development of, what Kopmels calls, the didactic approach, whether to integrate subjects or to teach each separately, as well as choice of activities and methods of evaluation. Zone four, which Kopmels sees as a key area involves the *organization of cooperation* among the teaching staff. This includes both school leadership and also the development of support and friendship among class teachers. Finally, the fifth zone deals with the links with *external contacts* such as the education authorities, parents and various support systems such as the psychological service.

Kopmels (1989) in analyzing the case study reports from the contact schools, identifies common themes among all twelve schools in relation to this five zones model. First, in zone one, schools were committed to what Kopmels termed 'active individualization' and a recognition of the import-ance of pupil autonomy and cooperation. By the former term, Kopmels means that teachers should recognize that when attempting a particular task, such as working with construction materials, telling or writing their own story, children will accomplish such tasks in different ways. The teacher then needs to suggest complementary activities for each child to take the learning a stage further. Kopmels here is talking of something similar to the concept of 'match' as used by HMI (DES, 1978). All contact schools also encouraged children to take responsibility for their own learning but also to work cooperatively. Thus whilst pursuing their own ends a child should learn to respect other pupils' needs.

In the second zone, the organization of education, special attention was given by all schools to the formative evaluation process which was necessary to ensure that these active learning strategies were effective. Programmes were designed specifically to avoid the kinds of 'intermittent working' iden-tified in the ORACLE studies (Galton *et al*, 1980) and also in other similar observations of primary schools in the United Kingdom (Galton, 1989). What was most striking in some of these continental schools was the way in which teachers deliberately set out to give priority to those activities which research indicates are likely to maximize learning. Thus, in The Netherlands contact school, teachers concentrated on maximizing the time when they could en-gage in challenging questioning with pupils and also provide feedback. Monitoring of more straightforward activities, such as spelling, grammar and computation, were carried out, independently of the teacher, through the use of computer programmes devised by a local parent with expertise in software development. Pupils would bring a summary print out of their performance to the teacher so that particular problems could quickly be identified.

Use was also made of audio-tape recordings for language work and pupils were again encouraged to summarize their progress and note any difficulty as a way of cutting time typically used by teachers to check details or to monitor individual pupils working methods. Again, in keeping with current research findings, a considerable amount of whole class work still took place during which children were encouraged to express themselves, share each other's successes and to plan future activities as well as evaluating past progress. Generally, each day had a fixed pattern which was considered by most of the teachers in the contact schools to promote feelings of security and confidence in the children.

Another important concept developed within the contact schools was that of diffused time. In the busy atmosphere of a modern primary classroom, background noise can often lead to increased stress levels in pupils so that their concentration falls away at certain periods. In The Netherlands school this was countered by providing listening booths where pupils could work individually with tape recorders and earphones, thereby shutting out the sounds of the rest of the class. For example, the parents made recordings of a large number of reading books which the pupils from the reception class could take away to a quiet corner. Once there they could listen to the stories while turning over the pages when instructed to do so by the voice on the audio-tape. In most contact schools considerable thought was given to ways of optimizing instructional time. Tape recorders were often used to present instructions so that pupils would not continually interrupt the teacher because they had forgotten what to do.

In the zone dealing with the content of instruction the similarities between contact schools related not so much to the subject areas covered, which were dependent on different national traditions, but to the principles governing the presentation of this content. First, many of the schools sought to present material, whenever possible, so that it was linked to aspects of daily life. Second, and of interest to the current debate now taking place in the United Kingdom, a majority of the schools broke with the tradition of having one teacher for each class towards the top end of the primary school so that teachers with different expertise were increasingly used to stimulate pupils in their particular subject specialism. However, it is important to stress that the specialist teachers' main task was to develop the process skills associated with the particular subject discipline rather than simply to increase the coverage of a particular subject area.

Most attention, however, was given to developing cooperation between teachers within the fourth zone. Kopmels (1989) in his analysis points out that in most European schools the organizational structure is unclear and that while this is not a crucial matter when schools operate in a fairly routine fashion it becomes crucial once innovation is required and staff have to cope with potential conflict. In such cases it is essential that satisfactory agreements are made about a system of procedures which are available to all staff within the decision-making process. In the contact schools such agreements were often worked out despite the presence of teachers who were ineffective or reluctant to change and in some cases despite the negative reaction from the local community.

Kopmels argues that in order that schools can cope with such problems without creating internal conflicts three conditions are necessary. First there must be a clarity in the structure of organizations so that teachers are aware of the tasks that are expected of them. Second, participants must have an understanding of what is taking place within the organizational structure. Many schools try to achieve this by having meetings with all teachers present. Kopmels concludes it is not necessary for this to happen and, further, that this kind of general staff meeting is often very ineffective as well as time consuming. Moreover, such meetings often act only as a 'rubber stamp' for a course of action already decided upon by the head teacher. It is necessary, however, for teachers who are not involved in a particular decision-making process to be aware that it is taking place and to have an opportunity to put their point of view if they wish to do so. Third, there must be consistency between the organizational model adopted and the other aims and practices within the school. By this Kopmels means that the system of cooperation between staff and the system of leadership must be very similar to that employed in other relationships involving teachers and children and teachers and parents.

In zone five, contact with parents was given a special emphasis. Unlike schools in the United Kingdom, most continental schools do not make much use of parents other than for fund-raising activities. In the contact schools, however, there was a deliberate effort to involve parents in the classroom, particularly in helping children read. Advisory Councils, the equivalent of parent teacher associations, were given opportunities to discuss ways of improving not only parent-teacher relationships but also the school's effectiveness.

Finally, all the contact schools, in one way or another, made considerable use of external consultants. For example, the school in Cyprus was adjacent to the Nicosia College of Education and the lecturing staff there were frequently called upon for help. However, some of the most interesting developments took place within the Dutch school which had close links with the Zeeland Pedagogic Centre. These links deserve closer scrutiny.

Creating a Climate for Effective Pedagogy

Looked at superficially, the Netherlands Regional Pedagogic Centres perform functions which are not unlike a mixture of Teachers' Centres and the Advisory Service in the United Kingdom. They run courses dealing with specific curriculum issues such as teaching new techniques in science. Their main function, however, is to support the improvement of teaching and learning within local schools. To do this they employ a staff of expert teacher advisers and also of psychologists whose role is not only to identify learning difficulties of individual pupils but also to help support school improvement and, in particular, increased teacher effectiveness.

As part of the 1985 reform of Dutch primary education, schools are now required to submit a school development plan every second year and one of the important functions of the Pedagogic Centre is to assist schools in drawing up this plan. In so doing, weaknesses are identified and courses of remedial action suggested and then implemented with the staff of the Pedagogic Centre offering support. The Centre draws its money not only from the Local Authority but also by bidding for central funds for specific projects. For example, the Zeeland Pedagogic Centre has undertaken a school improvement programme in small rural schools as part of a national initiative. As with any organization offering support of this kind there is a limit to the number of schools which can be assisted at any one time. The range of support services is, however, increased through a system of networking whereby schools who have successfully completed a programme of school improvement, based on the five zones model, are then used as 'mother schools' to support others following similar programmes. These networks are very important and much time is spent in cultivating and maintaining them with regular updating and training sessions for key staff from the 'mother schools'.

Evaluations of these teacher effectiveness programmes have demonstrated excellent results with over 80 per cent of respondents stating that there has been a marked improvement in their relationships with colleagues. With pupils, teachers reported they were better able to handle conflict without resorting to authoritarian solutions. Levels of motivation and work in the classroom improved. A key element in this improvement was a series of workshops entitled *Teacher Effectiveness Training* based upon the work of Gordon (1975). During this training teachers learnt to become better listeners, to discriminate between problems they could solve by changing their own behaviour rather than the childrens' and, in general, were better able to express their point of view without antagonizing colleagues. Other contact schools have also followed the same programme.

Within the Zeeland Pedagogic Centre the work of the psychologists seemed to be particularly rewarding. Instead of concentrating exclusively on the identification and treatment of learning difficulties, they taught teachers to do much of this work, leaving themselves free to engage in collaborative activities with teachers in which psychological theories about teaching and learning were integrated into the effectiveness programmes. The psychologist also had a role to play during the innovation process when conflict arose. They were able to help teachers handle such conflict creatively.

Thus, in summary, the emphasis within these programmes is on the improvement of teaching and learning rather than on the development of coherence and continuity of subject coverage. This is an aspect of work in the United Kingdom which traditionally has been neglected so that as Simon (1981) observes the lack of any interest in pedagogy dictates that the debate about primary teaching methods should remain a sterile one and be conducted in terms of 'catch all' phrases such as 'progressive' and 'traditional' or 'formal' and 'informal'. The interest generated in teaching methods, following Alexander's (1991) Report, has raised the issue of how we should teach children in the primary school once more. This time if the debate is to be advanced beyond popular conceptions of teaching methods then practitioners, as well as researchers, will need to open themselves to the influence of current thinking now taking place among our European neighbours.

References

ALEXANDER, R. (1991) *Primary Education in Leeds, Final Report from PRINDEP Project*, Leeds, University of Leeds.

ALEXANDER, R., WILLCOCKS, J. and KINDER, K. (1989) *Changing Primary Practice*, Lewes, Falmer Press.

BENNETT, N. (1976) *Teaching Styles and Pupil Progress*, London, Open Books.

BLYTH, A. (1989) 'Organization, policy and practice of primary education in Europe' in GALTON, M. and BLYTH, A. (Eds) *Handbook of Primary Education in Europe*, London, David Fulton.

CALLAGHAN, J. (1976) 'Towards a national debate — The Prime Minister's Ruskin speech', *Education*, 22 October, pp. 332–3.

COX, C.B. and DYSON, A.E. (Eds) (1969a) Fight For Education: A. Black Paper, *Critical Quarterly Society*.

COX, C. and DYSON, A. (Eds) (1969b) Black Paper Two: The Crisis in Education, *Critical Quarterly Society*.

DECS/EGT [83] 64 *Primary Education in Western Europe: Aims, Problems, Trends*, Project No 8 Conference, Liechtenstien, Vaduz.

DECS/EGT [85] 44 *The use of Microcomputers in Primary Schools in Bar-le-Duc*, Bar-le-Duc, France. Report by R. Dieschbourg, Luxembourg.

DECS/EGT [86] 36 *Coordinated School Work in Iceland — Icelandic Primary Schools*, Report by Professor M. Galton, United Kingdom, Strasborug, CDCC.

DECS/EGT [86] 59 *Symposium on Science and Technology in the Primary School*, Council of Europe Project No 8, Cambridge, United Kingdom.

DECS/EGT [87] 33 *Implementation of Innovation in Primary Education at the Local Level*, Stockholm, Sweden.

DENHAM, C. and LIEBERMAN, A. (Eds) (1989) *Time to Learn*, Washington, DC, Department of Health, Education and Welfare, National Institute of Education.

DES (1978) *Primary Education in England: A Survey by HM Inspectors of Schools*, London, HMSO.

DES (1985) *The Curriculum from 5–16, Curriculum Matters*, London, HMSO.

DES (1986) *Education in the Federal Republic of Germany*, London, HMSO.

DES (1987) *Aspects of Primary Education in The Netherlands*, London, HMSO.

ELLIOTT, J. (1989) 'Educational theory and the professional learning of teachers', *Cambridge Journal of Education*, 19, 1, pp. 81–101.

ELSTGEEST, J. (1985) 'Encounter, interaction, dialogue' in HARLEN, W. (Ed) *Primary Science, Taking the Plunge*, London, Heinemann.

GALTON, M. (1989) *Teaching in the Primary School*, London, David Fulton.

GALTON, M. and BLYTH, A. (1989) (Eds) *Handbook of Primary Education in Europe*, London, David Fulton (with CDCC).

GALTON, M., FOGELMAN, K., HARGREAVES, L. and CAVENDISH, S. (1991) *Rural Schools Enhancement: A National Evaluation*, Report to the DES, London, HMSO.

GATHER-THURLER, M. (1989) 'Continuity: A necessity in education' in GALTON, M. and BLYTH, A. (Eds) *Handbook of Primary Education in Europe*, London, David Fulton.

GORDON, T. (1974) *Teacher Effectiveness Training*, New York, Peter Wyden.

HILLGATE GROUP (1987) *The Reform of British Education*, London, The Claridge Press.

JANSEN, M. (1989) 'New Basics in primary education in Europe: literacy' in GALTON, M. and BLYTH, A. (Eds) *Handbook of Primary Education in Europe*, London, David Fulton.

JANSEN, M., JACKSON, R. and ERIKSON, P. (1978) *The Teaching of Reading Without Really any Method: An Analysis of Reading Instruction in Denmark*, Copenhagen, Munksgaard.

KOPMELS, D. (1989) 'Innovation and practice in education' in GALTON, M. and BLYTH, A. *Handbook of Primary Education in Europe*, London, David Fulton.

MOON, R. (1986) *The New Maths Curriculum Controversy*, Lewes, Falmer Press.

Maurice Galton

NEAVE, G. (1987) 'Challenges met: Trends in teacher education 1975–85' in *New Challenges for Teachers and Their Education*, Council of Europe Study Conference of European Ministers of Education: Fifteenth Session, Helsinki, Iceland. (MEd.-15–4) CDCC, Strasbourg.

ROSENSHINE, B. (1987) 'Direct instruction' in DUNKIN, M. (Ed) *Teaching and Teacher Education*, Oxford, Pergamon Press.

SIMON, B. (1981) 'Why no pedagogy in England?' in SIMON, B. and TAYLOR, W. (Eds) *Education in the Eighties*, London, Batsford Educational.

THOMAS, N. (1989) 'Aims of foreign education in member states of the Council of Europe' in GALTON, M. and BLYTH, A. (Eds) *Handbook of Primary Education in Europe*, London, David Fulton.

VANDENBERGHE, R. (1989) 'School improvement: An European perspective in PARKAY, F. (Ed) *Improving School for the 21st Century: Research and Development Centre of School Improvement*, Gainesville, FL, University of Florida.

Notes on Contributors

Mike Ashton is Headteacher of Liscard Primary School, Wirral, one of the largest primary schools in the country. He has been a tutor with the Open University on Educational Management and a consultant tutor at the North West Management Centre, Padgate.

Geva Blenkin's work and interests lie in the field of curriculum studies in general and the early years curriculum in particular. She was formerly Head-teacher of an infant school in the East End of London. Her current work at Goldsmiths' College is focussed on the higher degree programmes in early childhood education and curriculum studies, and on the provision of short INSET courses for early years teachers. Her publications include *The Primary Curriculum* (Harper and Row, 1981), *Early Childhood Education* (Paul Chapman, 1988), and *Assessment in Early Childhood Education* (Paul Chapman, 1992).

Jim Campbell is Professor of Education at the University of Warwick, where he directs the MA in Primary Education and the Policy Analysis Unit. He is editor of the journal *Education 3–13* and his books include *Developing the Primary School Curriculum* (Holt Rinehart & Winston, 1985) and *Humanities in the Primary School* (Falmer Press, 1989).

Ray Derricott is Reader and Director of Continuing Education at the University of Liverpool. He is also Director of the Liverpool Evaluation and Assessment Unit. His recent work includes the appraisal of teaching in higher education and the development of work-based learning in undergraduate courses.

Maurice Galton has been Professor of Education at the University of Leicester since 1982. He has conducted a number of large-scale observational studies of primary classrooms, and his latest book, *Group Work in the Primary Classroom* is the final book in the ORACLE series. From 1982 to 1988 he was Consultant to the Council of Europe's project on primary education, and his chapter is based upon material collected during the course of this programme.

Vic Kelly is Professor of Curriculum Studies at Goldsmiths' College. Within the field of curriculum studies he has a particular interest in encouraging a higher level of conceptual clarity within the planning of the school curriculum, and more appropriately intellectual forms of debate than are evident in many current publications and pronouncements. His publications include *The Curriculum: Theory and Practice* (Paul Chapman, 1989), *Knowledge and Curriculum Planning* (Paul Chapman, 1986) and *The National Curriculum: A Critical Review* (Paul Chapman, 1990).

Bill Marsden is Reader in Education at the University of Liverpool. His books include *Evaluating the Geography Curriculum* (Oliver and Boyd, 1976), *Unequal Educational Provision in England and Wales: The Nineteenth Century Roots* (Woburn Press, 1987) and *Educating the Respectable: A Study of Fleet Road Board School, Hampstead, 1897–1903* (Woburn Press, 1991).

Jennifer Nias is Visiting Professor of Education at the University of Plymouth. Her books include *Primary Teachers Talking* (Routledge, 1989), *Staff Relationships in the Primary School* (Cassell, 1989) and *Working and Learning together for Change* (Open University Press, 1992).

Andrew Pollard is Professor of Education at The University of the West of England. He taught in primary schools for ten years before moving into teacher education and research. His books include *The Social World of the Primary School* (Holt Rinehart & Winston), *Reflective Teaching in the Primary School* (Cassell 1982) and *Learning in Primary Schools* (Falmer Press, 1987).

Colin Richards, HMI, is Assistant Director of Inspection (primary phase) in the Office for Standards in Education (OFSTED). He was previously a primary school teacher and university lecturer. He has published widely on aspects of primary education. His books include *New Directions in Primary Education* (Falmer Press, 1982) and *The Study of Primary Education: Source Books 1–4* (Falmer Press, 1990).

After a training in the Social Sciences, **Alistair Ross** taught in Inner London primary schools for ten years, including a period as advisory teacher for social studies and history in primary schools. He joined the Polytechnic of North London in 1985 and has had a particular interest in social studies/industry and economics education in primary years, and directs the Primary

Schools and Industry Research Centre there. He was made a professor in 1991.

Norman Thomas taught in primary schools for fourteen years. He then joined HMI, retiring in 1981 as Chief Inspector for Primary Education. He has since acted as consultant to a number of LEAs and the House of Commons Select Committee, and lectured and written on primary education. He was a member of TGAT. He is Honorary Professor to the University of Warwick and Visiting Professor to the University of Hertfordshire. His book, *Primary Education from Plowden to the 1990s*, was published by Falmer Press in 1990.

Index